THE HIDDEN AUTHORSHIP
OF SØREN KIERKEGAARD

The Hidden Authorship
of Søren Kierkegaard

Jacob H. Sawyer

Foreword by Murray Rae

WIPF & STOCK · Eugene, Oregon

THE HIDDEN AUTHORSHIP OF SØREN KIERKEGAARD

Copyright © 2015 Jacob H. Sawyer. All rights reserved. Except for brief quotations in critical publications or reviews, no part of this book may be reproduced in any manner without prior written permission from the publisher. Write: Permissions, Wipf and Stock Publishers, 199 W. 8th Ave., Suite 3, Eugene, OR 97401.

Wipf & Stock
An Imprint of Wipf and Stock Publishers
199 W. 8th Ave., Suite 3
Eugene, OR 97401

www.wipfandstock.com

ISBN 13: 978-1-4982-0892-5

Manufactured in the U.S.A.   09/17/2015

Dedicated to Miriam, who helps me in my struggle to author these words in my life.

Contents

Foreword by Murray Rae | ix
Preface | xi

0.1 Introduction | 1
0.2 Kierkegaard's Task and How He Sought to Accomplish It: An Explication of the Thesis | 15

Part I: The Content
1.1 The Problems of Outwardness and Direct Communication | 25
1.2 "The Single Individual" | 39
1.3 The Gospel Truth | 52

Part II: The Form
2.1 "The Single Individual" as Authorial Form: The Outward Dimension | 79
2.2 An Overview of Kierkegaard's Authorship | 89
2.3 Kierkegaard's Reception Today | 110

Part III: Kierkegaard as an Example of a Christian Communicator
3.1 The Inward Dimension of Kierkegaard's Authorship | 131
3.2 Pseudonymous Authorship as Reduplication | 145
3.3 Kierkegaard's *Point of View* | 152

Conclusion | 159

Bibliography | 167
Subject Index | 173
Names Index | 179

Foreword

The published works of Søren Kierkegaard are endlessly fascinating, profound, witty, deeply moving, and enigmatic. While the individual works present numerous hermeneutical challenges for the reader, so too does the corpus as a whole. Kierkegaard published a good number of his works under the names of pseudonymous authors. Sometimes he named himself as "editor" of these works, while at other times he published under his own name. Although there are very clear thematic relationships across the whole corpus, and while the works sometimes refer to each other, Kierkegaard was adamant that nothing published under the name of a pseudonym should be attributed to him. And yet his *Journals* give evidence of his own agreement with many of the things penned by his pseudonyms, and reveal that on more than one occasion he decided only at the eleventh hour whether to publish particular works pseudonymously or under his own name. What is the reader to make of this complex mix of disclosure and concealment?

Scholarly practice and opinion on this matter has diverged widely. For over a century, virtually no heed was paid to the pseudonymity of Kierkegaard's works. The views expressed in pseudonymous works were assumed to be Kierkegaard's own. Then, in 1993, Roger Poole declared that this tradition of reading Kierkegaard had produced only "a useless corpus of secondary comment."[1] While that is far too harsh a judgement, and while not all have agreed with Poole's insistence that Kierkegaard's pseudonymous literature be viewed as a forerunner of deconstructivism, few scholars now deny that the pseudonymity is a matter of considerable hermeneutical importance. There remains, nevertheless, much dispute over the nature and content of Kierkegaard's works, and over the purpose that Kierkegaard's "indirect communication" serves.

1. Poole, *Indirect Communication*, 7.

Informed, quite rightly in my view, by the conviction that Kierkegaard's project is, above all, a theological one, Jacob H. Sawyer charts a course through the turbulent waters of Kierkegaard scholarship and offers a compelling account of what theological purpose is served by the pseudonymous concealment of Kierkegaard himself. The content of the authorship itself, Sawyer contends, directed as it is toward the edification of the reader through a personal encounter with God, requires of Kierkegaard that he "hide" himself as author. His intent as an author is not to win admirers for himself; nor is it to encourage attention to his own struggles; his intent rather is to provide opportunity for his readers to recognize that they exist before God and to respond to that reality with appropriate contrition, obedience, and joy. In service of that goal, Kierkegaard must hide away and leave his readers alone with God.

The evidence in support of Sawyer's reading of Kierkegaard's works is carefully assembled in this volume and is presented in a way that is consistent with the case made. Readers of this work too will be encouraged to consider anew their own existence before God, and to ponder again what may be required of them in response. Sawyer thus provides us with an astute and faithful reading of Kierkegaard's works, a reading that serves well the great task to which Kierkegaard devoted himself, the task of making clear what it is to be a Christian.

Murray Rae
University of Otago

Preface

This book was originally written as a thesis to obtain a Masters degree in theology from Laidlaw College in Auckland, New Zealand. In between submitting it and seeing it published, my wife and I travelled to Canada so that I could have the privilege of working as a pastor for the children and youth of Spring Garden Church in North York, Toronto. This experience brought to light many difficulties that arise from attempting to embody the ideas I have outlined here from my reading of Kierkegaard. The propensity and temptation to abstraction is always real in any work on behalf of people, and my family at Spring Garden helped to work with me to ground theology in life. I am grateful for having been a part of this community.

But before this, many people in many different ways are responsible for creating the space for me to grow into a theologian and an author: my teachers Mark Strom, David Williams, Rod Thompson, and my supervisor Nicola Hoggard-Creegan; my peers of the More's The Pity Society: Jimmy Harvey, Brendon Neilson, and Kyle Duncan, along with Christian Parker; various mentors and encouragers throughout the years, who have, I believe, shaped my life for the better: Malcolm Irwin, Gene Tempelmeyer, and various teachers, friends and family at The Salvation Army, Browns Bay. I am also thankful to Murray Rae for encouraging me to get this published and supporting me in this process.

And I am thankful to my mother, for her constant support and encouragement through editing and discussion, along with the rest of my family, who have been forced to journey with me through my endless outward processing. Lastly, of course, I am thankful to my wife, Miriam, with whom life is an ongoing adventure and joy, as we strive to know as we are known.

Jacob H. Sawyer
November, 2014

0.1 Introduction

SØREN KIERKEGAARD IN HISTORY

Isaiah Berlin famously commented on Leo Tolstoy's authorship as being one of "a fox trying to be a hedgehog"—that is, one who saw the infinite value in being about "one thing," but could not himself be like this because he was constantly attempting to chase many diverse ideas at the same time, attempting to write a complex pluriform of social commentary in a single work.[1] On the surface (the *outward* appearance), Kierkegaard could be accused of the same thing. In fact, Kierkegaard's pluriformity is so *outwardly* overwhelming that it seems that one would be hard-pressed to see any kind of big idea behind it. His construction of multiple layers of pseudonymity, genre, and subject matter is so diverse that it makes finding explicit links between them difficult. However, according to Kierkegaard himself, there is indeed unity, *one big idea*: becoming a Christian.[2] This is a *hidden* unity, and this *hiddenness* will be the main theme of this paper. Firstly, a brief introduction to Kierkegaard is in order.

---

1. Berlin, "The Hedgehog and the Fox," 436–98.
2. Kierkegaard, "The Point of View for My Work as an Author," 23; Holmer's emphasis of "subjectivity" over "objectivity" and the reworking of both is the central theme of the complex and varied authorship is complementary to my view, since they are effectually the same issue. See his *On Kierkegaard and the Truth*, 24–26, and ibid., 57: "Almost all of Kierkegaard's writings are both an occasion for, as well as an illustration and kind of defense of the thesis that 'truth is subjectivity.'"

THE MELANCHOLY DANE

Søren Kierkegaard was brought up in the midst of a bleak home life. In particular his father Michael was the source of much anguish for young Søren, as in his strict pietism he enforced high demands on his children. The guilt that came from Michael cursing God as a poor shepherd boy followed him to his grave. He "continued to be haunted by the suspicion that a curse lay upon his family,"[3] seeing evidence for this curse in the death of his first wife, along with five out of his seven children, all in his lifetime.[4] This fear seemed to have been passed onto Søren, who, after an "aesthetic" period in his youth, took up his life with determined vigor in the belief that his life would be short.[5] He was determined to find a direction for his life beyond his own worldly success, and realized that the mere acquisition of knowledge was not enough:

> . . . the crucial thing is to find a truth which is truth *for me, to find the idea for which I am willing to live and die*.[6]

Such thinking is indicative of Kierkegaard's emphasis on subjectivity and his critique of his society's obsession with objectivity. These are key themes that Kierkegaard adopted throughout his authorial task, and in a sense, they became the very "life-view" for which he was looking. He came to name his calling in life to be one that was evangelistic: to reacquaint his society with the truth of the gospel of Christianity, since he perceived that his entire age had lost the understanding of what it meant to be a Christian.[7] Armed with a considerable inheritance from his father, it was to this task that Kierkegaard applied himself unreservedly and without worldly constraint.[8]

Kierkegaard claimed that to be a Christian, a believer must be a "single individual." "The single individual" is a key concept in the authorship of

---

3. Barrett, *Kierkegaard*, 8.

4. Rae, *Kierkegaard and Theology*, 7–8.

5. Ibid., 8–10; Barrett, *Kierkegaard*, 12.

6. Kierkegaard, *Journals and Papers*, 5/5100, 1 A 75, August 1, 1835, emphasis author's own.

7. This is most clearly the case in Kierkegaard, *The Point of View*; see also Malantschuk, *Kierkegaard's Thought*, 113–14 etc.

8. "Few men have been motivated by such evangelical zeal as Kierkegaard" (Holmer, *On Kierkegaard and the Truth*, 16).

Kierkegaard. It was the first step in achieving his task of "reintroducing Christianity to Christendom."⁹

> The single individual—*this category has been used only once, its first time in a decisively dialectical way, by Socrates, in order to disintegrate paganism. In Christendom it will be used a second time in the very opposite way, to make people (the Christians) Christians. It is not the missionary's category with regard to the pagans to whom he proclaims Christianity, but it is the missionary's category within Christendom itself in order to introduce Christianity into Christendom. When he, the missionary, comes, he will use this category . . .*¹⁰

Kierkegaard saw himself as the Socrates of Christendom, the "gnat" of his home town of Copenhagen, Denmark, in the first half of the nineteenth century.¹¹ Influenced by his family's dual involvement with the mainstream Danish state church alongside the fringe anti-institutional Moravian church, Kierkegaard saw his fellow Danes as being oppressed with the illusion of Christendom.¹² He believed that his neighbors thought themselves indeed and unquestionably Christian by default, and so would not see themselves in need of Kierkegaard's evangelistic "task." Kierkegaard understood this obstacle and took up the illusion of being an aesthetic writer through employing various pseudonyms in order to gain an audience with his neighbors.¹³ It was by this deception that he was able to be an effective witness, in an attempt to subvert and circumvent the illusion of a Christian identity in his readers.¹⁴ Specifically how he was able to accomplish this is a key part of the concern of this book.

---

9. See Kierkegaard, *Journals and Papers*, 6/6271, IX A 390, n.d., 1848; cited in Evans, *Kierkegaard*, 2 n. 2; also Kierkegaard, *Practice in Christianity*, 36.

10. Kierkegaard, *Point of View*, 123–24, emphasis author's own.

11. Ibid., 24 and the translator's footnote on 314–15.

12. Barrett, *Kierkegaard*, 9–10.

13. "Aesthetic" being that which pertains to the senses, so an "aesthetic author" is one who resembles a poet, and writes beautifully and popularly for the sake of moving readers.

14. ". . . Thus in a certain sense I began my activity as an author with a falsum [deception] or with a pia fraus [pious fraud]. The situation is that in so-called established Christendom people are so fixed in the fancy that they are Christians that if they are to be made aware at all many an art will have to be employed. If someone who otherwise does not have a reputation of being an author begins right off as a Christian author, he will not get a hearing from his contemporaries. They are immediately on their guard, saying, 'That's not for us' etc." (Kierkegaard, *Journals and Papers*, 6/6205, IX A 171, n.d., 1848; cited in Kierkegaard, *Point of View*, 161–62).

Because Kierkegaard understood Christianity to be primarily an inward relation to God, he saw the kind of automatic nominalism in Danish culture and its institutional church as an evil that must be challenged. Such thinking to Kierkegaard was a powerful obstruction that inoculated his neighbors against the gospel which spoke to the *individual*[15]—that is, that each person is at all times "directly before God."[16] Kierkegaard sought to upset and disarm the comfortable presuppositions and clichéd understandings of Christianity possessed by the everyday Dane, in an effort to push them into taking responsibility for their own faith and not rely on outward factors such as the faith or the intellectual systems of others. Kierkegaard labeled the oppressive, one-size-fits-all hegemonic system of Danish Christianity, "Christendom." He spent the final years of his life in a vehement offensive against this religious empire, publishing a series of tracts which were posthumously compiled as *Attack Upon Christendom*.[17]

Kierkegaard's theology was largely in accord with the orthodoxy of the Western church.[18] Its distinctive lay in its emphasis on *lived life*; hence his work is often regarded as the foundation of existentialism. He did not seek to develop a systematic theology that was abstract, exhaustive, and objectively certain (thereby irrelevant to life), but was instead concerned with the lived life of "the single individual."[19] Thus his articulation of the role of a believer (and his definition of a self) was one of continual evolution—that of striving after Christ, who was seen as both the prototype and savior of the Christian.[20] Being a Christian was a *becoming* which necessitated an ongoing balance between many extremes.[21] It is for this reason (among others) that Kierkegaard did not focus on developing theology as a comprehensive system, since what mattered was life. For instance, it was less important for him to *explain* faith as both a gift and a responsibility

---

15. ". . . when the gospel speaks it speaks to the single individual" (Kierkegaard, *Works of Love*, 31).

16. Kierkegaard, *The Sickness Unto Death*, 111.

17. Kierkegaard, *Attack*.

18. Rae, *Kierkegaard and Theology*, esp. 166; see also Gouwens, *Kierkegaard as Religious Thinker*, 142–43.

19. E.g., the concept of "pure thinking" in relation to essential truth: Kierkegaard, *Concluding Unscientific Postscript*, 310–11, etc.

20. Ibid., 80.

21. Kierkegaard, *Sickness*.

than it was for him to communicate *how* faith was taken up and used in the life of a Christian.²²

Much of what Kierkegaard was responding to in Copenhagen was his view of the public being dominated and easily swayed by the intellectual fashions of the day. He frequently labeled the phenomenon of this collective tide as "the crowd" in contradistinction to the individual,²³ and this evil was directly opposed to the realization of "the single individual."²⁴ A key feature of Kierkegaard's thought was the dimension of choice and responsibility, which "the crowd" removed from the individual.²⁵ Kierkegaard understood that this abdication of responsibility could be either intentional or unintentional, and outlines this via his pseudonym Anti-Climacus in *Sickness Unto Death*.²⁶

In Kierkegaard's view, the most notable intellectual influence on the Danish public was the German philosopher Georg Wilhelm Friedrich Hegel. Hegel's task was so vast that it included a summary of history up to that point, setting forth his contemporary German culture (including German Christianity) as the apogee of human civilization.²⁷ His analysis of the development of philosophy and schools of thought claimed to incorporate all intellectual and cultural shifts into his great "system," as Kierkegaard's pseudonym Johannes Climacus has called it.²⁸ Climacus claims that Hegel had arrogantly drawn a line around the world, reducing life to an innumerable number of cogs in a cosmic machine, leaving no room for freedom, choice, the individual, and therefore for life itself. Hegel carried this out through a dialectical form which worked two opposite concepts (thesis,

---

22. "Kierkegaard's overriding interest in what it means to be a Christian means that we do not find in him anything remotely resembling a systematic presentation of Christian doctrine" (Rae, *Kierkegaard and Theology*, 3).

23. Holmer comments on the theology of Kierkegaard's day: that "the homogeneity becomes almost overpowering," i.e., a crowd mentality (*On Kierkegaard and the Truth*, 38).

24. "[A] crowd . . . is untruth, since a crowd either makes for impenitence and irresponsibility altogether, or for the single individual it at least weakens responsibility by reducing the responsibility to a fraction. See, there was no individual soldier who dared to lay hands on Caius Marius . . . [but a] crowd is an abstraction, which does not have hands . . ." (Kierkegaard, *Point of View*, 107–8).

25. Crabtree and Gutenberg College, *Kierkegaard*.

26. See 1.2: "The Single Individual: A Dialectic of Being" below.

27. Crabtree and Gutenberg College, *Kierkegaard*.

28. In particular, see Kierkegaard, *Concluding Unscientific Postscript*.

antithesis) into a synthesis, thus eliminating contradiction.[29] Kierkegaard argued that such an approach worked from the assumption that nothing was beyond its grasp, but its fundamental weakness was its own impossibility, since it only survived in the fantastic realm of objectivity and thus had no traction in actual existence. The irony was that Hegel had effectively philosophized *himself* out of existence, thus creating an impossibility which completely negated his work, for how can such an author see or speak (let alone with any authority) if he himself does not exist?[30]

In such fashion, Hegel and his followers negated existence for the sake of "pure being" and "pure thinking."[31] Kierkegaard understood these ideas as illusory (and at the very least useless) for a human being. A person's condition is always constituted by existence in time which is a process that eludes finality (hence Kierkegaard's emphasis on *becoming* and *striving* as opposed to static being).[32] So Kierkegaard sought to remove such illusions that enslaved his fellow Danes to untruth in the form of a kind of intellectual mob mentality, and instead sought to re-emphasize the responsibility and spiritual reality of every person as an *existing* "single individual." It would not do for him to mimic the systematic and coolly logical form of Hegel (or much of modern scholarship for that matter), for he would just be replacing one illusory system for another (fighting fire with fire)[33] and would be at risk of becoming a victim of Hegelian synthesis himself. Instead, he sought to subvert the formal conventions of writing in order to

---

29. Holmer, *On Kierkegaard and the Truth*, 32.

30. See especially Kierkegaard, *Concluding Unscientific Postscript*, 301–18. For instance: "But abstraction does not care about whether a particular existing human being is immortal, and just that is the difficulty. It is disinterested, but the difficulty of existence is the existing person's interest, and the existing person is infinitely interested in existing. Thus abstract thinking helps me with my immortality by killing me as a particular existing individual and then making me immortal and therefore helps somewhat as in Holberg the doctor took the patient's life with his medicine—but also drove out the fever" (ibid., 302); "pure thinking, in mystical suspension and with no relation to an existing person, explains everything within itself but not itself . . ." (ibid., 313); "But for an existing person pure thinking is a chimera when the truth is supposed to be the truth in which to exist" (ibid., 310); "To think existence *sub specie aeterni* and in abstraction is essentially to annul it, and the merit of it resembles the much-heralded merit of canceling the principle of contradiction" (ibid., 308).

31. Ibid., 304, 308.

32. For instance, see Kierkegaard, *Practice in Christianity*, 205–7.

33. "Within the realm of pure thinking many, many objections can perhaps be made against Hegelianism, but that leaves everything essentially unchanged" (Kierkegaard, *Concluding Unscientific Postscript*, 309–10).

help realize his task of awakening "the single individual" in his reader. He achieved this through *hiding* himself in his authorship.[34]

This *hiddenness* was undertaken in the hope that his reader would, as we presume of Kierkegaard himself, meet God in the hiddenness of her own heart. Therefore, my thesis is this:

> *It was through Kierkegaard's understanding of the gospel that his authorship took the form of hiddenness.*

The underlying question that has driven me in this research of Kierkegaard and his work is to do with the appropriate relation between form and content: How does the nature of truth affect or impinge on its communication? In particular, how does the Christian claim of Jesus as truth affect a person who attempts to speak truthfully? What does it mean to speak as a Christian? If Christ is the truth, how is a believer to speak (or write) of him? Through examining Kierkegaard's authorship, I will present him as one who understood this tension and attempted to embody Christian truth in his own authorship.

Although the writing of this book is undertaken in the pretense of demonstrating a level of "mastery" over the subject material (that being the work of Søren Kierkegaard), I will attempt to undertake this work *in truth* by inverting this expectation, instead demonstrating its mastery over myself and this book. As has been noted most gracefully in the foreword and preface to the recent posthumous publication of Paul Holmer's work *Kierkegaard and the Truth*,[35] Holmer recognized the existential difficulty in attempting to write about Kierkegaard. Such anguish is indicative of a Kierkegaardian commentator's faithfulness *to* Kierkegaard. As one attempting to be Kierkegaard's reader, and therefore more than this—a penitent before God,[36] I myself am wrestling over the writing of this book. So in light of

---

34. Kierkegaard's relation to Hegel is very complicated and my brief treatment here is no doubt incomplete. My particular interest here restricts me to Kierkegaard's understanding of Hegel and his followers, and then how he counteracts or circumvents what he sees as the weaknesses of Hegel's approach. I have attempted to refrain from making judgments as to the fairness of Kierkegaard's critique of Hegel (or "Danish Hegelians"), and Hegel's influence on Kierkegaard (not an exclusively negative one) is worth investigating. However, this is beyond the scope of this work. Those interested should consult the influential book: Stewart, *Kierkegaard's Relations*; and also the following: Aumann, "Kierkegaard's Case," 221–48.

35. By Stanley Hauerwas, David J. Gouwens, and Lee C. Barrett III in Holmer, *On Kierkegaard and the Truth*, ix–xxii.

36. As Kierkegaard named himself. See Kierkegaard, *Point of View*, 62.

this, I will attempt to communicate Kierkegaard's form of communication in a way that is likewise "in truth."

This work is not written in an attempt to summarize Søren Kierkegaard's life or thought, nor to dissect him as an object of interest on the altar of objective, universal knowing. Rather, it is an attempt to learn from Kierkegaard's works as they addressed his context and to present him as an example of a Christian communicator. Through demonstrating Kierkegaard's literary genius on behalf of the gospel, I hope that we may learn how to communicate "in truth."

METHODOLOGY

> *The beginning is not what one begins with but what one arrives at, and one reaches it by going backward.*[37]

This book will not employ a systematic description or definition of terms and ideas used by Kierkegaard. To do so would be to import a philosophical or academic system that is foreign to his work.[38] Instead, as a demonstration of my *mastery* "over" the "subject matter" of Kierkegaard's authorship, I will seek to emulate (in the fashion also adopted by Ludwig Wittgenstein)[39] Kierkegaard's tendency to *demonstrate* a term's meaning by its *use*.[40] In this way, I will attempt to read Kierkegaard according to his own terms.[41] However, in saying this, an outline of my own pre-understandings of the following terms could be helpful:

- "Hiddenness" and its derivatives are being used in this work in a sense similar to Kierkegaard's use of these words, especially in his concept "hidden inwardness." These words carry the sense of something being kept from direct observation or understanding.

- "Authorship" is typically in reference to Kierkegaard's "authorship proper": those works outlined in *Point of View*,[42] along with the works of Anti-Climacus, which contribute to Kierkegaard's task.

---

37. Kierkegaard, *Spiritual Writings*, 184.
38. See Rae, *Kierkegaard and Theology*, 3; and Barrett, *Kierkegaard*, 5.
39. See especially Wittgenstein, *Philosophical Investigations*; Creegan, *Wittgenstein and Kierkegaard*.
40. See also Rae, *Kierkegaard and Theology*, 3.
41. Holmer, *On Kierkegaard and the Truth*, 42.
42. See Kierkegaard, *Point of View*, 29 and its accompanying footnote by Kierkegaard

- "Believer," "learner," "reader," "hearer," "student," etc. have been used throughout as interchangeable terms for a person engaging with either Kierkegaard's works, truth, or a matter presented to them by another.
- "Truth" is largely being used throughout as a reference to essential truth—that is, truth concerning ethics and religion.[43]

Much of what is written here presumes Christian faith, and Kierkegaard argues that a true depth of knowing Christianity requires the passion of faith. I therefore hope to demonstrate here the importance of an *inside* reading of Kierkegaard.

The reader will also come to notice the layered and repetitive form of this book. The themes we will explore cannot be easily argued in a linear fashion but must be approached by many different routes.[44] This is a common characteristic of Kierkegaard's work, and I will employ such repetition also. This approach carries the advantage that it fosters a greater understanding in the reader, for by going too quickly we can miss something.[45] My book therefore is less a linear argument, and more of an exploration that paints a picture, the parts of which are interdependent and cannot be accurately understood apart from the whole.

STRUCTURE

In this work I attempt to pay closer attention to the *how* of Kierkegaard, rather than the *what*.[46] I therefore explore and emphasize the communication strategies and out-workings of Kierkegaard's writings, working from what is said in his own *explicit* articulation of his authorial task in *Point of*

---

and endnote by the translators.

43. See Kierkegaard, *Concluding Unscientific Postscript*, 199 and its footnote.

44. C. Stephen Evans also shares this difficulty due to the interrelation of many of Kierkegaard's concepts, though I would not go as far as he does in linking Kierkegaard's concepts of "indirect communication," the "spheres of existence," "subjectivity" and his pseudonymity. I would argue that the "spheres" in particular are not as central in Kierkegaard's thought, since "subjectivity" in the God-relationship is primary. The "spheres" are helpful in elucidating such subjectivity under God, but are not necessary for "subjectivity" to be used in an effort to understand Kierkegaard's work. See Evans, *Kierkegaard's Fragments and Postscript*, 6.

45. Kierkegaard, "Philosophical Crumbs," 94 n. 1.

46. See Kierkegaard, *Journals and Papers*, 3/3684, X3 A 431, n.d., 1850; and Kierkegaard, *Concluding Unscientific Postscript*, 202.

View.[47] In order to do this, I touch on many key concepts found throughout the content of the authorship in order to elucidate the overall form of his authorial task. The focus will be on *form* rather than content, but will proceed through the content in order to get to the form.[48]

Another way of understanding this is to see Kierkegaard's authorship as consisting of three layers. The first layer is *what* is said explicitly (content). The second is *how* it is said, in terms of the use of pseudonyms or its veronymity along with its literary form,[49] in order to elicit a response in the reader—that is, the *outward* dimension. The third is a deeper *how*; that which pertains to Kierkegaard himself; the *inward* dimension. This layer also involves the issue of pseudonyms, along with connections to Kierkegaard's own life, both literary and otherwise. It is vital to understand Kierkegaard's authorship as a multifaceted venture in communicating the gospel through being hidden "in the truth." It is a matter involving not only concepts, but also the embodied relation of such concepts to the reader and the author. In this work we will give primary consideration to Kierkegaard's use of pseudonyms in order to come to understand this layering.[50]

We begin with a brief explication of my thesis statement by way of introducing Kierkegaard's task, and will propose a christological understanding of "hiddenness" as the basis for the form of his authorship. This will then be the foundation for demonstrating such hiddenness being outworked in the authorship in a multilayered fashion. Three sections correspond to those layers mentioned above, each contributing to a progressively deeper demonstration of Kierkegaard's *hidden* authorship:

Part I outlines some key concepts that are explicit throughout the authorship and are important in understanding Kierkegaard's task. Chief of these are "the single individual" and essential truth, and the concept of hiddenness is discussed throughout.

---

47. Ironically, this is similar to Climacus' confession as to how he is "reviewing" the other pseudonymous works. See Kierkegaard, *Concluding Unscientific Postscript*, 283.

48. As we will find throughout, though, such a dichotomy between form and content is a false one, and is used here only as a preliminary understanding in order to eventually make clear the error of such an understanding.

49. Such as the pathetic (in the sense of "pathos," or *passion*) tone, argumentative structure, etc.

50. This leaves unexplored how exactly this takes place in the more detailed factors regarding literary form. I have unfortunately no space to give enough attention to factors such as the use of genre, argumentative styles, formatting, etc. in this work. I will instead restrict my discussion to Kierkegaard's use of pseudonyms.

Part II discusses how the very *form* of the writing was an attempt to awaken such concepts within the reader herself through indirect communication.[51] Here we will particularly focus on how Kierkegaard's works were designed to impact his reader, looking at how the concepts of "the single individual" and "indirect communication" were outworked in the form of his writing. It is here that we will come to see how understanding Kierkegaard's authorial form as *hidden* becomes apparent and useful.

Part III considers Kierkegaard as an example of a Christian communicator and evaluates his authorship against his own critique of Hegel, the author who wrote himself out of existence. This section seeks to address how Kierkegaard overcame the problems inherent in the work of Hegel and his followers through *hiding* himself. We then discuss Kierkegaard's concepts of existence-communication and reduplication, and how they can be understood to relate to Kierkegaard himself, as well as how his own explanation of his authorship impinges on his task.

This book will demonstrate the presence of hiddenness throughout Kierkegaard's authorship as a whole, and how this was derived from his understanding of the gospel of Christianity.

My Use of Kierkegaard's Pseudonymous and Signed Works

In this essay I regard Kierkegaard's pseudonymous works as expressing views that he himself often agreed with and found useful as representative of his own words.[52] I will give hermeneutical priority to Kierkegaard's signed works, seeing these as the authoritative works through which to understand his pseudonymous works. I will do this in light of his warning that "in the pseudonymous books there is not a single word by me."[53] However, we must keep in mind that the goal is *not* merely to understand Kierkegaard's view, since this would risk objectivizing his work and reducing it to "a

---

51. In this book, I will use the feminine singular in reference to "the ideal reader." It is singular in keeping with Kierkegaard's concept of "the single individual," and feminine for the sake of the link to Regine Olsen. See Kierkegaard, *Journals and Papers*, 6/6388, X1 A 266, n.d., 1849. See also section 3.3: "That Single Individual, My Reader" in McDonald, "Kierkegaard, Søren." It can also be seen to be in keeping with the New Testament use of the feminine in regard to the Christian church (e.g., Eph 5:25).

52. This is made possible through the correlation between the themes in the pseudonymous and veronymous works, including the journals, as is common practice amongst Kierkegaardian scholarship.

53. Kierkegaard, *Concluding Unscientific Postscript*, 626.

paragraph in the system."[54] Instead we will attempt to engage with his works on their own terms.[55]

These pseudonymical voices are understood to be various points of view, each carrying an important function (particularly as demonstrations) in the overall task to which Kierkegaard employed them: That is, "to the issue: becoming a Christian, with direct and indirect polemical aim at that enormous illusion, Christendom, or the illusion that in such a country all are Christians of sorts."[56] This will become clearer as we explore these matters further.

Primary Works Consulted

Because of the limited amount of time rather than the limited scope of my work, it was necessary for me to limit the number of works written by Kierkegaard with which I engaged. In this work, I have found it crucial first to consult the collection of Kierkegaard's direct works on his authorship compiled in *Point of View*.[57] I will also assume this veronymous,[58] posthumous work as the hermeneutical key for understanding the strategies employed in his authorship.[59]

From there I have sought to include a range of Kierkegaard's books from his own analysis of what he understood to be his "authorship proper."[60] These include, from the first division (aesthetic writing): *Fear and Trembling*,[61]

---

54. Ibid.; see also Gouwens, *Kierkegaard as Religious Thinker*, 1.
55. I will discuss this in my critique of "psychoanalytic interpretations" of Kierkegaard in 3.1 below.
56. Kierkegaard, *Point of View*, 23.
57. Kierkegaard, *Point of View*.
58. I am following Joel Rasmussen in his use of "veronymous" in reference to Søren Kierkegaard's signed works. See Rasmussen, *Between Irony and Witness*, 9; he states here that he gained the term from Strawser, *Both/And*.
59. I will address Joakim Garff's critiques on the historical reliability of this work further below ("The Eyes of Argus," 75–102).
60. Kierkegaard, *Point of View*, 29 n.
61. Kierkegaard, *Fear and Trembling*.

Philosophical Fragments,[62] and portions of *Either/Or*,[63] additionally I examine a limited selection of the concurrent *Upbuilding Discourses* which accompanied such works.[64] *Concluding Unscientific Postscript*[65] was consulted as the bridge between the aesthetic and religious works, and from the third division ("only religious writing"), *Works of Love*,[66] as well as a selection of other *Upbuilding Discourses in Various Spirits* and *Christian Discourses*.[67] Furthermore I have also consulted both *Practice in Christianity*[68] and *The Sickness Unto Death*,[69] which were written after "The Point of View for My Work as an Author" and therefore not included in Kierkegaard's divisions above, but can be understood to fit with the religious works. I have also engaged with portions of *Concept of Irony*[70] and various entries from his *Journals*[71] as other direct sources for understanding Kierkegaard's authorship. References to other works by Kierkegaard are largely derived through secondary sources, and will be referenced accordingly.

62. In the body of the text and in the footnotes I will refer to the better known title "Philosophical Fragments," and will reference the version translated by M. G. Piety, who chose to translate the title "Philosophical Crumbs." Kierkegaard, "Philosophical Crumbs."

63. Kierkegaard, *Either/Or*.

64. Chapters 1–4 and 11–12 compiled by George Pattison in *Spiritual Writings* were originally from 1833–34's *Eighteen Upbuilding Discourses*. Chapter 10 of this work was originally published as *The Lily of the Field and the Bird under Heaven* in 1849 to accompany the second edition of *Either/Or*.

65. Kierkegaard, *Concluding Unscientific Postscript*.

66. Kierkegaard, *Works of Love*.

67. Kierkegaard, *Spiritual Writings*, chapters 5–7 were originally from *Upbuilding Discourses in Various Spirits* of 1847, chapters 8–9 were originally from *Christian Discourses* of 1848, chapter 13 was from 1850's *An Upbuilding Discourse*, chapter 14 was from 1849's *The High Priest, the Tax Collector, and the Sinful Woman*, and chapters 15–6 were originally from *Two Upbuilding Discourses* in 1851. Also Kierkegaard, "Two Discourses at the Communion on Fridays," 418–26. All of these works appear to have been stand-alone religious works, rather than accompaniments for the aesthetic works.

68. Kierkegaard, *Practice in Christianity*.

69. Kierkegaard, *Sickness*.

70. Kierkegaard, *The Concept of Irony*; This work also lies outside the above list since it was his university thesis, and not part of his "authorship proper." See Kierkegaard, *Point of View*, 315 n. 9.

71. Kierkegaard, *Journals and Papers*.

My Use of Personal Pronouns in Relation to God

Regretfully, there is no unisex personal pronoun in the English language by which I can refer to God that retains the warmth and gravity of personhood. Thus, I will use masculine pronouns in referring to God where I feel that it would be too inappropriate to use the cold and detached "God" or "Godself," instead opting for "him" or "himself." I have simply chosen the masculine for the sake of my own preferred language in speaking of and to God without intending to offend. I hope that my reader will afford to me the goodwill of which Joakim Garff speaks.[72]

---

72. See 2.3 below.

0.2 Kierkegaard's Task and How He Sought to Accomplish It
An Explication of the Thesis

INTRODUCTION

This chapter serves to outline the task that informed and directed Kierkegaard's authorship. We consider here how the Christian belief of the incarnation can be seen to be fundamental to Kierkegaard's understanding of the correlation between form and content.[1] We can then see how Kierkegaard outworked this understanding through his authorship, an authorship characterized by *hiddenness*.

Søren Kierkegaard dedicated his literary talents to reacquaint his fellow Danes with Christianity. He believed that his society had seriously misunderstood what it meant to be a Christian to the point of distorting it, and so sought to do what he could as an author to "reintroduce Christianity into Christendom." To begin with, Kierkegaard wrote in order to awaken his reader from being a mindless number in "the crowd" to being confronted by what he understood to be each and every person's human duty and joy: to be a "single individual."[2] Kierkegaard believed that such a realization was

---

1. "Kierkegaard's conception of his authorship and his incarnational view of God in Christ should be understood together . . ." (Rasmussen, *Between Irony and Witness*, 2).

2. Kierkegaard understood that "The Glory of Being Human" consisted of being an individual. As he explains in his own name, "God set human beings apart and made each human being this one individual being . . ." and to neglect this fact by a person associating herself with "the crowd" is a negation of such glory: "The individual animal is an individual only in a numerical sense and belongs to what the most renowned of pagan thinkers called the attribute of animality: the mass. In this way, those who despairingly

a necessary first step for a person to know herself as a "single individual" *under God*—that is, a Christian.³ This was because he understood that the gospel of Christianity addressed people only as individuals, and required a personal decision from each and every human being.⁴ Therefore, a society's presumption that all within it are Christians, under the illusion that it is a Christian society, is antithetical to Kierkegaard's understanding of Christianity.⁵ Kierkegaard labeled such erroneous thinking as "Christendom."

As he practiced throughout his authorship and reiterated most directly in his posthumous "The Point of View for My Work as an Author," he claimed: "I am and was a religious author, that my whole authorship pertains to Christianity, to the issue: becoming a Christian, with direct and indirect polemical aim at that enormous illusion, Christendom, or the illusion that in such a country all are Christians of sorts."⁶

This was his task: to reintroduce Christianity as a demand on individual persons, into a society which believed Christianity to be a matter of an impersonal, objective status.⁷ But *how* was he to do this?

Kierkegaard understood that his task must be internally coherent: his *form* needed to complement his *task*. Such a conviction was not merely an

---

turn away from those elementary thoughts in order to plunge into the mass element of comparison make themselves into mere numerical individuals, regarding themselves as if they were animals, whether they emerge from the comparison at the top or at the bottom of the pile" (Kierkegaard, *Spiritual Writings*, 121–22).

3. It is important to realize though that for Kierkegaard there was actually no such thing as a "single individual" apart from under God. See Rae, *Kierkegaard's Vision of the Incarnation*, 145. But this category is important for a preliminary understanding of what Kierkegaard wanted his reader to be aware of in order to truly consider Christianity, and could be a good summation of the goal of the pseudonymous authorship before *Postscript*, as we shall explore below.

4. Kierkegaard, *Works of Love*, 31.

5. Kierkegaard could be critiqued along the lines of his thought being a Westernized preoccupation with the individual, and one that does not take into account non-Western, communal ways of thinking. Even the New Testament could be cited in the recorded events of mass conversion, such as that of the Philippian jailer's family in Acts 16:33–34.

6. Kierkegaard, *Point of View*, 23.

7. I assume that Kierkegaard is through-and-through a religious author, that the main concern of Kierkegaard's authorship is Christianity, and that there is no good reason for not accepting Kierkegaard's direct accounts of his authorship—particularly those given in the collection of Kierkegaard, *Point of View*. Views which attempt to argue otherwise are at best unhelpful. I believe I am in good company in making such an assumption; see also Rae, *Kierkegaard and Theology*, 1–2; Rae, *Kierkegaard's Vision of the Incarnation*, 1 n. 1; Holmer, *On Kierkegaard and the Truth*, 22 n. 10; cf. Garff, "Eyes of Argus." I will give a critique of Garff's article further below.

0.2 Kierkegaard's Task and How He Sought to Accomplish It

artistic or stylistic one, but was rooted in the gospel, receiving theological support from the Christian claim that God's Word became flesh. This complementarity between form and task is related to his understanding of the Christian belief in the incarnation, which lead Kierkegaard to adopt the form of *hiddenness* in his authorship.[8]

THE KING WHO LOVED A HUMBLE MAIDEN

In this parable we are given an insight into Kierkegaard's understanding of the gospel.[9] Although Kierkegaard distances himself from this work by employing a pseudonym to articulate it,[10] Kierkegaard's veronymous writings as well as his own authorial practice are sympathetic to such an analogy. Through examining this analogy we will suggest how this can be understood to give rise to the form of Kierkegaard's authorship.

As a way of portraying the love of "the god" for "the learner" in Christianity,[11] Climacus employs an analogy in the form of a fairytale. Beyond mere unity of the parties concerned, love requires *understanding*. Climacus endeavors to suggest how the love of God for an individual becomes understood in Christianity.[12] In this illustration, the King could not make his love for the maiden known to his subjects because they would force the maiden into meeting the King's desires. Such love would become "unhappy" and distorted in this lack of equality. Likewise, the King *elevating* the maiden to an equal status with himself would also result in the

---

8. This is similar to the thesis expounded by Joel Rasmussen, who convincingly demonstrates that Kierkegaard undertakes a "Christomorphic poetics," that is, that Kierkegaard's emphasis of the correlation between form and content is derived from Christ embodying the ideal sought after in human attempts at the poetic. See Rasmussen, *Between Irony and Witness*, e.g., "The theological heart of Kierkegaard's reinterpretation and harmonization of the Romantic ideal of 'living poetically' and the traditionalist understanding of 'true art,' therefore, is that the reconciliation of the actual to the ideal to which poetry purportedly attests finds its fulfillment not in any human art, but in God's poem" (ibid., 10–11).

9. Kierkegaard, "Philosophical Crumbs," 102ff.

10. The significance of such distancing we will explore below in Part II and III.

11. This view, as we will explore below, is part of Climacus' "thought project" which contrasts the Socratic view of truth and the conditions through which it is "acquired," and a view that is presented as logically derived in opposition to the Socratic, which is easily recognized by the reader as an articulation of the gospel of Christianity.

12. Kierkegaard, "Philosophical Crumbs," 101. Also, "[t]he poet's task is to find a solution, a point of union where there is true understanding in love," (ibid., 104).

misunderstanding of his love, as the maiden would be compelled—both internally and externally—to be in the debt of her lover. This would not elicit a genuine love that is concerned with the King for his own sake. The maiden would cease to be herself, and would instead become conscious of her debt to the King. Although the maiden would be satisfied in forgetting herself and in serving the King in all his glory, this would not satisfy the King "because he does not wish his own glorification, but the girl's."[13]

Climacus sees the solution as one where the King would come down to the level of the maiden, where the King would disguise himself as a lowly commoner and attempt to win her affection on an equal footing—free from the trappings of power-relations, thus steering away from demand or coercion by the King, and emphasizing the risky and vulnerable invitation in which all the power of the decision is given to the humble maiden. In this sense, the *form* of such an invitation becomes vital. It is here that Climacus uses the New Testament phrase "in the form of a servant" to establish in the mind of the reader a direct link to the incarnation of God in Jesus Christ.[14] It is here that we begin in our understanding of the key concept of "hiddenness."

Although this "thought experiment" is undertaken in the name of a pseudonym, this account of the gospel can easily be seen to be consistent with Kierkegaard's own belief as is illustrated in his explicit emphases on "the single individual" and "hidden inwardness."[15] More significantly, this concept of hiddenness is outworked in the *form* of Kierkegaard's authorship. Because God did not primarily demand allegiance through appearing *directly* in all his glory, but instead sought to win the genuine love of each and every person through *hiding* himself and making himself our equal (or even less than this),[16] Christianity is a humble and vulnerable invitation from God. The shift here is from Christianity being seen as a matter of status or intellectual ascent, to it being understood as God inviting each and every person into a subjective (i.e., *personal*) relationship with himself. In order for the individual to understand this in such an intimate way, the *form* of the gospel becomes the all-important emphasis for Kierkegaard.

---

13. Ibid., 104.

14. Ibid., 106–7, cf. Phil 2:7.

15. Two brief examples of Kierkegaard conveying (in his own name) a similar understanding of the gospel are Kierkegaard, *Journals and Papers*, 2/1389, X1 A 408, n.d., 1849 and ibid., 1/301, IV A 33, n.d., 1843.

16. See Phil 2:6–8 especially.

0.2 Kierkegaard's Task and How He Sought to Accomplish It

This is the theological basis for Kierkegaard's paying special attention to the *form* of communicating the gospel. This led him to realize that the form his evangelistic authorship must take was that of *hiddenness*.

THE HIDDENNESS OF THE GOSPEL—GOD HIDDEN IN CHRIST

For Kierkegaard, the idea that God became a human being was, paradoxically, a revelation of the hiddenness of God.[17] This *hidden* revelation was not simply a subsidiary characteristic of the Christian gospel.[18] As Kierkegaard attempted to demonstrate through Climacus, the *means* through which God revealed himself in Christ was necessary for God to win humanity (each person as a "single individual") to himself. What appeared to deeply concern Kierkegaard was God's love for humanity. He was attempting to explain that God revealing himself directly in all his glory would be incompatible with God's *telos* of love.[19] Such directness appeals to the ability of human reason to grasp God's love for the human learner, but this is impossible. Through both Climacus and Anti-Climacus, Kierkegaard strove to show how an understanding of God's love requires the precondition of faith to understand and believe that the particular, lowly human being of Jesus is God.[20] Such a fact is paradoxical to human reason. Climacus therefore calls it "the Absolute Paradox" which transcends worldly ways of knowing, and is only recognizable by those who have the eyes of faith.[21] It is only through faith that a person can come to know God's love for herself and this very faith relies on the hiddenness of God.[22] Even separated by two thousand

---

17. Craig Hinkson suggests that there was an "affinity" with Luther's thought in Kierkegaard during the time of the writing of *Philosophical Fragments*, and direct influence only came three years afterward in 1847. See Hinkson, "Luther and Kierkegaard," 29–30. Hinkson uses the following journal entry in support of this: Kierkegaard, *Journals and Papers*, 3/2463, VIII1 A 465, n.d., 1847. A key difference is that for Luther, hiddenness is related to Christ crucified rather than the wider event of the incarnation, which Kierkegaard emphasizes. See McGrath, *Luther's Theology of the Cross*, 161–75.

18. As Murray Rae helpfully articulates: "Kierkegaard insists that 'the surroundings of actuality' are not incidental to but constitute the truth itself" (Rae, *Kierkegaard and Theology*, 63).

19. See Kierkegaard, "Philosophical Crumbs," 100–101.

20. Ibid., 119; cf. Kierkegaard, *Practice in Christianity*, 125–36, etc.

21. Chapter 3 in Kierkegaard, "Philosophical Crumbs," 111–25.

22. Hinkson, "Luther and Kierkegaard," 32, cf. Kierkegaard, "Philosophical Crumbs,"

years, the same faith is required to recognize God in Christ. As Climacus explores further in *Concluding Postscript to Philosophical Fragments*, such historical categories of knowing are irrelevant to knowing God "in truth."[23] To be contemporaneous with Christ is not a relationship that concerns history—it is only through faith that a person is made contemporary with Christ.[24]

Therefore, Kierkegaard understood that the *form* of the gospel is absolutely vital to it being understood correctly and believed that the particular form intrinsic to the gospel is "hiddenness." As one who sought to communicate this gospel he endeavored to undertake this form in his own authorship.

POUL MARTIN MØLLER

The impact of Professor Poul Martin Møller on the development of Kierkegaard's interest in the relation between form and content is important to recognize. Møller was an unconventional teacher whose admiration of Socrates was influential for Kierkegaard. Møller sought to embody his belief in the importance of a life's relation to what was taught, so his philosophy "was lived out in conversations in the market square and with ordinary people."[25] However, this method presented a problem for Kierkegaard as his follower, who "feared, not without reason, that when Møller was no longer able to support his ideas with his own living personality—and thereby *demonstrate* their legitimacy—posterity would be unable to sense the scope of his contribution to a philosophy of living."[26] Kierkegaard embraced similar convictions to Møller in terms of the importance of form and subjective pathos (passions) in communication but, just as Kierkegaard extended his friend's Socratic ideas, he also extended Møller's form of communicating them.[27] Kierkegaard sought to improve on Møller's method of indirect,

---

107, 131–34.

23. E.g., Kierkegaard, *Concluding Unscientific Postscript*, 95–96.

24. This is the main subject of the latter part of Kierkegaard, "Philosophical Crumbs," 125–73; see also Anti-Climacus' discussion in Kierkegaard, *Practice in Christianity*, 62–66 especially.

25. Rae, *Kierkegaard and Theology*, 20.

26. Garff, *Søren Kierkegaard*, 91.

27. ". . . they were equal but their roles quite different: Møller as a Socratic deliverer of ideas that seemed perhaps to be there already, and Kierkegaard developing them further"

0.2 Kierkegaard's Task and How He Sought to Accomplish It

lived communication, shifting it from being outworked primarily through the medium of live performance to literature.[28]

Whatever Møller may have encouraged or even initiated in Kierkegaard, it is the New Testament that led Kierkegaard to see a more substantial foundation for understanding the significance of the relation between form and content in the Christian event of the incarnation. This theological foundation gave rise to Kierkegaard pursuing a form of authorship that was characterized by *hiddenness*.[29] By being roused to the importance of form's relation to content through Socrates and Møller, Kierkegaard found the fulfillment of such congruence in the gospel. The particular shape this congruence took was the *hidden* invitation of God to the individual.

BEING HIDDEN "IN THE TRUTH"

In summary, Kierkegaard saw *form* (not merely content) as being a vital factor in communication. He ultimately saw such congruence between form and content as being embodied in the incarnation of the God-Man, who came *hidden* "in the form of a servant."[30] Thus in communicating the gospel, Kierkegaard understood that his communication must likewise be undertaken in hiddenness in order to complement and preserve the subjective invitation of God. Before we conclude this chapter, one final point of clarification is necessary.

Søren Kierkegaard fundamentally understood that his entire life was *hidden* in Christ, and that Christ himself was the truth.[31] Therefore, attempting to undertake his authorial task through the form of hiddenness was not only necessary for his outward communication, but was itself an

---

(Jensen, "Poul Martin Møller," 116–17).

28. I do not have space to defend this suggestion here or to look into it further, but I put it forward as a helpful view for further research. A good place to start would be ibid., section C: "Fragments on Irony and Nihilism," starting on p. 128.

29. The influence of Møller on Kierkegaard's authorial form is one that I regret I have not had the time to investigate further.

30. "Form" and "content" relate to Kierkegaard's categories of "actuality" and "ideality," used well by Joel Rasmussen in his discussion of Kierkegaard's "Christomorphic Poetics," in Rasmussen, *Between Irony and Witness*, e.g., 48: "If poetry reconciles an imperfect actuality to its perfect ideal in a merely imaginative fashion, then a reconciliation between an individual's imperfect actuality and the divine ideal for that individual should be achievable not through writing poetry but by living poetically."

31. Kierkegaard, "Two Discourses," 418–26.

outworking of his own Christian discipleship.[32] Striving after Christ is to strive after the truth, who is also the way: "only then do I in truth know the truth, when it becomes a life in me."[33] For Kierkegaard, the truth is embodied: it is characterized by a congruence between form and content, where the believer strives to be who she is, that is, hidden in Christ.[34] And because Christ is the only truly congruent one, the *communication* of his truth is to be *in* the truth: that is, to be *hidden* in Christ.

Thus, this is my thesis:

> *Through Kierkegaard's understanding of the gospel, his authorship took the form of hiddenness.*

CONCLUSION

In this chapter we have sought to establish a link between Kierkegaard's understanding of Christianity and his own life's task as an author. Through examining his understanding of the Christian doctrine of the incarnation, we have seen that this formed the basis for his understanding of the necessity of the congruence between form and content. So we have seen that Kierkegaard's belief of God being *hidden* in the particular person of Jesus necessitated Kierkegaard's own authorial form of *hiddenness*. Now we turn to look in greater detail at that which Kierkegaard was reacting to.

---

32. Kierkegaard, *Practice in Christianity*, 202–7.
33. Ibid., 206, cf. John 14:6.
34. This will become clearer through our discussion below in 1.3: "Christomorphic Poetics."

Part I: The Content

This section gives an overview of some key concepts of Kierkegaard's that are common themes throughout the authorship. I will survey the concepts of outwardness, "the single individual," and truth in particular, giving special emphasis to how the concept of hiddenness relates to each. Because Kierkegaard valued the congruence between form and content, we cannot understand the form of Kierkegaard's authorship apart from its content. Like the analogy of the "circle" or "spiral" in hermeneutics where there is an ongoing interaction between pre-understandings and encountering a text, the student of Kierkegaard must constantly go between *what* is said and *how* it is said in order to approach a full understanding.[1] Firstly, we will briefly explore these concepts themselves in order to illustrate how they impact Kierkegaard's authorship of hiddenness.

---

1. In this way, what the student engages with is not only the subject matter, but also the form in which it is presented. For a critical engagement with the concept of "hermeneutical circle" in relation to Friedrich Schleiermacher, see Thiselton, *The Two Horizons*, 103–14; see also Gadamer, *Truth and Method*, 292–93; though such an understanding needs to be broadened to include considering language as a "form of life," where the entire communicative act is considered. For instance, see Wittgenstein, *Investigations*, 19, §11; and Wittgenstein, "Philosophy of Psychology," in *Philosophical Investigations*, 327, §235, as well as the field of pragmatics and speech-act theory. This matter is far beyond the scope of this work.

1.1 The Problems of Outwardness and Direct Communication

INTRODUCTION

Kierkegaard's task was directly opposed to outwardness. Therefore, he saw direct communication as being unhelpful and largely opposed to his task. In this section we begin with an overview of Kierkegaard's use of the terms "Christendom" and "the crowd" and how he used them in reference to his outwardly focused society. To illustrate, we will contrast these ideas with Kierkegaard's use of Abraham, in order to understand the dangers of outwardness in regard to making oneself understood. We will then explore in greater detail Kierkegaard's problem with outwardness in his critique of Hegelian thought, contrasting this with Kierkegaard's understanding of the *inwardness* of a person's relation with God. This chapter concludes with a discussion of the incompatibility of direct communication with Kierkegaard's task of hiddenness.

CHRISTENDOM AND THE CROWD

For Kierkegaard the most problematic manifestation of the danger of outwardness was the religious culture of Denmark which claimed to be Christian, named by him as "Christendom." This social phenomenon perpetuated the illusion that outward ritual and Christian practice (particularly the collective identity of Denmark naming itself "a Christian nation") established a member of the Danish public as Christian and that relating to God occurred *en masse*.¹ Kierkegaard saw outwardness being valued in Christendom, with little thought given to inward subjectivity.² In contrast, Kierkegaard understood Christianity to be *entirely* a matter of inwardness, and therefore such a fixation on the outward was antithetical to the gospel.³

As Climacus' caricature comically portrays, there was little acceptance for those who doubted their automatic Christian status:

> If [a doubter] were married, his wife would tell him, "Hubby, darling, where did you ever pick up such a notion? How can you not be a Christian? You are Danish, aren't you? Doesn't the geography book say that the predominant religion in Denmark is Lutheran-Christian? You aren't a Jew, are you, or a Mohammedan? What else would you be, then? It is a thousand years since paganism was superseded; so I know you aren't a pagan. Don't you tend to your work in the office as a good civil servant; aren't you a good subject in a Christian nation, in a Lutheran-Christian state? So of course you are a Christian."⁴

In his short essay "For the Dedication to 'That Single Individual,'" Kierkegaard named "the crowd" as untruth.⁵ This is particularly in reference to the press-culture of Copenhagen in his day where feuds of the literary elite were fought using various pseudonyms—the most destructive of which Kierkegaard claimed was "Anonymous."⁶ With this disembodied mask, any person could say whatever he wished, abdicating all responsibility of bearing what was said in his own life.⁷ As Kierkegaard went on to explain, such a surrender of individual responsibility gives up one's birthright to be a "single individual"⁸—to be their own person before God—and instead reduces himself to a member of "the crowd." Such a fracture between form

---

1. See especially Kierkegaard, "For the Dedication," 105–12.

2. That Kierkegaard later saw his fellow Danes using his concept of hidden inwardness to justify their own outward inaction will be discussed below in 1.2: "Hidden Inwardness As Individualism?"

3. Kierkegaard, *Works of Love*, 31.

4. Kierkegaard, *Concluding Unscientific Postscript*, 50–51.

5. Søren Kierkegaard, "For the Dedication," 105–12.

6. See Storm, "II: Kierkegaard's Authorial Dialectic"; Pattison, "Kierkegaard as Feuilleton Writer," 126 n. 2; see also Mackey, *Kierkegaard*, 247.

7. Kierkegaard, "For the Dedication," 110–11.

8. This concept of Kierkegaard's is to be taken at face value, and will be discussed further below.

and content, actuality and ideality, words and life was not only restricted to the press, but was the criticism which Kierkegaard leveled at his entire society, especially the intellectual elite.[9]

"The crowd" was Kierkegaard's most vulgar reference to the problems of the outwardness of his society. It is here that a person measured himself according to the perceptions of his peers and does his best to make himself *intelligible* to those who surround him. Kierkegaard strove to show that this was sinful, in two key ways. The first was that it replaced God with the idol of "the crowd," where the world became a person's object of concern.[10] Instead of deriving ethics, truth, and their identity from God, "the crowd" became the authority for the person.[11] It also abdicates responsibility—for Kierkegaard this was particularly in the form of negating the importance of integrity between one's words and actions. For Kierkegaard, this was a definition of sin.[12]

ETHICS AND UNDERSTANDING

In *Fear and Trembling*, Kierkegaard explored the biblical story of Abraham being called by God to sacrifice his only son. Kierkegaard suggested to the reader that she has likely forgotten the real "shock-factor" of the story—that is, that Abraham went beyond ethics and therefore beyond intelligibility in order to be obedient to God and become "the father of the faith."[13] His "risk of obedience" meant that he was willing to be seen as the murderer of his own son.[14] Kierkegaard reminded his reader that Abraham's role within this story is too often only seen retrospectively as the exemplary undertaking of a test of faith, without seeing the depth of anxiety and horror that Abraham experienced in order to be obedient to God.[15] Kierkegaard sought to reveal the incompatibility of Christian scripture (and its hold-

9. This is most clearly seen in the pseudonymous *Concluding Unscientific Postscript*.

10. See "The Anxiety Caused By Being in Two Minds," originally from 1848's *Christian Discourses*, published as chapter 9 in Kierkegaard, *Spiritual Writings*, 165–77.

11. Kierkegaard, "For the Dedication," 109.

12. Rasmussen, *Between Irony and Witness*, 52, 58, 71; see also Kierkegaard, *Concept of Irony*, 280–81.

13. "There were countless generations that knew the story of Abraham by heart, word for word. How many did it make sleepless?" (Kierkegaard, *Fear and Trembling*, 28).

14. The phrase "risk of obedience" is taken from Rae, "The Risk of Obedience," 308.

15. "Kierkegaard intends the reader to experience in Fear and Trembling the tension of truly Christian ethics" (Hall, "Self-deception," 40).

ing up Abraham as an heroic example) with that of Kant's *Religion Within the Limits of Reason Alone*.[16] Abraham cannot be understood through the universal language of ethics; Abraham is alone before God.[17]

The horror with which Kierkegaard sought to reacquaint his reader was already in the biblical story: how Abraham was called to sacrifice his only son, "Isaac whom he loved," by the very God who had given him. Abraham could not make this command (which was *hidden* in his own heart) intelligible to others, as they would simply dismiss this call as a dangerous construction of an unhealthy mind and attempt to stop him from fulfilling this command. Abraham was utterly alone before a terrible God, and the journey to Mt Moriah took three days riding on the back of a donkey.[18] As Kierkegaard's pseudonym Johannes De Silentio comments, "no one was as great as Abraham; who is able to understand him?"[19]

De Silentio discusses this story in terms of a "teleological suspension of the ethical." Abraham did not simply dismiss his understanding of what was right and wrong and all reason in favor of a "higher" ethics of divine command,[20] but instead put this understanding on hold.[21] De Silentio's portrayal of Abraham is that he somehow believed that God would make this action right, but could not foresee how. Abraham therefore acted in faith that *God* would be the one who would make things right; he acted out of the belief that justice was fundamentally in the hands of God and not in his own.[22] He did not abandon ethics, but instead left ethics in the hands

16. See Rae, "The Risk of Obedience," 313.

17. Cf. Kierkegaard, *Fear and Trembling*, 139.

18. "Some understand the story of Abraham in another way. They praise God's mercy for giving him Isaac once again, the whole thing was just a trial. A trial—that can say a lot or little, yet the whole thing is as quickly done with as said. One mounts a winged horse, that very instant one is on the mountain in Moriah, the same instant one sees the ram. One forgets that Abraham rode on an ass, which can keep up no more than a leisurely pace, that he had a three-day journey, that he needed time to chop the firewood, bind Isaac, and sharpen the knife" (ibid., 59–60).

19. Ibid., 13.

20. See John J. Davenport on an introduction to a (mis)reading of *Fear and Trembling* by Alasdair MacIntyre and others, who reduce "Kierkegaardian faith to blind fanaticism" in "Faith as Eschatological Trust in Fear and Trembling," 196–98.

21. "Problema I" in Kierkegaard, *Fear and Trembling*, 62–79.

22. Contra the humanistic ethics of Kant: "The implication of Kant's confidence is that the deliverances of practical reason enable us to know good from evil with incontrovertible assurance, and further, that this is just the same thing as seeing with the eye of God. One might imagine it possible to claim the support of Genesis 3.5 for Kant's

1.1 The Problems of Outwardness and Direct Communication

of God, trusting that he would receive Isaac back from the dead, whether in his own lifetime or not.[23] John Davenport therefore argues that "the main point of *Fear and Trembling* . . . is to present the essence of 'faith' as *eschatological* trust."[24]

The key point is that Abraham's anguish was *hidden*—it was an inward reality which could not be justified outside of his own *subjective* call by God. Abraham was alone. He could not appeal to the universal common ground of ethics to make himself understood by anyone, unlike De Silentio's portrayal of "the tragic hero." For such a tragic hero, to make a sacrifice for "the greater good" (e.g., for the salvation of an entire people) is all too understandable and praiseworthy to the onlooking public. It is an outward act of heroism and easily gains the sympathy and admiration of "the crowd."[25] The anguish of Abraham's faith (that he "believed God, and it was credited to him as righteousness")[26] was completely subjective: it was *hidden*.

FEAR AND TREMBLING AND THE SPHERES OF EXISTENCE

A key series of concepts from Kierkegaard are his three "spheres of existence" which permeate his literature.[27] They are a way of categorizing different "life-views" according to a person's *telos*. The first sphere is the aesthetic: that pertaining to the immediate and the sensory. It is not necessarily vulgar, but is limited to being concerned with the surface experiences of life. The second is the ethical: those who are concerned with doing what is right, that which is required of them either by God, society or both. The

---

position, 'when you eat of the tree of the knowledge of good and evil your eyes will be opened, and you will be like God.' But that, of course, is the serpent's argument." (Rae, "The Risk of Obedience," 313).

23. Cf. Heb 11:19.

24. Davenport, "Faith as Eschatological Trust," 198, italics author's own.

25. "When at the decisive moment Agamemnon, Jephthah, and Brutus heroically overcome their pain, have heroically given up the loved one, and have only the outward deed to perform, then never a noble soul in the world will there be but sheds tears of sympathy for their pain, tears of admiration for their deed" (Kierkegaard, *Fear and Trembling*, 68).

26. Rom 4:3, cf. Gen 15:6.

27. The work dedicated to these "spheres" or "stages" is Kierkegaard, *Stages on Life's Way*.

third is the religious: that "single individual" who is concerned with God and God alone.[28]

In light of our discussion on *Fear and Trembling*, the sphere called "the ethical" can be dangerous to "the religious" because it can take a person away from her own subjective relationship with God. This happens when an individual substitutes their own "hidden inwardness" with the values and expectations of society: thus pursuing the idol of the outward, rather than God alone. In this sense, ethics based on the conventions of society can often be marred by self-righteousness, or the need to be esteemed by either the self or a neighbor, rather than by God. This is the danger of the ethical sphere for Christianity: the danger of outwardness. The ethical is understandable, justifiable, visible—*outward*. But *it has no necessary link to what is inward*. For Kierkegaard it was this *inwardness* that is everything for the Christian. Kierkegaard used Abraham to illustrate the radical nature of living out of the "religious" sphere of life, in which one is answerable to God alone, and which thus carries substantial risks. To be a Christian is to be alone; to be *hidden* from the understanding of others. To reduce Christianity to a matter of outwardness is to destroy what really counts and to reveal to others what must remain hidden in God.[29]

THE DANGER OF WORLDLINESS

A persistent theme throughout Kierkegaard's religious works is the danger of worldliness and fearing "the world" instead of fearing God.[30] That is, the danger of living according to the logic and expectations of "the world" or "the crowd" rather than according to what God requires of an individual.[31]

---

28. Sylvia Walsh helpfully points out that each progressive stage of existence does not exclude matters of the lower, but reforms them. Therefore, the religious is concerned with such things as art and doing what is right, but such things are reworked and reoriented to the ultimate ends of serving God. See her *Living Poetically*. For a more detailed introduction into Kierkegaard's "spheres" or "stages of existence," see Evans, *Kierkegaard's Fragments and Postscript*, 11–16.

29. Such aloneness and an inability to make oneself understood is what Kierkegaard himself claims to have experienced in his authorial task. See Kierkegaard, *Point of View*, 75.

30. E.g., Kierkegaard, *Works of Love*, 124, 187; and Part II in ch 10: "Silence, Obedience, and Joy," in Kierkegaard, *Spiritual Writings*, 196–213 originally published in 1849 as *The Lily of the Field and the Bird Under Heaven*.

31. "To know God requires that we become 'Godly.' We must learn to fear him, to be observant in his presence, and then we also realize what he is. For the God of Abraham,

1.1 The Problems of Outwardness and Direct Communication

Kierkegaard saw his society as a mob, chasing what was fashionable intellectually. He advocated for each person to take responsibility for owning her own beliefs and understandings. Instead of measuring herself by others and popular philosophical positions, Kierkegaard claimed that true selfhood was found in relating to God and God alone.[32]

Kierkegaard typically named Hegel as the figurehead of the trend of systematic speculative thought and the pseudo-Christianity that was derived from it. Followers in the Danish public were more concerned with making Christianity comprehensible to fashionable thinking than they were with God himself. They sought security in "the crowd" rather than their own hidden relationship with God which was completely removed from public concerns. As a corrective, Kierkegaard sought to emphasize the gospel which he understood to speak to the individual and *not* "the crowd."[33] That is, the individual is to live in the religious sphere by being concerned with the approval of God alone.

Kierkegaard frequently discredited attempts to establish Christianity externally, such as through appeals to the historical sciences.[34] This is true also of his signed *Works of Love*, where he often commented on the illusion of the external in terms of ethics. For instance, he wrote that the act of mercy is an internal matter of the heart and is completely irrelevant to the external ways in which it manifests itself. The act of mercy is equally available to the poor as well as to the rich, and the external manifestation of this inwardness is an illusion and can only serve to distract and tempt one away

---

Isaac, and Jacob, and of our Lord, Jesus Christ, is not truly known if he is not feared. This is why Kierkegaard said, and I believe truly, that Christianity requires inwardness. For fearing God means that the fears of others and of the world are cast out; but more, it becomes plainly silly to defy the Almighty God in any respect whatsoever" (Holmer, *The Grammar of Faith*, 211).

32. C. Stephen Evans rightly argues that Kierkegaard advocated for a selfhood being relational, but only through the God-relationship: "Not only is God the ontological foundation of the self; God is also the highest ethical task, in the sense that the highest form of selfhood requires a conscious relation to God." This then forms the basis for a healthy relating to others: ". . . though the God-relation is not merely a means to bettering human social arrangements, it ultimately must be seen as functioning so as to humanize those arrangements." It is in this way that Evans successfully deals with the critique of individualism so frequently leveled against Kierkegaard, such as that by Buber and others (Evans, "Who Is the Other?," 272–73).

33. " . . . when the gospel speaks it speaks to the single individual" (Kierkegaard, *Works of Love*, 31).

34. This is most particularly the case in Kierkegaard, *Concluding Unscientific Postscript*.

from the inward truth of mercy.[35] Kierkegaard's concept of "the single individual" is completely inward (subjective), and the only relevance or truth of Christianity is one that is true for "the single individual." The reduction of Christianity to the outwardness of doctrinal, intellectual or systematic forms is fundamentally flawed. Christianity is only rooted and grounded in faith—hidden in the heart of the individual believer. Pathos (the appropriate movement of the heart) must accompany and characterize the Christian life. As Holmer claims: "to have knowledge of God you must fear him and you must love him. There is no knowledge of God otherwise."[36]

HEGEL AND THE HEARTLESS SYSTEM

Søren Kierkegaard was deeply disturbed by the way in which Hegelian thought was being used to subsume Christianity within itself.[37] Such "speculative thought" placed its emphasis on the construction of an exhaustive, all-inclusive system which could understand all things—including human existence and the actions of God.[38] Kierkegaard saw in this the danger of reducing all of reality to the outward, with no space left for inward reflection and a person's own subjective existence.

Kierkegaard linked outwardness with immediacy, and saw immediacy as an illusion which inhibited interaction with the deeper reality of the eternal—that which only could be reached by subjective inwardness.[39] Kierkegaard understood that speculative thought with its emphasis on objectivity had its place in particular disciplines such as science and history. However what he saw as being fundamentally important (an individual's relation with God and her own self—*essential* truths concerning existence) could only be taken up and known by each person as a "single individual." In contrast to this, Kierkegaard saw how the Danish Hegelians were seeking

---

35. See part 2, chapter 7: "Mercifulness, a Work of Love, Even if It Can Give Nothing and Is Capable of Doing Nothing," in Kierkegaard, *Works of Love*, 292–305.

36. Holmer, *The Grammar of Faith*, 25; also: "Being religious is, however, being involved, being concerned, being a qualitatively different person. If a language claim, even about God, is believed to be true, there is nothing in that kind of assent to its claim that is productive of religiousness" (Holmer, *On Kierkegaard and the Truth*, 69).

37. Many scholars now see that the primary target of Kierkegaard's satire are Danish Hegelians, not so much Hegel himself. For instance, see Poole, *Kierkegaard*, 2; and Stewart, *Kierkegaard's Relations*.

38. See Rasmussen, *Between Irony and Witness*, 100.

39. See Kierkegaard, *Practice in Christianity*, 124–25.

1.1 The Problems of Outwardness and Direct Communication

to incorporate Christianity into their systems, moving "beyond" simplistic faith for the sake of progress.[40] This was the main target of Kierkegaard's attack on outwardness: the marriage of Hegelian thought and the church (or the church playing the harlot with Hegel), where philosophy was transgressing its limits.

Kierkegaard was advocating for theology to be recognized as a separate and vital realm of knowing for ethical and religious matters. He sought to remove the confusion that such personal knowing was contingent on scientific, objective knowledge such as that espoused by Hegelian thought.[41] Paul Holmer suggests that such rationalistic thinking was common to the point of being "almost indigenous to the intelligentsia" and that Hegel was targeted by Kierkegaard merely as the one who expounded this "intellectualist-myth" in "technical language and with the help of erstwhile dialectical and logical tools." In contrast to such literary practice, Kierkegaard sought to talk "sensibly and truly about concepts and behavior in . . . various areas," instead of subsuming all things under the rubric of science or history.[42] All of human life cannot be reduced to the descriptive "about," it must also contain the "of"; theology is the kind of knowing that must be embodied in a life.[43] This is Kierkegaard's point about the importance of subjectivity for "the single individual," and no amount of *outward* knowing "about" can summon the inwardness that Christianity demands.

Knowing "of" is the knowing which embodies what is known.[44] A characteristic of such knowing is no mere change of mind, but is "a transi-

---

40. Kierkegaard, *Fear and Trembling*; see also Antony Aumann on the work of the Danish Hegelian H. L. Martensen in "Kierkegaard's Case," chap. 2: "The Speculative Project."

41. There are innumerable parallels here with Michael Polanyi's thought, though he does not refer to Kierkegaard in his major work: *Personal Knowledge*. Such a link could be made via the thought of Bernard Lonergan, who shares affinities with both Polanyi and Kierkegaard. See Fitzpatrick, "Subjectivity and Objectivity," 64–74; Morelli, *Anxiety*.

42. Holmer, *On Kierkegaard and the Truth*, 120.

43. Holmer, *The Grammar of Faith*, 25. "In so far as Christianity can be 'said' at all, theology and Scripture say it. But what is therein said, be it the words of eternal life, be it creeds, or be it the words of Jesus Himself, we must note that like grammar and logic, their aim is not that we repeat the words. Theology must also be absorbed, and when it is, the hearer is supposed to become Godly."

44. As a negative example: "Therefore an understanding of evil (however much one tries to make himself and *others* think that one can keep himself entirely pure, that there is a pure understanding of evil) nevertheless *involves* an *understanding with* evil" (Kierkegaard, *Works of Love*, 266, emphasis author's own).

tion in existence" which is "pathos-filled."[45] Johannes Climacus is a pseudonym which Kierkegaard employed to ridicule Hegelian thought and the "intellectualist-myth." His *Concluding Unscientific Postscript* carries the subtitle "a mimical-*pathetical-dialectical* compilation,"[46] suggesting it to be "a study of both passions and concepts."[47] Climacus was against outward objectivity at the point when it excluded subjectivity, and fundamental to subjectivity was pathos, or the passions.[48] Kierkegaard used Climacus to argue that when it came to fundamental matters of existence, the ideal of having an "informed opinion" was both impossible and inhuman: a person must *choose* how she will live. This is because the goalposts are always shifting; a person cannot abstract herself outside of her own existing in order to see what she is to do *with* her existing.[49] Climacus argues that a distinctive of humanity is the need for impassioned commitment that functions *alongside* reasoned knowledge and gives direction to it in relation to essential matters.[50] This is why Climacus' writing, although carefully logical, is also filled with the pathos appropriate to his use of the subject matter,[51] for instance Climacus' illustration of the madman who sought to prove himself sane by continually repeating the universal objective truth claim "The earth is round." Such humor is an appropriate companion to Climacus' argument

45. Evans, *Kierkegaard's Fragments and Postscript*, 46.
46. Kierkegaard, *Concluding Unscientific Postscript*, 1, my emphasis.
47. Holmer, *On Kierkegaard and the Truth*, 4.
48. Kierkegaard's use of "passion" is articulated by C. Stephen Evans as being akin to the notion of "value": an enduring care that "must be developed and acquired," rather than a fleeting feeling. "The individual does decide for himself, but he cannot value what he knows is valueless; there must be a basis or root for his caring concern. Passions must be 'called forth'" (*Kierkegaard's Fragments and Postscript*, 39).
49. Hence Kierkegaard's repeated repudiation of the attempt to view humanity *sub specie aeterni* ("from the aspect of eternity"). See also Kierkegaard, *Concluding Unscientific Postscript*, 196: "Here it is not forgotten, even for a single moment, that the subject is existing, and that existing is a becoming, and that truth as the identity of thought and being is therefore a chimera of abstraction and truly only a longing of creation, not because truth is not an identity, but because the knower is an existing person, and thus truth cannot be an identity for him as long as he exists..."; this necessity of choice is also the big idea behind Kierkegaard's first key work *Either/Or*.
50. Just as mistrust is "a misuse of knowledge ... Love is the very opposite of mistrust, and yet is initiated in the same knowledge. In knowledge the two are, so to speak, not distinguished from each other (in the ultimate understanding knowledge is indifferent); only in conclusion and decision, *in faith* (to believe all things, to believe nothing), are they directly opposite to one another" (Kierkegaard, *Works of Love*, 214–16).
51. However, as we shall see, this is not a demonstration of a Christian use.

1.1 The Problems of Outwardness and Direct Communication

against those "assistant professors" who would demand a purely objective basis for any knowledge.[52]

Although Climacus affirms the necessity of pathos, he cannot (as an unbeliever) bring himself to have faith, which another pseudonym regards as "the infinite passion" or "the passion of infinity."[53] In knowing that "no conviction warranted by detached and rational argument [can] simultaneously move the thinker from detachment to attachment, from disinterestedness to interestedness,"[54] and that faith is given by God alone, the reader of Climacus is left waiting. This author can draw his readers out of the illusion of outwardness, but he cannot give them what is fundamentally necessary. Kierkegaard understood this gifting to be the work of God alone. Therefore, this is the primary reason for Kierkegaard's rejection of the use of direct communication in matters relating to essential truth.

AUTHORSHIP AND OUTWARDNESS: THE PROBLEM OF DIRECT COMMUNICATION

Direct communication was incongruent with Kierkegaard's task for a number of reasons. Firstly, as we have discussed in regard to *Philosophical Fragments*, Kierkegaard saw that the nature of the gospel lends itself to a form of *hiddenness*. The invitation of Christianity is fragile and personal.[55] Therefore, to announce it "directly" transfers the purely subjective and intimate relation of God and the individual into the realm of impersonal objectivity. In other words, it misdirects the direct communication of God as it interferes and reroutes God's relation to the individual through the speaker. For instance, it becomes possible for a well-intentioned believer who mediates God's un-mediatable invitation to become a false prophet, *even if what they say is true*: their *speaking* reduces Christianity to a matter of outwardness.

---

52. Kierkegaard, *Concluding Unscientific Postscript*, 194–95.
53. As voiced by De Silentio: "Faith is the highest passion in a human being" (Kierkegaard, *Fear and Trembling*, 151).
54. Holmer, *On Kierkegaard and the Truth*, 3.
55. In Kierkegaard's words, "infinitely gentle" (*Point of View*, 16).

PART I: THE CONTENT

Thus, the speaker becomes one who speaks in untruth, and the believer believes through untruth.[56] The "how" of Christianity is everything.[57]

In order for a person to speak on God's behalf and to directly announce the invitation of God in Christ, Kierkegaard understood that such a speaker must have divine authority, which he himself did not have.[58] As we saw in the illustration of the King and the humble maiden, only the King could approach his love in order to make himself understood; any interference from the royal courtier would occasion a fatal distortion of the invitation. This is how direct communication misrepresents and ultimately distorts Christian truth.[59]

Additionally, there is the problem of the illusion of "Christendom." That is, the people whom Kierkegaard was seeking to address thought themselves to be already Christian. He feared that a direct communication of Christianity would be dismissed by his readers as irrelevant to themselves, so for the sake of "reintroducing Christianity into Christendom," he abandoned direct communication and instead "approached from behind."[60] The first step of Kierkegaard's task was to remove "the illusion that in such a country all are Christians of sorts" by employing *indirect* communication.[61]

---

56. "Just as important as the truth, and of the two the even more important one, is the mode in which the truth is accepted, and it is of slight help if one gets millions to accept the truth if by the very mode of their acceptance they are transposed into untruth" Kierkegaard, *Concluding Unscientific Postscript*, 247.

57. Cf. Ibid., I:202; Kierkegaard, *Journals and Papers*, 3/3684, X3 A 431, n.d., 1850.

58. E.g., Kierkegaard, *Point of View*, 12 n. 32. This phrase itself acted as an indirect critique of the institution of ordinancy in the Danish state church. For a more extensive discussion of Kierkegaard's concept of authority and its relation to existence-communication in ethico-religious matters, see Whittaker, "Kierkegaard on the Concept of Authority," 83–101; Cf. Kierkegaard's understanding of "witnessing." See Kierkegaard, *Journals and Papers*, 1/670, X1 A 235, n.d., 1849.

59. To use an example from modern day Christianity, we can see the problems of such direct communication of Christianity when a speaker gives a direct invitation to another person. The minister says, "Christ stands at the door of your heart: repent and believe! Put up your hand; come up the front and declare Jesus as your own personal savior!" and the church-goer feels a quickening of his heart, tears in his eyes, and submits to this invitation. If the minister is not commissioned by the spirit of God, then these symptoms are merely *outwardness* and have no correlation to the inward work of God within the individual.

60. Kierkegaard, *Point of View*, 42–43. As he helpfully illustrates elsewhere, if a person is starving to death but their mouth is so full of food that she cannot eat, the first thing to do is not to give her more food but rather to remove the food in her mouth. Kierkegaard, *Concluding Unscientific Postscript*, 275.

61. We shall explore this strategy further below in 2.1.

1.1 The Problems of Outwardness and Direct Communication

Direct communication was also incongruous for Kierkegaard because it discouraged the critical discernment that he saw as being necessary for those who read his work to become "single individuals." As a society which reduced life to a matter of "results," their interest was rather with the views of intellectual giants such as Hegel, who gave such results.[62] The hiddenness that Kierkegaard sought to communicate, however, was concerned just as much with the *how* as the *what*, and such a focus on results was therefore at odds with Kierkegaard's task. If Kierkegaard was to *directly* communicate arguments which opposed such objectivity and perhaps argued against Hegel by employing a similar didactical form to him, there would be a violent incongruence between the content and form of Kierkegaard's communication. He would fundamentally contradict *what* was communicated in *how* he communicated it. So in order to advocate for subjectivity and to overcome the difficulties of communicating Christianity, Kierkegaard sought to communicate the truth of hiddenness in a suitably hidden *form*: that is, *indirectly*.[63]

CONCLUSION

In this chapter I have outlined a number of problems which Kierkegaard associated with outwardness in relation to Christianity. For Kierkegaard, the outwardness of "Christendom" and "the crowd" were incompatible with the (infinitely) high demands of Christianity and actually served as temptations or distractions from living and communicating essential truth. Kierkegaard emphasized, through the story of Abraham and Isaac, the demand of inwardness for the believer and the incommunicable mystery of one's own hidden relationship with God as a "single individual." He also emphasized the need for an embodied knowing regarding Christianity and therefore rejected the "intellectualist-myth," and its form of direct

---

62. This can be seen most clearly in his discussion of subjectivity in *Concluding Unscientific Postscript*. For example, "objective thinking invests everything in the result and assists all humankind to cheat by copying and reeling off the results and answers, subjective thinking invests everything in the process of becoming and omits the result, partly because this belongs to him, since he possesses the way, partly because he as existing is continually in the process of becoming, as is every human being who has not permitted himself to be tricked into becoming objective, into inhumanly becoming speculative thought" (73).

63. See also "§ 3: The Impossibility of Direct Communication," in Kierkegaard, *Practice in Christianity*, 133–36.

communication. In order to "reintroduce Christianity into Christendom," Kierkegaard understood that his task must not only address these dangers of outwardness, but actively oppose them in the very *form* that his corrective took: that is, a form of hiddenness.

1.2 "The Single Individual"

INTRODUCTION

Kierkegaard's corrective to his outwardly driven society was to emphasize the absolute claim that Christianity makes on each and every person *inwardly*. This point was summed up in Kierkegaard's phrase "the single individual," which constituted the key concept for Kierkegaard's reintroduction of Christianity into Christendom. We will explore this concept and how it was used as a contextual corrective by Kierkegaard. Out of this understanding of Kierkegaard's view of a human person, we will then consider a critique frequently made of Kierkegaard because of his concept of "the single individual": the critique of individualism.

"THE SINGLE INDIVIDUAL": A CONTEXTUAL RESPONSE

It is important to note that Kierkegaard's authorship and its accompanying concepts were not an absolute and definitive account of what he believed or understood. His works were always *in response to* the context in which he found himself. Much like Wittgenstein, who believed that philosophy was a tool to use in relation to something and not a goal or thing *per se*, Kierkegaard's thought cannot be removed from that with which he was concerned, i.e., the realization of "the single individual."[1] Therefore one should not be too quick to judge Kierkegaard as being overly individualistic, with no place for human interrelations and society—his work was a polemic corrective for the "mob mentality" that plagued his Copenhagen.[2] But more

---

1. Cf. Creegan, *Wittgenstein and Kierkegaard*, 12.
2. "[Kierkegaard's] authorship is a polemical corrective to the problems of the age.

than this, Kierkegaard anticipated such critiques and attempted to address them within his work.

As George Pattison helpfully articulates, "Kierkegaard is not just a debating partner for Hegel and Co."[3] That is, Kierkegaard did not merely isolate himself within the concerns and conversations of academic philosophers, but sought to dialogue with a raft of popular literature and art in an attempt to address the concerns of the public. He commented on popular novels, plays, actors, and music, as well as the latest and most influential philosophical works. Pattison calls him a "feuilleton writer": one who was concerned with reflecting on popular culture in the hope of influencing it.[4] As we have seen in the previous chapter, Kierkegaard was concerned with the lack of inward reflection that characterized his society, and sought to redirect his fellow Danes away from the distractions of outwardness and toward a consideration of their own lives as individuals. Kierkegaard's ultimate desire was evangelistic—for his reader to meet God in the "hidden inwardness" of her own heart—but this was not immediately achievable for him, as we shall see. So instead, as a first and necessary step, he sought to awaken "the single individual" apart from "the crowd."

Such a task was not therefore an attempt at a universally viable philosophical system, but arose out of a perceived need. Kierkegaard's "single individual" is thus a deeply contextual tool which was the product of its time, and should be considered as such.

"THE SINGLE INDIVIDUAL": A DIALECTIC OF BEING

The key idea of "the single individual" was fundamental to Kierkegaard's entire task, as he saw this as the true reality of what a human being was, as opposed to "one" who was swallowed up in anonymity and the untruth of "the crowd." "The single individual" was a person who had been stripped of this illusion of Christendom and was free to take responsibility for her own existence. Johannes Climacus' argument for the importance of subjectivity, ethics and the need for others to take note of their own existence

---

It may be recognized as such because it is opposed to the 'evil of the age.' Kierkegaard's championing of 'the individual' is a polemical result of the crowd mentality which he perceived in his age. Any good that there may be in that mentality (from a balanced view) is not his concern as a polemical, religious author" (ibid., 33).

3. Pattison, "Kierkegaard as Feuilleton Writer," 129.

4. Ibid., 125.

1.2 "The Single Individual"

is therefore an argument for "the single individual."[5] But Murray Rae notes that for Kierkegaard, "the single individual" is never *autonomous*, as if a human being could know truth within herself, but she is always "the single individual" *before God*.[6] Therefore, such attempts at greatness by an individual's own efforts is possible for an unbeliever like Climacus, but utterly antithetical to Kierkegaard the Christian. A casual (mis-)reading of the earlier pseudonymous works[7] can lead to an emphasis on "the single individual" as being apart from societal conventions, but to remain here is to miss the point of Kierkegaard's authorship as a whole.[8]

This is particularly the case with the work by the pseudonym Johannes De Silentio. This pseudonym was likely created by Kierkegaard to be a person who believed in God, but such a knowledge was primarily through the ethical.[9] This is why he repeatedly states that he cannot understand Abraham; from his own *human* capacity (i.e., without the eyes of faith), he elevates Abraham to be an unreachable figure, far above the possibility of emulation by others.[10] Such a presentation can therefore lend a casual surface-level reader to dismiss the story as an irrelevant impossibility.

Abraham is portrayed as a mysterious figure in *Fear and Trembling*. He is not presented as an example of a fear*less* individual, railing against

---

5. E.g., Kierkegaard, *Concluding Unscientific Postscript*, 319.

6. "What then, is the point of Kierkegaard's apparent isolation of the individual if it is not to emphasize the self-sufficiency of human beings in their efforts to know the Truth? The answer emerges when we recognize that there is really no such category as 'the individual' in Kierkegaard's work. It is rather 'the individual before God' who is the focus of Kierkegaard's concern" (Rae, *Kierkegaard's Vision of the Incarnation*, 145).

7. I.e., the pseudonymous works bar those by Anti-Climacus.

8. "The single individual" is roughly equivalent to Kierkegaard's use of "an existing individual," and as Holmer explains, it is not a "philosophical concept" that gives free license to any and all human activity. Instead, Kierkegaard "uses it to call attention to the man (not 'the average man') that each of us is when we love and hate, think and rusticate, argue and dream, and talk and imagine" (Holmer, *On Kierkegaard and the Truth*, 135). Also, as Gouwens rightly argues against volitionism: "Kierkegaard has a very different understanding than Sartre or for that matter Bultmann of human freedom and of the self. To be a 'self' ethically and religiously includes the will for Kierkegaard, but the self is hardly self-created by daily exercise of the will" (Gouwens, *Kierkegaard as Religious Thinker*, 10).

9. See Kierkegaard, *Journals and Papers*, 3/3130, X2 A 594, n.d., 1850.

10. As Daniel W. Conway helpfully notes, "Johannes also takes comfort in his inability to understand the faith of Abraham. As we have seen, the unavailability of Abraham frees him to locate the limitations of his own spiritual quest external to his striving" ("Abraham's Final Word," 194).

oppressive ethical systems. Abraham does not assert his own higher, *individual* moral code above that of his world by seeking to sacrifice his son. Instead, his actions respond to a command from God and, as Rae argues, Abraham's "absurd" behavior must be seen in light of the relationship between Abraham and God throughout Abraham's life. Such a backdrop is able to make Abraham's actions intelligible, but only to a point.[11] What Abraham knew of the faithfulness of God prior to the infamous episode on Mount Moriah became the *subjective*, rather than the universally objective (i.e., the ethical) grounds for undertaking such an unreasonable action by human standards. *Faith* became the basis of which to transcend society in favor of the religious, not Abraham's self-determination. So Kierkegaard's ammunition of "the single individual" can only be seen as "the single individual" in relation to God: being "the single individual" is to be elevated to be under God alone. So an individual's taking up of responsibility was only the first half of the equation. Søren Kierkegaard was convinced that Christianity was the only means by which "the single individual"—a true human self under God—could be fully realized. An individual could not simply become a self on her own terms; she must receive her true existence from God in fear and trembling.

For Kierkegaard, "the single individual" was derived from the ultimate paradox of the gospel—that God became a man. He frequently emphasized the Christian orthodox understanding of the incarnation as the paradoxical unification of the Divine and the Human—the absolute to the finite, the everything to the nothing. This tension (defying Hegelian synthesis) was understood by him to be essential to lived life, thereby providing the basis for Kierkegaard to pursue the fundamental importance of paradoxes in human existence. This is most notably the case in *Sickness Unto Death* written under the pseudonym of the super-Christian Anti-Climacus.[12] "The single individual" was, for Kierkegaard, the key idea of the true identity of a person—one who lived amongst the paradoxes of existing. In light of the

---

11. "Had Abraham heard the command of God to sacrifice Isaac 'out of the blue' as it were, apart that is from a history of relationality between God and Abraham characterized as it was by love and trust, then it is much less likely that Abraham could have regarded the word he heard as a command from God. The context of Abraham's covenantal relationship lends a degree of intelligibility to the command. It is not complete intelligibility of course . . ." (Rae, "The Risk of Obedience," 318).

12. The tensions between finitude and infinitude, the temporal and eternal, the possible and the necessary, not wanting to be oneself or wanting to be oneself etc. are all examined throughout this work.

1.2 "The Single Individual"

ultimate paradox of the gospel, each person is simultaneously nothing and yet everything. This can be seen in an early journal entry of Kierkegaard's:

> I felt at one and the same time how great and how insignificant I am; then those two great forces, pride and humility, joined compatibly.[13]

Kierkegaard goes on to name this "state of mind" as "humility," and the believer encounters this in nature, removed from society and under an awareness of God: "Here he feels himself great and small at the same time."[14] Here we can see Kierkegaard's understanding that in relation to God a person is nothing, and yet it is precisely the gospel that raises humanity (each and every person as "a single individual") to the heights of communion with God himself—the ultimate existence of the ultimate gravity. So a Christian is a person who understands herself as "a single individual" under God at all times, meaning that she is simultaneously nothing and yet everything—and is hence herself a paradox, akin to Luther's description of a believer as *simul justus et peccator* ("simultaneously justified and a sinner").[15] It is in this way that the Christian comes to resemble the "Absolute Paradox" of the God-Man[16] when she comes to understand herself in terms of her being "a single individual."

Kierkegaard's dialectical authorship also reflects this existential paradox.[17] In it, both the aesthetic works and the religious works carry the idea of "the single individual," but with the tendency to emphasize opposite factors of this paradox. It could be claimed that the aesthetic works largely play the part of emphasizing the *greatness* of "the single individual," and the

---

13. The entry continues: "Fortunate is the man for whom this is possible at all times in his life, in whose breast these two factors have not only come to terms with each other but have reached out a hand to each other and have been married ... these fruits ... avoid the attention of the masses and only the solitary searcher discovers them and rejoices in his find. His life will flow on calmly and quietly, and he will drain neither the intoxicating glass of pride nor the bitter cup of despair. He has found what the great philosopher—who by his calculations was able to destroy the enemy's implements of war—desired but did not find: that Archimedean point from which he can lift the whole world, that point precisely for that reason must lie outside the world, outside the restrictions of time and space" (Kierkegaard, *Journals and Papers*, 5/5099, 1 A 67, n.d., 1835).

14. Ibid., 5/5099 1 A 67 (1835).

15. McGrath, *Luther's Theology of the Cross*, 133–34.

16. The key place in which Kierkegaard refers to the incarnation as "the Absolute Paradox" is in chapter 3 of "Philosophical Crumbs," 111–20.

17. The following is derived from Kierkegaard's own direct account of his authorship in Kierkegaard, *Point of View*, 115.

reader is indirectly enticed to realize herself as a great "single individual" (for example in the likes of Abraham, 'A,' Judge William or Climacus), to realize her own life-view apart from mindless assimilation into "the crowd." The religious works, however, tend to emphasize the need for the reader to be humble under God: "Be Satisfied with Being Human" is a title of one of Kierkegaard's signed "Upbuilding Discourses."[18] Here in this (non)sermon is another plea to retreat to nature in order to quell anxieties.[19] After knowing herself as being distinct from "the crowd," nature directs the individual toward the *humility* of knowing that she is always before God. She can come to know this by "learning from the lilies and the birds."[20]

Having such anxieties regarding the individual's own security in life calmed by observing the world under God happens through her *voluntarily* giving up her natural tendency to self-establishment, self-justification and survival, and instead entrusting God with her life. Kierkegaard reminds us that just as God clothes the lily of the field and feeds the bird of the air, so will he meet the needs of "the single individual." And unlike the bird or lily, it is the privilege, responsibility, and worship of a human being as a "single individual," to choose God.[21] In other words, she no longer attempts to control or poeticize her world by placing herself above it, but instead lets herself be "poetically composed" by the "divine poet" by surrendering to God in the realization that she is also one of God's glorious creations.[22]

---

18. Chapter 5 in Kierkegaard, *Spiritual Writings*, 85–112, originally published in *Upbuilding Discourses in Various Spirits* from 1847. The notable exception is the sermon at the end of the first "aesthetic work": Kierkegaard, *Either/Or*, 595–609.

19. For a discussion as to why Kiekegaard's religious works were not named "sermons," see Hong and Hong, "Translator's Introduction," xix–xx.

20. ". . . if just two of us talk together—and all the more if we are ten, or more—it is so easily forgotten that you and I, we two, are before God. But our lily, our teacher, is deep. It doesn't let itself get involved with you; it keeps silent, and by keeping silent it indicates to you that you are before God and are to remember that you are before God, so that you, too, in all seriousness and in truth might become silent before God" (Kierkegaard, *Spiritual Writings*, 191).

21. Ibid., 142–49; also: "To be Spirit—that is human beings' invisible glory. So when the anxious stand out there in the fields surrounded by all those witnesses, when every flower says to them, 'Remember God,' a human can answer, 'That I shall, little one, for I shall worship Him, which you, poor things, cannot do.' The one who stands upright is thus a worshipper" (ibid., 124–25).

22. For a reference to God as poet and Christ as God "introducing himself into his work," see Kierkegaard, *Journals and Papers*, 2/1391, X1 A 605, n.d., 1849; for a reference to being "composed poetically," see Kierkegaard, *Concept of Irony*, 280; see also Walsh, *Living Poetically*, 9, 57; see also Rasmussen, *Between Irony and Witness*, 10–11. Both

1.2 "The Single Individual"

Such a position is one of *humility*—that is, the happy marriage of being simultaneously great and nothing under God.

These two factors are vital—to be *under God* is for a person (in *humility*) to acknowledge her own nature as a human creature in space and time, with the boundaries of the self being finitude, temporality, necessity and so on. But this needs to be balanced with the nature of the self as being created by God to be his glory *in the world*. Again, being a "single individual" means to be a person who embraces her paradoxical existence as one created to be great under God: ". . . having a self, being a self, is the greatest, the infinite, concession that has been made to man, but also eternity's claim on him."[23]

Sickness Unto Death is a pseudonymous work that presents Kierkegaard's understanding of the Christian view of a self, and is prefaced by the quote of one Bishop Albertini: "Lord! Give us weak eyes for things of no account, and eyes of full clarity in all your truth."[24] This work is about the supreme urgency of Christianity, where it is not the outward and the immediate about which humanity should be concerned, but the inner spiritual life. Kierkegaard's Anti-Climacus talks about the need of being a self under God, and suggests that when this is not embraced, two equal and opposite dangers are likely.

The first is "in despair wanting to be oneself"—that is, an individual being a self on her own terms and not submitting to God. Such arrogance of "strength" derives a (false) identity from the individual herself, and seeks to control and shape the world around her to her own ends. Such a person sees herself as a "single individual," but as needing to maintain her self on her own, and ends up "severing the self from any relation to the power which has established it."[25] In this way, through her own suffering, caused by her being unable to be her own ideal self apart from God, such an individual ends up destroying herself.[26] The second danger is when the person is "in despair not wanting to be oneself"—that is, an individual, in "weakness" abdicating her responsibility and privilege to be who she has been created to be by God. She does not derive her identity from him, but instead allows herself to be blown by the winds of fashionable society. Such

---

Walsh and Rasmussen are very helpful in their analysis of Kierkegaard's work under the rubric of the poetic.

23. Kierkegaard, *Sickness*, 51.
24. Ibid., 33.
25. Ibid., 99.
26. Ibid., 98–105.

a person lives for the immediate, and fundamentally denies her own privilege and responsibility to be a "single individual," even to the point of not being aware of who she is.[27]

In both extremes there is the focus on the outward. The first sees the outward as a plaything to manipulate for her own ends; the second sees the outward as the basis for her identity. The exception here is when the latter comes to a realization that such immediacy has robbed her of herself. This despising of the outward, followed by a turn to reflection is a necessary first step, but becomes stuck in inward self-loathing unless she turns *further inward* to God.[28]

"HIDDEN INWARDNESS" AS INDIVIDUALISM?

As has been discussed above, any primary significance given to outwardness is a hindrance to the realization of "the single individual." Instead, Kierkegaard claimed that true selfhood is achieved through reflection, where a person is not merely subject to the outward conditions of the world (as is the case with the rest of creation) or interested in subjugating all that is outward for her own ends, but comes to be herself through meeting God in "hidden inwardness." Kierkegaard thus seems an easy target for the accusation of individualism, for if "hidden inwardness" is the priority and outwardness is seen as a danger, where does that leave human society? C. Stephen Evans names Martin Buber along with "numerous other writers" as those who accuse Kierkegaard of "being an arch-individualist who failed to appreciate fully the importance of community for selfhood."[29] But as we have seen throughout, Kierkegaard's concept of "the single individual" cannot strictly be understood as being individualistic because it is fundamentally relational: it is a self in relation to God, and out of this fundamental God-relation a true self is formed.[30]

---

27. Ibid., 84.

28. Ibid., 91–99.

29. Evans, "Who Is the Other?," 268–69; see also Rae, *Kierkegaard's Vision of the Incarnation*, 133 n. 2, 144–45.

30. "Kierkegaard makes clear in *Works of Love* that those who would live faithfully and love truly must face God's demand that each of us relate to God as individuals. The most fundamental relationship for which I exist and for which my beloved exists is the relationship to God" (Hall, "Self-deception," 40); see also Rae, *Kierkegaard's Vision of the Incarnation*, 144–48.

1.2 "The Single Individual"

Evans outlines two assumptions of those who accuse Kierkegaard of individualism by engaging with *Sickness Unto Death*: "One is that the 'other' to whom the self is said to relate is thought to be exclusively God. The second is that God somehow does not count as a real other or at least does not make the self part of a real community."[31] Evans is on safer ground in arguing against the latter assumption, but his first is somewhat confused. He quotes passages in both parts of *Sickness Unto Death* which suggest that a self can be formed in relation to other beings, and that the "other" throughout part one can easily stand for a human person instead of God.[32] This does indeed point to a relational view of a person for Kierkegaard, but such an argument is ultimately irrelevant since, as Evans himself says, "God is the ontological ground of the self."[33] Kierkegaard (through Anti-Climacus) claims that for a person to make anyone *but* God the criterion for their self is mistaken because it is impossible. Whether or not there are higher or lower "gradations" of a self is irrelevant because "the quality of the relation is insufficient to give the individual a criterion that makes for selfhood."[34]

Thus, against Evans, Kierkegaard does *not* advocate for "the importance of community for selfhood," at least in terms of *human* community. Kierkegaard is arguing for true selfhood to be grounded *only* in God, thereby rejecting the notion that a person becomes a true self through their relations with others. But if this is the case, how then does a person come to realize herself as a "single individual"? If it is purely the work of God through the divine interruption of faith, why then is there a need for others to communicate what is only the work of God?

Kierkegaard understood the people of his society to be living largely superficial lives. The level of inwardness or subjectivity required for each of Kierkegaard's three stages of existence increased accordingly. So the religious was the stage of deep inwardness and personal reflection, whereas the aesthetic person lived a life fundamentally concerned with the superficial—the immediate reality around her as she perceived it.[35] Christianity was distorted in catering to the lower views, so the aesthete related to

31. Evans, "Who Is the Other?," 269.
32. Ibid., 269–72.
33. Ibid., 271.
34. Ibid.
35. See, for instance, chapter 3: "Existence and Existence-Spheres: Climacus' Reading of Kierkegaard's Pseudonymous Literature," in Evans, *Kierkegaard's Fragments and Postscript*, 33–54.

God primarily through immediate experience, while the ethicist tended to see God as a divine judge. In order to address this, Kierkegaard sought to communicate Christianity in a way that appealed to those living out of the first two stages but then drove them deeper inwardly, to meet God in the "hidden inwardness" of their own hearts (the religious stage). The problem for those in these lower stages was a lack of *awareness*, a forgetting and being distracted by the immediate, when God could only be known through deep, inward reflection. It was in "hidden inwardness" that Kierkegaard understood God to act and to instil faith in the individual. Kierkegaard believed that it was his task to help his reader to reflect, because this was when a person became a "single individual" and when faith in God took root.

But later in his authorship, Kierkegaard came to see that this concept of "hidden inwardness" was being used by Christendom as an excuse for outward indifference, and as a justification for their aligning themselves with the "Church triumphant," rather than the "Church militant."[36] That is, "hidden inwardness" was cut off from all outwardness, and the gospel was emasculated from its existential demands on the way a believer went about in the world.[37] Kierkegaard sought to address this problem by outlining how "hidden inwardness" does not then necessitate privatism. Although it is the case that any *outwardness* (e.g., speech, actions, outward displays of emotion) does not have any *causal* link to the inward, hidden reality of a person, it does not then follow that such hiddenness is unsocial. In fact, Kierkegaard understood that the encounter with God which takes place in the "hidden inwardness" of "the single individual" manifests itself in a life.

Works of Love was written especially to anticipate and counteract such accusations made against him, and to dispel the notion that he "[knew] nothing about sociality."[38] In the opening chapter of this work Kierkegaard stated: "[L]ove itself is in a certain sense in hiding and therefore can only be known by its revealing fruits."[39] The source of love for "the single individual" is hidden in God, and is therefore eternal,[40] but is not introspective: it is concerned with the world, as this is its natural outworking.[41] But words

---

36. See Gouwens, *Kierkegaard as Religious Thinker*, 213.

37. Kierkegaard, *Practice in Christianity*, 214ff.

38. Kierkegaard, *Journals and Papers*, 5/5972, VIII1 A 4, n.d., 1847; quoted in Hong and Hong, "Translator's Introduction," xxvi.

39. Kierkegaard, *Works of Love*, 26.

40. Ibid., 27.

41. Ibid., 28.

or actions carry no intrinsic proof of the presence of love in a person, since the truth of their origin lie hidden: "works of love" are only true when they are, in fact, undertaken in love, but this motive is concealed.[42]

Therefore, the problem here lies in the tendency to assess the inward (the hidden) on the basis of the outward (what is revealed). Kierkegaard moved beyond this by focusing on the dispositions of his reader, rather than external particulars (i.e., quantifiable practices such as how much money a person should give to the poor).[43] In this movement, he simply echoed how Christ inverted the question "And who is my neighbor?"—the focus is on the inwardness of "the single individual" situating herself properly in the world.[44] Instead of seeking to change the world, the Christian is to change herself, *but for the sake of the world*. Similarly, although love is *hidden* within the heart, Kierkegaard suggested that his reader should be concerned with making her works recognizable as "works of love," since "it is more blessed to believe in love." This recognizability, then, is a *gift* toward the other and is a disposition that exists *for* the other.[45] Lastly, just because Kierkegaard advocated for a blindness toward "worldly" social distinctions does *not* mean a rejection of others altogether, quite the opposite: because social distinctions can hinder true neighborly love (Danish *Kaerlighed*),[46] they need to be disregarded by the Christian for the sake of equality *in the world*.[47] This is absolutely the opposite of "an unbiblical commitment to abstraction."[48]

We can therefore see that what Kierkegaard was concerned with here and throughout *Works of Love* was not prescribing specific outward practices, but rather giving strategies to his reader which sought to encourage

---

42. Ibid., 30.

43. See especially part 1, chapter 7: "Mercifulness, a Work of Love, Even if It Can Give Nothing and Is Capable of Doing Nothing," in ibid., 292–305.

44. ". . . in the answer the question is first turned around to mean essentially: in what manner is one to ask the question?" (ibid., 38).

45. See part 1, chapter 1: "Love's Hidden Life and Its Recognisability by Its Fruits," in ibid., 23–33. We will attempt to keep this chapter in mind as we read Kierkegaard here.

46. See Pattison, "Foreword," xi.

47. See, for instance, the parallel of the banquet in Kierkegaard, *Works of Love*, 90–92, e.g., "He who feeds the poor but yet is not victorious over his own mind in such a way that he calls this feeding a feast sees in the poor and unimportant only the poor and unimportant. He who gives a *feast* sees in the poor and unimportant his neighbours—however ridiculous this may seem in the eyes of the world" (ibid., 92).

48. Adorno, "On Kierkegaard's Doctrine of Love" cited in Ferreira, "Other-Worldliness," 66. Ferreira's whole article makes this point well.

the development of inward dispositions of faith, hope and love: Christian ways for the reader to situate herself in the world. Such inward dispositions are *not* private, but, in fact, *only exist socially*: love can only be loved forth, and a loving heart only exists in its being *for* others.[49] So although such dispositions are *hidden*, they are not private but instead are fundamentally outward.[50]

So we can see that despite the point of departure being inward, the goal is outward: a lived life, or "reduplication" (meaning for a person to *be* what she *says*—a concept we will explore further below). For Kierkegaard, the self was established through being *hidden* in God, and can *then* be recognized through existing for others. But because of the fundamental hiddenness of an other's faith, there was no *necessary* link between the inward and the outward: this was brought about by God alone. Because of this, there was always the possibility of deception—even (or particularly!) self-deception—and for this reason, a Christian hesitated from judging, and lived *out* her salvation in fear and trembling.[51]

CONCLUSION

We have seen in this chapter that the concept of "the single individual" was key for Kierkegaard's reintroduction of the gospel into Denmark. In a manner of speaking, this concept was the *content* of Kierkegaard's task, because "the single individual" was one who stood apart from "the crowd" and took responsibility for her own existence. Such a stance would lead a person to see the importance of her own *inward* relation to God, and come to see herself as a paradox of greatness and nothingness by virtue of her being raised to an infinite height under God. This understanding of a person in terms of "hidden inwardness" did not, however, entail individualism or a withdrawal from society, quite the opposite: Kierkegaard understood that a self grounded in God alone was the means of appropriate engagement with the world. It was Kierkegaard's task to lead his reader to understand herself in this light, but precisely because such a realization was infinitely

---

49. Kierkegaard, *Works of Love*, 206–7 and "Love is not an exclusive characteristic, but it is a characteristic by which or in virtue of which you exist for others" (ibid., 211).

50. See also Holmer, *On Kierkegaard and the Truth*, 131. For a further treatment of these themes in regard to Kierkegaard and sociality, Gouwens is indispensable. See his *Kierkegaard as Religious Thinker*.

51. See Hall, "Self-deception," 41.

inward and hidden, it could not simply be prescribed by Kierkegaard. This, then, leads us to a consideration of the need for an appropriate form of communicating the truth of Christianity that is *indirect*. But first we must pause to consider the nature of such truth.

1.3 THE GOSPEL TRUTH

INTRODUCTION

We have explored Kierkegaard's understanding of the proper nature of the self as a "single individual," and that it is through this stance which emphasizes "hidden inwardness" in which the reception of faith is made possible. But what then is the *object* of such faith, and what does the life of such a person look like? To answer these questions, we need to explore that to which "the single individual" is directed: truth. In this chapter we will be exploring the nature of truth according to Christianity and how it differs from the Socratic understanding, drawing primarily on *Philosophical Fragments* by Johannes Climacus. In this work Kierkegaard illustrated that the fundamental understanding of Christ being the truth reorients the learner away from disembodied objectivity and toward a subjective embodiment of her relationship with the truth. Such a relationship is characterized by a continued striving "in the truth"—that is, to follow Christ the prototype by attempting to marry ideality and actuality, form and content.

THE SOCRATIC AND CHRISTIANITY: PHILOSOPHICAL FRAGMENTS

Kierkegaard's pseudonym Johannes Climacus presents a book which takes the form of a "thought experiment," looking at the nature of essential truth and an individual's relation to it.[1] It begins with the question: "How can the truth be learned?" and introduces this problem by recounting Socrates'

---

1. "Essential truth" being that which is used in regard to matters pertaining to existence, namely the ethical and religious.

1.3 The Gospel Truth

conversation with Meno—if a person lacks the truth, how then could she recognize it if she came across it? Climacus then outlines the Socratic position: chiefly, that the learner already has the truth through anamnesis—an *a priori* familiarity with what is true through her pre-existent soul—and therefore can recognize or remember the truth due to her eternal familiarity with it.[2] Thereby, the teacher is one who resembles a midwife (hence the Greek "maieutic"), and is insignificant to the learning of truth. Likewise, the moment is insignificant, since it is merely an occasion when the individual re-collects herself into the eternal, and the situation of the learner is merely one of ignorance or lack of knowledge.[3]

"If it is to be otherwise," speculates Climacus, the truth must have "an historical point of departure": a moment that divides the individual between being in untruth and being in truth. According to this "logical" alternative, the learner does *not* have the precondition for recognizing the truth. The truth is not something innate within her soul, long forgotten, but the learner is instead completely alien to the truth. And more than this, Climacus argues, she is *hostile* to the truth. Hence the problem is not simply one of deficiency, but utter opposition—what he names as the condition of *sin*. Under this alternative, *faith* is named as the precondition—the eyes to re-cognize the truth—and this precondition must be given by the teacher himself. This then provides the capacity in the student to receive truth, and thus be redeemed from the sin of being in untruth. The teacher is therefore also the Savior. The moment (now of *absolute* importance) is named "the fullness of time," and can be understood to be the event of conversion.[4]

It is now possible for the reader to recognize with Climacus that the real problem in the initial question lies in its conception of truth.[5] According to the Socratic paradigm, truth is abstract, objective, timeless; it exists in complete disregard of human existence and relationships, and is a commodity or status to be obtained. Christianity, however, names Jesus Christ *as truth*. For the Christian, then, truth is fundamentally relational and demands the *whole person* in time, not just an intellect that relates to

---

2. "SOCRATES: And if the truth of all things always existed in the soul, then the soul is immortal" (Plato, "Meno," n.p.).

3. Kierkegaard, "Philosophical Crumbs," 88–91.

4. Ibid., 91–95.

5. "[The] concept of truth at work here is the utterly wrong one" (Holmer, *On Kierkegaard and the Truth*, 19).

the eternal.[6] So Christian truth requires an *embodiment* of truth, that is, a whole-person knowing in which she is *captured by* the truth, not merely in her mind but in her heart also. Being known by the truth is a matter of cognitive understanding which is accompanied by the passions appropriate to it, and Kierkegaard's word for this embodiment is *subjectivity*. This notion of "passionate reason"[7] is why Climacus then elaborates on his point, not primarily with an *intellectual* argument, but with a fairytale (and a love story at that!).

As is clear from the journals, Kierkegaard's understanding of the gospel was that God had come to humanity in Christ.[8] More than that, it is God with *me* which is incommunicable—it is *hidden* and *subjective*. Kierkegaard emphasized that God cannot be bought and sold like a commodity, or expounded as an idea. Christianity is not an intellectual system that can be used to win others by means of "speculative reason"[9] or an entertaining work that can win a person over by means of romantic pathos; it is the secret invitation of God himself. It is the Absolute Paradox:[10] that God has become a particular human being in history in order to reveal that God *knows* each and every person, that God desires communion with each person as "*a single individual.*"[11] This is the marrying of finitude with infinity, which a human cannot grasp apart from abandoning herself to God in the simple humility of faith, that phenomenon which De Silentio calls "the highest passion in a human being."[12] This gospel was not, for Kierkegaard, an event that could be reduced to something less than subjectivity and analyzed at an impersonal distance. The gospel was *the way, the truth, and the life* for Kierkegaard—Christ was not merely another teacher or Socratic midwife, he *is* the truth, and therefore the only criterion *of* truth.[13]

---

6. For a consideration of Kierkegaard's "relational epistemology," see Rae, *Kierkegaard's Vision of the Incarnation*, 144–48.

7. A phrase borrowed from Evans' *Passionate Reason*.

8. E.g., Kierkegaard, *Journals and Papers*, 1/284, II A 595, n.d., 1837; ibid., 1/297, II A 473, July 7, 1839.

9. The thesis of Johannes Climacus in Kierkegaard, *Concluding Unscientific Postscript*.

10. Kierkegaard, "Philosophical Crumbs," 111ff; Cf. Anti-Climacus' "sign of offense" Kierkegaard, *Practice in Christianity*, 35 etc.

11. Kierkegaard, *Point of View*, 105–12.

12. Kierkegaard, *Fear and Trembling*, 150.

13. Kierkegaard depended heavily on John 14:6 throughout his religious works especially. See for instance *Practice in Christianity*, 207.

1.3 The Gospel Truth

But as can be seen, this is a world apart from the Socratic understanding of truth, which was likely to have been adopted as intellectual orthodoxy by Kierkegaard's "enlightened" readership.[14] In Kierkegaard's understanding of the gospel, the only recipient of truth (that is, the person of Jesus Christ; the God-Man) was "that single individual" who humbled herself to receive the precondition that was necessary to recognizing and knowing truth himself; that is, the precondition of faith.[15] Christianity *en masse* was no Christianity at all and was therefore in "untruth."[16]

This truth (as illustrated through the analogy of the King who loved a humble maiden[17]) is fundamentally concerned with freedom and mutual understanding, with *subjective relationality*. Kierkegaard understood Christian truth as *existential* (*essential*) truth; in the irreducibly human realm of actuality and lived life, it is characterized by contradiction and the inescapable necessity of radical choice.[18] Therefore, what was most important for someone from a Christian point of view was the stuff of lived life (the *how* more than the *what*[19]) rather than abstract ideas in the *non-existent* realm of objectivity. In this view of truth-in-life, how a person *chose* to commit and live in existence (the development of what Kierkegaard called a "life-view"[20]) was impossible to come to an "informed decision" about, for the conditions of existence perpetually elude objective certainty.[21] So in *Philosophical Fragments* Kierkegaard was seeking to point out the ludicrousness of examining matters which concerned existence objectively. Instead, Christ was to be the key in understanding life.[22]

---

14. Holmer, *On Kierkegaard and the Truth*, 120.

15. See Kierkegaard, "Philosophical Crumbs," 91–97 especially.

16. Kierkegaard, *Point of View*, 105–12.

17. Kierkegaard, "Philosophical Crumbs," 102ff.

18. This is in contrast to the realm of objectivity, which Hegelians were right to point out that contradiction and choice had no place in. But Climacus ridicules the possibility of an existing individual (a "single individual") seeing any relevance, use or reality in such thinking. See Kierkegaard, *Concluding Unscientific Postscript*, 304–6.

19. Ibid., 323.

20. See Kierkegaard on his critique of Hans Christian Andersen, "From the Papers of One Still Living," in Kierkegaard, *Early Polemical Writings*.

21. Kierkegaard, *Concluding Unscientific Postscript*.

22. "What is happening is that the literature in a variety of ways presents cases that make one doubt that the concept 'objective truth,' for example, is a particularly useful expression with which to handle ethical and religious difficulties" (Holmer, *On Kierkegaard and the Truth*, 25).

Part I: The Content

Analogous to this perspective of Christian truth and how it differs from Socratic truth is love, and it is for this reason that Climacus uses a fairytale to illustrate this difference. Objectivity is completely out of place regarding love—speculative reason seeks to *quantify* the truth of love by attempting to measure it. This is absurd and completely inappropriate to the subject matter: love cannot be reduced to, say, a husband giving flowers to his wife every Wednesday. So what Climacus is advocating for in *Philosophical Fragments* is a "paradigm shift"[23] so radical that it changes the very conditions by which something is recognized *as* truth, or what it means to be consistent (or *faithful*) *to* truth. Therefore, such a fundamental paradigm shift is either met with offense or openness—it cannot be "true to a certain degree."[24] Kierkegaard sought to correct what he saw as a fundamental error in the thinking of Christendom—that is, the reduction of Christ to a mere Socratic teacher of "truth" when in fact Christ himself *is* the truth: "But in our day everything is made abstract and everything personal is abolished: we take Christ's teaching—and abolish Christ. This is to abolish Christianity, for Christ is a person and is the teacher who is more important than the teaching."[25]

When truth is understood to be a person, and this truth is therefore concerned with "the single individual" in existence, it can only be known *subjectively*; it cannot be understood to be compatible with objectivity and cannot be *objectively understood*.[26] As Climacus argues in *Concluding Unscientific Postscript*, the realm of existence is not objective, and existing individuals (i.e., human beings who are living according to the reality of their being creatures under God)[27] do not have the luxury of examining life at an objective distance which reduces choice to simply cause and effect.[28]

23. I am using this term tentatively in light of Rae's critique of C. Stephen Evans use of "paradigm." Because of its tendency to lessen the gravity of the gap between human knowing and revelation, Rae instead argues that "metanoia" in the New Testament sense is a more appropriate term. See Rae, *Kierkegaard's Vision of the Incarnation*, 140–41.

24. Kierkegaard, *Concluding Unscientific Postscript*, 229.

25. Kierkegaard, *Practice in Christianity*, 124.

26. For Kierkegaard, "'subjective' and 'subjectivity' are linked with 'truth' (not in logic or contexts where we talk science) in expressions like 'I am the truth' or 'the truth shall make you free,' where nothing scholarly or intellectual is being proposed at all" (Holmer, *On Kierkegaard and the Truth*, 25–26).

27. What Kierkegaard describes as to "Be Satisfied with Being Human," originally from 1847's *Upbuilding Discourses in Various Spirits*, but published as chapter 5 in Kierkegaard, *Spiritual Writings*, 85–112.

28. See especially Kierkegaard, *Concluding Unscientific Postscript*, 305–7.

The realm of existence is the realm of life and truth, and therefore also of paradox: it is incompatible with objective understanding.[29] Kierkegaard successfully circumvents this fracture of truth in the need to explain his position by using the pseudonym Johannes Climacus to undertake his argument. We will explore this further in the next section on Kierkegaard's authorial form.

CHRIST AS THE ABSOLUTE PARADOX

Johannes Climacus suggests in *Philosophical Fragments* that the gospel is the Absolute Paradox. The claim of Christianity, that God entered into history as a human being, is absolutely impossible to understand from an objective point of view. This is the thought which cannot be thought of.[30] Along with the initial discussion regarding Christian truth as opposed to Socratic truth, this understanding of the gospel as the Absolute Paradox did much to confront popular philosophical thought in Kierkegaard's time. This is particularly so in its understanding that the learner is alienated from truth and has no capacity in herself to know or recognize the truth, since both the rationalism and romanticism prevalent in Kierkegaard's Denmark saw no limits to an individual learning the truth by herself.[31] In contrast to this, Kierkegaard claimed that the learner is not one who discovers the truth by herself through reason or by some sort of Feuerbachian projection,[32] but is

---

29. The irony here of course is that I, as an author, am speaking objectively—an issue which I will have to confront further below in the conclusion.

30. Kierkegaard, "Philosophical Crumbs," 107–11, 119.

31. Kirmmse, *Kierkegaard in Golden Age Denmark*, 35–39.

32. Feuerbach claimed that theology was merely anthropology, and that all human knowledge of God was derived from itself. Murray Rae suggests that chapter two of Philosophical Fragments was Kierkegaard's critique against such thinking. See Rae, *Kierkegaard's Vision of the Incarnation*, 41; see also Malesic, "Illusion and Offense," 43–55. Malesic argues that Kierkegaard's relation to Feuerbach isn't altogether negative, but recognizes the value of Feuerbach's critique which he saw as helpful in "ridding European Christian thought of its tendencies to accept ideology and to idolize the human" (ibid., 54).

instead, in a manner of speaking, discovered *by* it.³³ The truth is no longer something to be grasped, instead, the truth grasps the learner.³⁴

In other words, it is not enough to simply *cognitively* understand truth as God becoming a particular human being in history. Treating the gospel as anything less than subjective and existential is to castrate and domesticate it, remaking it in humanity's own image. This is why it was vital for Kierkegaard to point out that the God-Man did not overtly disclose himself as the god or the Lord of the cosmos, thus demanding allegiance and unquestioning loyalty to the absolute reality of his divine sovereignty. For God to expect such conformity would be a predictable human action, where God would merely act according to human ways of thinking.³⁵ But this was what Kierkegaard understood the gospel to have become for his society. He believed that God's revelation in Christ, and hence Christ as the truth, had been reduced, chopped down and confined to the procrustean bed of the Hegelian system. So to recover the shock-value of the gospel, Kierkegaard encouraged his readers to reacquaint themselves with how the Bible speaks of God in Christ "taking the form of a servant."³⁶ This attention to Christ's *form* became key for Kierkegaard's reintroduction of Christianity into Christendom.

In direct opposition to predominant Hegelian, Kantian, and other rationalistic logic, Kierkegaard sought to emphasize this paradoxical nature of gospel truth. Through Johannes Climacus, he voiced the *intellectual problem* of the gospel—arguing that Christianity cannot be understood logically, whilst through Johannes De Silentio, Kierkegaard pointed out the *existential mystery and agony* of the unintelligible faith of the Judeo-Christian

---

33. *Fear and Trembling* in particular is frequently seen as a polemic work against such rationalists as Kant, Hegel, and others, who were highly influential in Kierkegaard's Denmark. See Lippitt, "What Neither Abraham," 84 n. 6, 88; Rae, "The Risk of Obedience," 310; Hall, "Self-deception," 50; see also Kant's influence on J. P. Mynster, who appears to have been caught up in arguing for the historicity of the gospel. See Kirmmse, *Kierkegaard in Golden Age Denmark*, 101.

34. This becomes an important point to emphasize in defending Kierkegaard against the critique of irrationalism. For instance: ". . . in his attempt to reverse the rationalistic relationship between thought and faith, Kierkegaard poetizes Christian faith as something against or beyond cognition, and not reached by reflection" (Rasmussen, *Between Irony and Witness*, 11).

35. Rae helpfully points out that chapter 2 of *Philosophical Fragments* forms a satirical attack on Feuerbach. Rae, *Kierkegaard's Vision of the Incarnation*, 41; see also Rasmussen, *Between Irony and Witness*, 70 n. 86.

36. Kierkegaard, "Philosophical Crumbs," 106. See also Phil 2:7 and Isa 53:2.

father of the faith, Abraham.[37] Kierkegaard understood that the philosophy which dominated "the spirit of the age" was that God was the objective Lord of reason and morality, and that humanity had the ability within itself to determine logically what was right and what was moral.[38] Thus reason, morality and therefore God were universally accessible to all people at all times, and such thinking appealed to what Kierkegaard derided as "the crowd." Such universality carried a cut-and-paste logic which reduced God to a necessary cause in the Hegelian system and disregarded the delicate and profound specificity of the Christian gospel. So for Kierkegaard it was not at all the case that God was accessible by human reason, and this was because of God's "infinite qualitative difference"[39] from humanity: it was not humanity who approached God, but God who accommodated himself to humanity in order to become known.[40]

It was therefore also vital for Kierkegaard to note that God did not come to humanity with universal and self-evident glory in an hegemonic demand of truth, but instead that God *hid himself in the form of a servant.* Humanity's relation to "the god" was not then a matter of self-sufficient speculative thought, where this god was in the service of universally accessible objective truth; instead "the god" is himself truth, and is the teacher-savior who redeems "the single individual" from the sin of untruth at an infinitely personal and subjective level.[41] It is because of this *form* of the truth that Kierkegaard affirmed the subjective nature of the relation of "the single individual" *to* truth, where outward "proofs" had no bearing on the matter.[42] Therefore, speculative thought as a means of approaching such subjective truth was completely irrelevant and even harmful to the individual. Such an understanding constituted the most profound shift in

---

37. Kierkegaard, "Philosophical Crumbs"; Kierkegaard, *Concluding Unscientific Postscript*; Kierkegaard, *Fear and Trembling*.

38. See Rae, *Kierkegaard and Theology*, 168–70.

39. Kierkegaard, *Sickness*, 150, 159.

40. Ibid., 155. "God and man are two qualities separated by an infinite difference in kind. Every doctrine that ignores this difference is, humanly speaking, insane; divinely understood, it is blasphemy" (ibid., 159).

41. See Kierkegaard, "Philosophical Crumbs," 91ff.

42. As Holmer suggests in regard to Kierkegaard's discussion on the concept of immortality in *Postscript*: "... the interest to prove is not congruent with such a concept; in fact, the very quest for proof changes the concept altogether" (Holmer, *On Kierkegaard and the Truth*, 126).

knowing for humanity, most aptly named by the New Testament writers as *metanoia*.[43]

FAITH VS. HISTORY: THE INCOGNITO AND THE POSSIBILITY OF OFFENSE

The "incognito" is the emphasis of the super-Christian Anti-Climacus,[44] who repeatedly refers to Christ as "the sign of offense and the object of faith."[45] He states that "Jesus Christ is the object of faith; one must either believe in him or be offended; for to 'know' simply means that it is not about him. Thus history can indeed richly communicate knowledge, but knowledge annihilates Jesus Christ."[46] What Anti-Climacus means here is that *outwardly*, Jesus cannot be recognized as the God-Man but appears just as another human being: a carpenter's son from Nazareth. History is concerned with knowledge of what was the immediate, but Christ "exists only for faith."[47]

Both Climacus and Anti-Climacus point out that the gap of history is irrelevant to faith. Through these pseudonyms, Kierkegaard claimed that many people think that if they had only lived in Palestine in the first century and had been able to see Jesus and his working of miracles firsthand, then they themselves would believe in Christianity; that being an *historical* contemporary of Christ would give birth to faith in them.[48] But Kierkegaard pointed out that this is a false understanding, at the very least because there were witnesses to the historical person of Christ who did *not* believe (including, most obviously, those who crucified him). Therefore, Kierkegaard claimed that the intervening two millennia of church history are irrelevant to faith.[49] He instead claimed that those who place such an emphasis on history reveal themselves to be those who do not actually understand themselves, nor the demand of Christianity on them.[50] To rec-

---

43. See Rae, *Kierkegaard's Vision of the Incarnation*, 140–71.
44. See Kierkegaard, *Journals and Papers*, 6/6349, X6 B 48, n.d., 1849.
45. Kierkegaard, *Practice in Christianity*, 35.
46. Ibid., 33.
47. Ibid., 25.
48. See chapter 5: "The Disciple At Second Hand" in Kierkegaard, "Philosophical Crumbs," 154–73; see also Kierkegaard, *Practice in Christianity*, 128.
49. Kierkegaard, *Concluding Unscientific Postscript*, 46–49.
50. ". . . there is no direct and immediate transition to Christianity, and that therefore

ognize Christ is to proceed through the possibility of offense to come out the other side as one who accepts him as one who is absolutely beyond their own understanding. Because "contingent truths of history can never become the demonstration of necessary truths of reason,"[51] Christ cannot be apprehended as God except by faith. In *Philosophical Fragments* and *Postscript*, Climacus reminds us that there is no reason-*able* link between human experience or rationality (e.g., history) and the reality of God. We lack the ability in-and-of-ourselves to *think through* (Greek *diagnosis*) to the reality of who God is.[52]

Therefore, for Kierkegaard, faith was not primarily intellectual assent (such as the type of knowing that is appropriate to history), but a relational encounter which "the single individual" approaches *through* seeing Christ as "the sign of offense" and moves on *to* knowing him as "the object of faith."[53] And it is precisely because one cannot be in relationship with a dead person—even the greatest person in history—that faith must leap over the "gap" of history. A relationship outside history can only take place in the belief that Jesus is alive (i.e., resurrected)[54] and more than this—divine. This can be known through faith in the *hiddenness* of inwardness. This is where Kierkegaard's term "the incognito" becomes helpful.

Christianity claims that Jesus was fully human, and yet fully God; that the absolute, all-powerful creator and sustainer of all things became incarnate as a human. Kierkegaard's Anti-Climacus attempts to point out the intellectual absurdity of this claim by further emphasizing that it was not some abstract unity of God and the human race as some intellectual or metaphysical idea (*sub specie aeterni*), but it is God as *a single human individual*.[55] He says that this, humanly speaking, is impossible to comprehend and can only be grasped by faith—that is, in "hidden inwardness," which is the foundation of a believer's (subjective) relationship with God. Because it is precisely faith that God desires of humanity, God *hid himself* as a par-

---

all those who in that way want to give a rhetorical push in order to bring one into Christianity or even help one into it by a thrashing—they are all deceivers—no, they know not what they do" (ibid., 49); Also, Kierkegaard, *Practice in Christianity*, 144.

51. Kierkegaard, *Concluding Unscientific Postscript*, 97, quoting Lessing.

52. Torrance, *John MacMurray*.

53. Kierkegaard, *Practice in Christianity*, 35; "Faith is not a matter of intellectual assent but a mode of existence" (Rae, *Kierkegaard's Vision of the Incarnation*, 64).

54. Kierkegaard does not dwell on Christ's resurrection, preferring instead to dwell on the primary absurdity of the incarnation itself.

55. See Kierkegaard, *Practice in Christianity*, 123.

ticular individual known to history as Jesus of Nazareth. For a *subjective* relation to occur between Christ and the individual, the revelation of this subjective truth had to be *hidden*, to be revealed only in the inwardness of "the single individual." Kierkegaard emphasized this through an appeal to Isaiah, God came "in the form of a servant" and had "no comeliness to attract us to him," so that even those *historically* contemporaneous with Christ did not "in truth" see him at all if they did not look with the eyes of faith.[56] Christ *hid himself*—Christ was (and *is*) "the incognito" of God.[57]

As Anti-Climacus repeatedly reminds the reader in *Practice in Christianity*, it is not merely the *content* of Christ's teaching which is the essence of Christianity.[58] To think in this way is to reduce Christ to a human being in historical garb, and we are back to the Socratic. The *form* of Christ as the God-Man is what is of central importance. This God-Man is not some nice abstraction of the unity of God and humanity; Anti-Climacus reminds his reader that the God-Man is the unity of the all-powerful wonder of God with an *individual person*. This is "the incognito": that which is "a stumbling block to Jews and foolishness to Gentiles."[59]

Jesus is "the sign of offense and the object of faith."[60] For Jesus to be recognized *qua* sign is to realize that there is more to this man than what is immediately apparent (i.e., his worldly identity as a carpenter's son or a great teacher in history).[61] It is being open to the possibility that points to a *hidden* reality—that he, in fact, is God. But embracing the possibility that there is more to this man opens an individual to vulnerability and volatility. This is the possibility of offense—offense that *either* this man presents himself too highly *or* that God presents himself too lowly. This offense is one of impropriety according to the individual's own preconceptions—as if the individual is the final judge of who this man is, and what God can and cannot do.[62] This recognition of Christ *qua* sign is to then open the reader up to a conflict between God and her own control over her life—a conflict over the reader's spirit. Does the reader stick to her preconceptions,

---

56. See Kierkegaard, "Philosophical Crumbs," 106. See also Phil 2:7 and Isa 53:2.

57. See No. II, chapter 2: "The Form of a Servant is Unrecognizability (the Incognito)," in Kierkegaard, *Practice in Christianity*, 127–33.

58. Ibid., 123–24.

59. 1 Cor 1:23.

60. Kierkegaard, *Practice in Christianity*, 35.

61. Ibid., 124–27.

62. Ibid., 94–121; Kierkegaard, *Sickness*, 115–20.

or does she humbly surrender to the gospel? This conflict ("the possibility of offense") is made possible by the reader realizing herself as "a single individual," reflecting on the gospel for herself and considering what it means to be contemporaneous with Christ. For, as Anti-Climacus states, one can only be contemporaneous with Christ through the *hiddenness* of faith.[63] Faith gives the reader the eyes to see Christ as God incarnate.

If Christ is truth, then the individual is in untruth (a sinner), and she fundamentally lacks the capacity to know anything in truth apart from him.[64] All notions of self-sufficiency and autonomy must be sacrificed, and the believer's participation in "the world" of human society is reconfigured toward a radical dependence on God.[65] It is at this point that Anti-Climacus emphasizes Christ's suffering, and that one who embraces the gospel is to be one who "strives" to suffer with Christ for the sake of the truth.[66] To be given the eyes of faith is a costly gift, and converts the believer's primary reality *from* that which is outward (that is, the immediate, to be understood, to desire admiration and success in society, etc.) *to* what is inward (what is between the believer and God alone).

This is why Climacus plays with the idea of Christ as epistemological savior, since he is merely interested in the intellectual dynamics of Christianity, whereas Anti-Climacus adds to this the concept of Christ as the prototype or pattern.[67] For the Christian, "love is the fulfillment of the law": it

---

63. Kierkegaard, *Practice in Christianity*, 9.

64. "The contradiction is *Passional*; it is an affront to common conceptions of God, and also an affront against the assumption that one has the truth 'within'" (Gouwens, *Kierkegaard as Religious Thinker*, 130).

65. Here Kierkegaard could be critiqued as only representing a masculine view of sin and conversion, just as Niebuhr's understanding of "pride" being the fundamental sin has been criticized as not taking into account a more feminine tendency toward the sin of subsumation or weakness. See Niebuhr, *The Nature and Destiny of Man*, 186–240; cf. Creegan and Pohl, "Evangelical and Feminist Maps," 135–37. Although in *Sickness Unto Death* Anti-Climacus does contrast the sin of pride with the sin of weakness (see the despairs of "not wanting to be oneself" and "wanting to be oneself" in 1.2: "The Single Individual: A Dialectic of Being," above), by and large his emphasis is on the former. This then prompts him to commonly refer to "womanly" tendencies as a way out of sin, which could very well be critiqued as degrading to women.

66. E.g., "It is just as essentially a part of 'the truth' to suffer in the world as to be triumphant in another world, in the world of truth—and Jesus Christ is the same in his abasement as in his loftiness" (Kierkegaard, *Practice in Christianity*, 154).

67. See Rae, *Kierkegaard's Vision of the Incarnation*, 109 n. 3; and Gouwens, *Kierkegaard as Religious Thinker*, 127.

is a life of action that flows out of a full heart, rather than the cold, abstract speculation of those who determine their own steps.[68]

MIRRORS OF JUDGMENT OR JOY

> *"May it be to you as you have believed"*; *"he who is forgiven little loves little."*[69]

There are a number of places where Kierkegaard (veronymously) suggested the character of judgment in Christianity. He sought to undo commonplace notions of judgment that are extrinsic to the individual and replace them with a far greater "horror"—the reaches of love which extend to the depths of the individual's soul.[70] It is only then, when such a contrast is created against this love in the individual, that she comes to realize her own sin.[71] The need for forgiveness is accentuated to an impossible degree and yet this forgiveness is declared by the gospel, unconditionally available for all. This, again, is the moment of crisis when a decision is demanded of "the single individual": *either* offense and a preservation of self *or* joyful acceptance and an abandonment of self. Such a decision, of course, is not rational or objective but comes out of the condition of the heart—hence these words of Scripture can serve equally as words of judgment *or* words of comfort, depending on *how they are read by the reader*.[72]

Christianity is therefore the infinitely subjective, existential element, and Kierkegaard emphasized the need for the reader's decision in the present. For him this moment was the eternal *now*: the moment of existence, and this constitutes the basis for such judgment: "For it does not say that those who are forgiven *loved* little. No, it says they *love* little."[73] Therefore

---

68. See III A: "Love Is the Fulfilling of the Law" in Part One of Kierkegaard, *Works of Love*, 99–136; and the concluding sermon in Kierkegaard, *Either/Or*.

69. "Conclusion," in Kierkegaard, *Works of Love*, 344–53 cf. Matthew 8:13; *Two Upbuilding Discourses* from 1851, published as chapter 15: "Luke 7:47," in Kierkegaard, *Spiritual Writings*, 279–88.

70. Kierkegaard, *Spiritual Writings*, 283.

71. ". . . love's judgment is the most severe judgment of all. What was the most severe judgement ever pronounced on the world? Was it the Flood? Was it the ruin of the tower of Babel? Was it the destruction of Sodom and Gomorrah? Wasn't it rather the yet more severe judgment pronounced in Christ's innocent death, love's own sacrifice? And what was the judgment? It was that love was not loved" (ibid., 282).

72. Ibid., 279–88.

73. Ibid., 286.

it is also eternally hopeful *and* eternally condemnatory, since the decisive moment is always present. In another manner of speaking, "the Christian like-for-like is: as you do unto others, God does unto you in the very same mode."[74] In this way, Kierkegaard's works serve as mirrors, and just as Christ did not come to judge, it is not Kierkegaard who judges the reader: instead, the reader judges *herself*.[75]

Judgment was not a simple cause-and-effect relation for Kierkegaard, but he presented it as a subordinate reality that the individual may choose instead of God. If a person seeks out sin, he will find it, but this is not extrinsic, rather, it lies *within* the individual and *how* he sees. Kierkegaard was not saying that God judges on the basis of some external standard or law and the individual's ability to uphold it. Instead, judgment is a *subjective reality* which opposes love, and an individual has the ability to "opt out" of this reality and be ushered into the other.[76] In this way, Kierkegaard saw that God's forgiveness is given unconditionally, but one must have the eyes to see it. This "Look of Love" is the precondition of faith, which is the *hidden* gift of God.[77]

CLIMACUS AND ANTI-CLIMACUS

It is helpful here to point out that Kierkegaard demonstrated through both Climacus and Anti-Climacus the implications of such *metanoia,* as can be seen in their subtle but significantly differing treatment of Pilate's question in John's gospel. As well as coming to a further understanding of the nature

---

74. Kierkegaard, *Works of Love*, 351.

75. Kierkegaard, *Point of View*, 15 and "the one who passes judgment is disclosed by the way he judges" (ibid., 18 n.). Cf. Anti-Climacus describing the God-man as "the sign of contradiction" as "a mirror: as he is forming a judgement, what dwells within him must be disclosed. It is a riddle, but as he is guessing the riddle, what dwells within him is disclosed by the way he guesses. The contradiction confronts him with a choice, and as he is choosing, together with what he chooses, he himself is disclosed" (Kierkegaard, *Practice in Christianity*, 126–27).

76. E.g., Kierkegaard, *Spiritual Writings*, 252; Kierkegaard, *Works of Love*, 351.

77. "The Look of Love," from *Eighteen Upbuilding Discourses*, 1843–44, published as chapter 11 in Kierkegaard, *Spiritual Writings*, 227–42. We must also keep in mind here Climacus' contrast between the Socratic and the Christian accounts of a learner's relation to the truth. For the Socratic, the truth is extrinsic and impersonal; for the Christian, Christ is the truth and the learner must relate to him through subjectivity and faith. Kierkegaard, "Philosophical Crumbs."

of truth for Christianity, we also see demonstrated a use of the pseudonyms, which will be explored further in the next sections.

According to Climacus, "subjectivity is truth."[78] So for him, it is at the moment when Pilate asked the question "What is truth?" that he abdicated his own existence and collapsed into impossible abstraction.[79] This question thereby removed him from the perilous uncertainties involved in existence and its requirement on Pilate to make an *un*informed decision regarding his prisoner (in objective uncertainty).[80] In following "the crowd" and its thirst for objectivity, Pilate revealed his own alienation from the truth. It is the danger and irresponsibility of such abstract thinking that Johannes Climacus seeks to address, particularly in *Concluding Unscientific Postscript*. Although such abstraction carries the appearance of wisdom and is successful in winning admiration from "the world," it does not stack up to the reality of life—i.e., the "essential truths" with which Christianity concerns itself.[81] By retreating into abstraction and imposing an objective view of truth on life, Pilate cut himself off from his own subjective engagement with the God-Man as well as from existence altogether. In doing so, he became "the fantastical *I-I*": Pilate's *hermeneutical stance* excluded him from the truth.[82] This problem of abstraction would exist for Pilate even if he had released Christ, since *knowing the truth comes subjectively*. Conversely, even if Pilate took it upon himself to make the decision to crucify Christ, he would still be infinitely closer to the truth, since he still embraced his own subjectivity and took part in existence as a "single individual"; i.e., he at least embraced the *how* of the truth.[83] Thus for Climacus (a non-Christian

---

78. Kierkegaard, *Concluding Unscientific Postscript*, 189.

79. Ibid., 229, John 18:37–8.

80. Kierkegaard, *Concluding Unscientific Postscript*, 203.

81. Ibid., 199 n.

82. Ibid., 193; Kierkegaard's emphasis on a person's hermeneutical stance (the way a person judges or sees) rather than explicit actions is the main theme in *Works of Love*. See for instance, (as discussed above in 1.2) the opening chapter: "Love's Hidden Life and Its Recognisability by Its Fruits" in Kierkegaard, *Works of Love*, 23–33.

83. See also Kierkegaard, *Concluding Unscientific Postscript*, 247: "Just as important as the truth, and of the two the even more important one, is the mode in which the truth is accepted, and it is of slight help if one gets millions to accept the truth if by the very mode of their acceptance they are transposed into untruth"; and ibid., 201: "If someone who lives in the midst of Christianity enters, with knowledge of the true idea of God, the house of God, the house of the true God, and prays, but prays in untruth, and if someone lives in an idolatrous land but prays with all the passion of infinity, although his eyes are resting upon the image of an idol—where, then, is there more truth? The one prays in

"experimentalist" who "climbs" from below),[84] what was problematic in this story was the disposition of Pilate.

Interestingly enough, Anti-Climacus also discusses this episode from John's gospel to demonstrate very similar implications of the fundamental importance of subjectivity, but he does this from the opposite direction to Climacus. For Anti-Climacus, "Christ is truth."[85] He does not approach the situation from the unchristian starting point of the necessity of the individual (Pilate) relating himself *subjectively* to his situation (that is, to take responsibility for his own existence and thereby make a decision). From this position, the person of Christ is entirely irrelevant. Instead, Anti-Climacus starts with the Christian reality of Christ as the truth. For Anti-Climacus, Pilate then becomes a fool not primarily because of his objective stance toward his own existence, but because he did not recognize Christ as the truth. Whereas what Climacus sees in Pilate could perhaps be described as a lack of courage to be an existing individual,[86] Anti-Climacus sees a *lack of faith* in Pilate to recognize Christ as the truth. Thereby Pilate lacked the eyes to see that Christ could not answer his question *directly* ("What is truth") because his entire *existence* was truth, and therefore he could not *in truth* say anything more. The truth is what the truth is, and cannot be qualified, because it is its own qualification.[87]

It is in *this* way that Pilate was judged by his own judgment, and revealed himself to be a fool.[88] In other words, Climacus sees subjectivity as appropriate to humanity and Christianity as complementary to it ("climbs" from below), whereas Anti-Climacus derives his understanding from, and grounds his view in, the *prior* reality of the gospel (the infinitely high

---

truth to God although he is worshiping an idol; the other prays in untruth to the true God and is therefore in truth worshiping an idol."

84. Evans, *Kierkegaard's Fragments and Postscript*, 21–24; the name of this pseudonym was taken from that of a monk in the sixth century known for his work *Ladder of Divine Ascent*. See Rae, *Kierkegaard and Theology*, 36.

85. Kierkegaard, *Practice in Christianity*, 154.

86. Note the suggestion above that the *greatness* of being a "single individual" is emphasized in the early pseudonymous works (referred to by Kierkegaard as his "aesthetic works").

87. See Kierkegaard, *Practice in Christianity*, 203–7; also, "Christ was the fulfilling of *the law*. From him we should learn how to understand this thought, for he was *the explanation*. Only when the explanation *is* what it explains, when the one who explains is that which is explained, when the explanation is the transfiguration, only then is there the right relationship" (Kierkegaard, *Works of Love*, 108).

88. Kierkegaard, *Practice in Christianity*, 203–4.

vantage point of faith). The existential reality of Christ as truth leads Anti-Climacus to *preach* in such an authoritative way, whereas Climacus is still playing (ironically) with probabilities and speculative thought.[89] Climacus may *say* that Christianity is viable, but he does not truly *believe* it because he does not embody it in *how* he speaks (i.e., in his explicit logic or manner of writing).

But there is an important question to consider here. While Anti-Climacus and Kierkegaard himself wrote from "inside" Christianity, Climacus is an outsider.[90] So, as Rae helpfully points out, how is it that he can have such extensive knowledge about faith and yet is one who does not have it?[91] Rae is then right to point out that full Christian knowing is an *embodied knowing* (though he does not use this phrase), and so he concludes that this is why Climacus has to be "a 'fantastic figure' who does not really exist."[92] But this does not quite solve the problem, since there are many who can articulate accurate knowledge *of* Christianity.[93] The solution instead is to emphasize the difference between "knowing of" and "knowing with," which we will explore later in this chapter. But regardless of this, there is still a need for a *metanoia*—a radical conversion in knowing.

CHRIST THE TRUTH

Away from the objective idealism of Socrates, Kierkegaard argued that the truth was not something innate and familiar to all human beings but was in fact Jesus Christ. The incarnation constituted a radical break in all human knowing, exposing humankind's various attempts to "ascend" to

---

89. A quote of Climacus' at the end of his discussion on Pilate supports my view: "If, however, subjectivity is truth and subjectivity is the existing subjectivity, then, if I may put it this way, Christianity is a perfect fit . . ." His use of this initial "if," as well as his ordering of logic is revealing. Kierkegaard, *Concluding Unscientific Postscript*, 230; note also Climacus' own description of himself as a "humoristic, experimental psychologist" who is not a Christian. See Evans, *Kierkegaard's Fragments and Postscript*, 21–24.

90. Kierkegaard's veronymous analysis of Pilate's question is in Kierkegaard, *Works of Love*, 103–8 esp. Kierkegaard uses this situation to demonstrate the importance of love as action, rather than the paralyzing effects of the law.

91. Rae, *Kierkegaard's Vision of the Incarnation*, 4, 23.

92. Ibid., 4; quoting Kierkegaard, *Journals and Papers*, 6/6349, X6 B 48, n.d., 1849.

93. Consider also Kierkegaard's view on the neutrality of knowledge, where what counts is how a person approaches it. See Part 2, chapter 2: "Love Believes All Things—and Yet Is Never Deceived," in Kierkegaard, *Works of Love*, 213–30.

1.3 The Gospel Truth

God as bankrupt.[94] Instead, Kierkegaard understood that knowing the truth meant being in relationship with the truth: not to grasp the truth, but instead to be grasped by it. This relationship took place in the "hidden inwardness" (subjectivity) of each believer as a "single individual."

This relationship is not characterized by intellectual acquisition of knowledge, but rather a continued striving to be conformed to the truth. Kierkegaard explains this by emphasizing the orthodox understanding of "the Word made flesh": Christ's *words* were not only key, but these words taken up and lived in a particular life was *the* Word of God—that is, Christ himself.[95] Thus, for a person to be *in the truth* (i.e., "in Christ"), she must strive to *embody* truth. As the only one who married actuality and ideality, Kierkegaard pointed to Christ as the prototype for the believer in the way that he embodied the truth in word and deed.[96] So to be a person who is "in the truth" is to be someone who strives for congruence between what is lived and what is spoken.[97]

The theological importance of subjectivity for Kierkegaard becomes clear as he repeatedly stated in many ways: his concern was not the *what* of Christianity but the *how*.[98] By this, Kierkegaard was not advocating for "the single individual" simply to abandon Christian teaching for the sake of genuinely believing in whatever (as could be derived from consulting only Climacus), but instead he was advocating for the Christian to embody the truth in a form that is faithful to Christ. *This* is what is meant by being "in the truth": it is to be *hid in Christ,* the congruent one.

In summary, to know the truth is to know *Christ* in subjective relationship. This relational participation of being in the truth is characterized by an ongoing striving toward conformity *with* the truth, such conformity being chiefly characterized by the attempt at congruence between what the believer says and what she does: what is *inward* with what is *outward*. Thus, the truth of Christ must be hidden within the heart of the believer.

---

94. The reader should keep in mind here Johannes Climacus and his discussion of Pilate "from below."

95. E.g., Kierkegaard, *Practice in Christianity*, 123–24, 203–5 especially; and Kierkegaard, *Spiritual Writings*, 297: "He is the truth, not in such a way that you get to know from Him what the truth is and are then left to yourself but so as to remain in the truth only by remaining in Him."

96. Rasmussen, *Between Irony and Witness*, 52–53.

97. See Kierkegaard, *Practice in Christianity*, 201–9 esp.

98. See Kierkegaard, *Journals and Papers*, 3/3684, X3 A 431, n.d., 1850; see also Climacus in Kierkegaard, *Concluding Unscientific Postscript*, 202.

Part I: The Content

PATHOS: THE HEART OF THE MATTER

Understanding that the truth of Christianity must be known *subjectively* (i.e., hidden in the heart of the believer) led Kierkegaard to emphasize the role of pathos or *passion* in such knowing. As Paul Holmer explains, Kierkegaard was not putting all disciplines and forms of knowing "in a continuum with the sciences as foundational and more basic. Instead he argues that the difference between scientific truths and what he calls 'essential truth,' ethico-religious truth, lies not in data, but in the way we use what we have."[99] We "use" the truth of Christ by embedding it in our heart, to make the transition from "knowing of" to "knowing with."[100]

Just as we know love only through loving, so we know the truth only by "abiding" in him.[101] This is where the role of pathos became important for Kierkegaard: it is the interestedness which opposes the disinterestedness that is characterized by objectivity, with objectivity being inappropriate for understanding life.[102] To know essential truth is to know in the *deepest* sense: it is to know with a believer's whole being. This is the *only proper* knowing for such matters. It is not simply a knowing of knowledge in the merely cognitive sense, but is a knowing that carries the mood, seriousness, passion, love etc., that is appropriate to such matters.[103] So, "[to] the concept of sin corresponds the mood of seriousness,"[104] and "[only] he who

---

99. Holmer, *On Kierkegaard and the Truth*, 72.

100. ". . . [to] be aware of the concepts of faith and love is not the same as the ability to use them . . ." (ibid., 139); see also Holmer, *The Grammar of Faith*, 25.

101. See John 15 and Kierkegaard, "Two Discourses at the Communion on Fridays"; Also, "Christ as Pattern for discipleship in this way provides the transcendent revealed model for existence that offers the standard for an individual to stand against her or his culture, to embody and 'do the truth'" (Gouwens, *Kierkegaard as Religious Thinker*, 232).

102. "But religion and morality suppose that one has an 'infinite personal interestedness,' a masterful passion, that is the defining condition of a human subject's life" (Holmer, *On Kierkegaard and the Truth*, 71).

103. As Climacus says, "With respect to existence, thinking is not at all superior to imagination and feeling but is coordinate" (Kierkegaard, *Concluding Unscientific Postscript*, 346–47) and "All existence-issues are passionate, because existence, if one becomes conscious of it, involves passion. To think about them so as to leave out passion is not to think about them at all, is to forget the point that one indeed is oneself an existing person. . . . The subjective thinker is not a scientist-scholar; he is an artist. To exist is an art" (ibid., 350–51).

104. Søren Kierkegaard, *The Concept of Dread* quoted in Holmer, *On Kierkegaard and the Truth*, 75.

abides in love can recognise love."[105] This emphasis on the inward and the importance of actions being grounded in the heart is found most clearly in Kierkegaard's *Works of Love*, where he stated in his opening prayer: "heaven is such that no act can be pleasing there unless it is an act of love . . ."[106]

CHRISTOMORPHIC POETICS

Kierkegaard understood that a Romantic poet was one who articulated beauty and truth in a form that attempted to carry the pathos appropriate to what was presented: the poet sought to elicit an emotional reaction to what he created.[107] But because Kierkegaard saw German Romanticism as concerned with the imagination alone, it ultimately was an abstraction and had no basis in actuality (real life).[108] Kierkegaard sought to illustrate how the writing of Romantic ironists carries beauty in its form but becomes ethically irresponsible when considered in light of actuality. Kierkegaard's pseudonymous satire of Schlegel's *Lucinde* in *The Seducer's Diary* extends such irresponsibility to that of nihilistic depravity, where an innocent young girl is left high and dry for the sake of the aesthetic whims of a seducer.[109] Such ideas are untenable in actuality because they are self-centered: they disregard morality and ethics for the sake of ideals.[110] Kierkegaard sought to demonstrate through this satire the repulsive horror of such a view.[111]

As a corrective, Kierkegaard advocated for a return to Socrates—"the master of irony"—and the Greek notion that "irony's great requirement [is]

---

105. Kierkegaard, *Works of Love*, 33.

106. Ibid., 19; Holmer is again helpful here: "Here he is radical, proposing that there is a kind of analysis of concepts which cannot be justified if they are abstracted from personality and subjectivity but can only be justified if done within the context of the subject's concerns and interests. Unlike, then, some language analysts, who study the language without the user, Kierkegaard does the analysis but with the user" (Holmer, *On Kierkegaard and the Truth*, 112).

107. This section (and its use of *Concept of Irony*) is heavily indebted to Joel Rasmussen's excellent work *Between Irony and Witness*.

108. ". . . the ironist is the eternal I for which no actuality is adequate" (Kierkegaard, *Concept of Irony*, 283).

109. Kierkegaard, *Either/Or*, 243–376; See also Rasmussen, *Between Irony and Witness*, 21; and Kierkegaard, *Concept of Irony*, 289.

110. Kierkegaard, *Concept of Irony*, 283.

111. Rasmussen, *Between Irony and Witness*, 21; and Kierkegaard, *Concept of Irony*, 289.

to live poetically." This occurs "only when he himself is oriented and thus integrated in the age in which he lives, is positively free in the actuality to which he belongs."[112] To illustrate, Kierkegaard's veronymous *Works of Love* describes two artists: one who travels the world to find a face worth painting, but ends in despair having found none. The other, who does not "pretend to be a real artist," rather finds joy in painting the faces of those nearest and dearest to him. Kierkegaard found the latter to be the true artist, and it is also this one who could be said to be "living poetically" in contrast to the other "poetically composing" the world around his own ideal notions of beauty. At the conclusion of the illustration it is suggested that the Christian should focus on "how love should be in order that it can love."[113] It is about how to orient *oneself* to actuality.

For Kierkegaard, true irony must relate itself to *both* ideality *and* actuality—not merely to the former. Here we have a transition from a self-centered manipulation of actuality ("to compose oneself [and one's environment] poetically") to a "let[ting] oneself be poetically composed."[114] Instead of an exclusive interest in imaginative abstraction, the true ironist attempts to live out the ideals she believes in. Kierkegaard saw that the strength of Romanticism was its pathos, and he attempted to retrieve and redirect such interestedness toward real life: to ground such affective knowing in actuality. This is the *embodiment* of truth.

Kierkegaard's corrective did not end there: most decisively he sought to recontextualise irony "under a religious life-view."[115] What prevented a person "living poetically" was sin: the "distance between ideality and actuality."[116] For Kierkegaard, there is only one who truly lived poetically— Jesus Christ. This is because *God* is the true poet who introduced himself into his own poem of creation through the incarnation, and by this "God 'fulfils' in actuality what every other poet only achieves in imagination, namely, a 'reconciliation' between the actual world and the divine ideal"— hence, a "Christomorphic poetics."[117]

---

112. Kierkegaard, *Concept of Irony*, 326.

113. Kierkegaard, *Works of Love*, 156–57.

114. Kierkegaard, *Concept of Irony*, 283.

115. Rasmussen, *Between Irony and Witness*, 23; see also Walsh, *Living Poetically*, 53.

116. Rasmussen, *Between Irony and Witness*, 52. Rasmussen references Kierkegaard's pseudonym Haufniensis for the claim that sin is what inhibits the reconciliation of the ideal with the actual, but I have been unable to locate the precise reference for this.

117. Ibid., 55.

This is also a place where we can see Kierkegaard's understanding of the relation between subjectivity and objectivity. The incarnation is the means by which God interrupted human history (i.e., objective actuality) and gave humanity the ultimate ideality—that is, himself—and thereby "expand[ed] the boundaries of the imaginable."[118] Thus the objective reality of the incarnation is the beginning of subjectivity for Kierkegaard,[119] in which the believer strives to live poetically according to the ideality of Christ "the prototype."[120] Christ is the congruent one, whose words matched his life. To be in the truth, then, is to strive after Christ "the prototype": the *how* in accord with the *what*. The Christian does not attempt to poeticise herself, but instead strives to have her life be "poetically composed" by the divine poet.[121]

THE PLACE OF ABSTRACTION AND THE CHARGE OF IRRATIONALISM

It is important to iterate here that Kierkegaard was *not* advocating for a complete dismissal of abstract thinking to be replaced by subjective knowing, but was instead arguing that when it comes to matters of "essential truth"—that is, matters of ethics and religion—such objectivity should be kept in its place.[122] When it comes to matters of existence, as Kierkegaard argued throughout his authorship (though most explicitly through Johannes Climacus), subjective passion is both natural and necessary in order to know such matters truly. Abstract reasoning, by contrast, is both appropriate and necessary for abstract knowledge (such as scientific or historical matters). It was Kierkegaard's understanding that this one way of knowing should not trump all others. As Paul Holmer explains, "It is Kierkegaard's theme, sounded clearly, that concepts that fit everywhere

---

118. Gouwens, *Kierkegaard as Religious Thinker*, 127.

119. In Climacus' term, "A Historical Point of Departure." Kierkegaard, "Philosophical Crumbs."

120. See Kierkegaard, *Practice in Christianity*, 238 esp.

121. Rasmussen, *Between Irony and Witness*, 10; drawing on Kierkegaard, *Journals and Papers*, 2/1445, XI2 A 98, n.d., 1854 and ibid., 2/1391, X1 A 605, n.d., 1849.

122. Kierkegaard is not putting all disciplines and forms of knowing "in a continuum with the sciences as foundational and more basic. Instead he argues that the difference between scientific truths and what he calls 'essential truth,' ethico-religious truth, lies not in data, but in the way we use what we have" (Holmer, *On Kierkegaard and the Truth*, 72).

really fit nowhere":[123] that is, a universal epistemology is both impossible and unhelpful.[124] Like the concept of *fact*, the use of *truth* is multiform and context-bound.[125] Theological truth, therefore, "must be done in the appropriate moods of praise, repentance, admonition, and exhortation or it will devolve into nonsense."[126]

By now it should be clear to the reader that Kierkegaard was not an irrationalist—he was merely claiming that the use of abstract rationality which was present in his day (and still in ours!) was far too wide, and the understanding of the nature of knowing was far too narrow, thus leading to an incongruent use of language and life: a *form* that did not match the *content*.[127] By accentuating the difference between Christian truth and historical or scientific truth, Kierkegaard was seeking to demonstrate the impossibility of transferring one form of knowing into the sphere of the other.[128] In the case of Christianity, subjective faith gives proper use to reason: a person cannot *start* from immediate, observable physicality and conclude that Christ is God, as this vision takes the eyes of faith.[129] From there reason can be employed alongside faith and in its service, as the rigorously intellectual nature of Kierkegaard's works show.

Christianity cannot be *reduced* to rational matters of ethics, history, science, etc.—it is completely separate from them, and must be known *with* and *from* faith. Knowing *about* faith and knowing *with* faith are two infinitely different things: in the latter, knowing is contingent upon subjectivity.

---

123. Ibid., 53; cf. Wittgenstein, *Investigations*, 10e, §13; see also chapter 8: "Theology, Atheism and Theism," in Holmer, *The Grammar of Faith*, 159–78.

124. "A point to remember about 'knowing God' is that the concept 'knowing' is always context-determined . . . there is no general epistemology" (Holmer, *The Grammar of Faith*, 186).

125. For Holmer's discussion on the concept of "fact," see ibid., 101–10. See also chapter 7: "Theology and Concepts" in ibid., 136–58, for instance "When those religious concepts are proposed in an appropriate context and with due weight given them, then humility, contrition, repentance, hope, love, and joy are also demanded. These are part of, not just applications of, the force of these concepts" (ibid., 158).

126. Barrett, *Kierkegaard*, 71; see also Gouwens, *Kierkegaard as Religious Thinker*, 19.

127. "And to imagine a language means to imagine a form of life" (Wittgenstein, *Investigations*, 11e, §19).

128. For instance, *Fear and Trembling* was used to such an end as a polemic against Hegel and Kant's "procrustean trimming" of the gospel to suit their absolute forms of knowing. See Rae, "The Risk of Obedience," 310–11.

129. See Kierkegaard, *Practice in Christianity*, 124–27 etc.; also, Rasmussen, *Between Irony and Witness*, 11.

It is not *irrational* to know something in the way it is to be known, quite the opposite: it is foolishness to impose a universal epistemology upon all subject matter, in much the same way that love cannot be known through mathematics: "Like is known by like."[130] Thus, the *hidden* Christ must be known in *hidden inwardness*.[131]

Michael Polanyi could be helpful here in dialogue with Kierkegaard, since he puts forward the thesis that *all* knowing is personal—not just the ethical and religious, but science and mathematics as well. He subtly draws on the language of John's gospel—"indwelling"—to discuss knowing as an embodiment of the truth.[132] T. F. Torrance and his understanding of "scientific knowing" and knowing something in accordance with its "intrinsic logos"—that is, knowing something according to the manner in which it presents itself—could also be helpful here.[133] Unfortunately I lack the space to investigate these matters here, and in this book I have restricted my attentions to Kierkegaard himself.

CONCLUSION

For Kierkegaard, truth was the person of Jesus Christ, who "the single individual" knows by faith. Constituting a radical break or *metanoia* from the Socratic understanding of disembodied objectivity, Kierkegaard's Christian understanding concerned the relationship a "single individual" has with God in Christ. This was therefore fundamentally opposed to the learner being able to know essential truth autonomously, but instead depended on the knower being grasped by, or *hidden in*, Christ himself. Such a relationship was therefore characterized by the learner striving to remain in the truth through the congruence between the *how* and the *what* of her life, thus developing the "form of life" that was appropriate to Christianity.

So as we have seen throughout the first part of our research, because the truth is *hidden* ("the incognito"), an individual must herself also become *hidden* (subjective; a "single individual") to know him. This was the *content* of Kierkegaard's task.

130. Kierkegaard, *Works of Love*, 33.

131. "[T]o use [theology] supposes that we translate from the third-person the mood of being their knowledge and language 'about' God to becoming my language 'of' faith" (Holmer, *The Grammar of Faith*, 25).

132. See Polanyi, *Personal Knowledge*.

133. Torrance, *The Mediation of Christ*, 13.

PART II: THE FORM

In this second part we move on to look at how Kierkegaard's *form* of writing was itself an attempt at "indirect communication." We will see how Kierkegaard's concepts are put to work in the space between his texts and his reader, particularly his concept of "the single individual." We will come to see in greater depth how Kierkegaard's authorship took the form of *hiddenness*.

It is important to note that this area is one of the main roots of contention in Kierkegaardian scholarship. It is generally recognized that Kierkegaard employed "indirect communication" in his work, but the question is how far this *form* of communication extended: What does it mean when a work is pseudonymous and how should it be interpreted? Are the works which carry Kierkegaard's name to be taken as what Kierkegaard *really* thinks? To what extent are the various works subjective or objective? Was Kierkegaard simply deceiving his readers? As we shall see, none of these questions can be answered *truly* in a straightforward manner.

At the center of this debate is Kierkegaard's veronymous work "The Point of View for My Work as an Author," in which Kierkegaard, in his own name, claims to *directly* explain his entire authorial strategy. The fundamental question here is whether or not to take this work at face value. I have chosen to use this work as the hermeneutical key for Kierkegaard's authorship, and in this section I will use it under the assumption of its usefulness. Such a decision is not a simple one for scholars, who seek to weigh such matters under the pretense of objectivity. So the issue here does not so much concern the contents of this work, but rather the hermeneutical (in)capacities which readers bring to it. It is for this reason that we will look at various ways in which Kierkegaard is being read today and evaluate them using Kierkegaard's take on hermeneutics (drawing particularly on *Works of Love*) and leave a focused discussion of "The Point of View for My Work as an Author" to the following section (Part III), where we will consider the coherency of this work within Kierkegaard's authorship as a whole.

For now, we will see how Kierkegaard adopted a hidden form of authorship for the sake of "that single individual whom I will call *my* reader."[1]

---

1. Kierkegaard, *Christian Discourses*, 359, emphasis author's own.

2.1 "The Single Individual" as Authorial Form

The Outward Dimension

INTRODUCTION

Kierkegaard's understanding of Christianity as embodied truth as opposed to disembodied abstraction had profound implications for his authorship—implications for both his reader and himself. In this chapter we will explore the implications for Kierkegaard's readers. As we have established, to be hidden in Christ as Kierkegaard understood himself and other Christians to be, was to be hidden in the truth. Therefore, in terms of the outward dimension of his hidden authorship, Kierkegaard sought to communicate Christianity in such a way that encouraged and made space for his reader to meet God in the quietness of her own heart. Thus, Kierkegaard's authorship took the form of *hiddenness*.

As we have seen, Kierkegaard understood that the true task of humanity was to become *subjective*—that is, for each person to follow and to participate in Christ (both as savior and prototype) by living according to the faithful realization that each person is a "single individual" under God.[1]

---

1. Kierkegaard, *Journals and Papers*, 1/334, X1 A 279, n.d., 1849. In regard to Christ as both savior and prototype, Gouwens notes that Climacus focuses on the idea of the former, while Anti-Climacus introduces the latter. This is because Climacus is not so much concerned with the ethical implications of Christianity, but rather the ideas. Anti-Climacus, as a super-Christian, is one who emphasizes the necessity of both conversion and the new life of the believer. See *Kierkegaard as Religious Thinker*, 127 and "In contrast to Luther, who stressed Christ as the atoner against 'a too zealous and too enthusiastic desire to make Christ only the prototype,' Kierkegaard's emphasis on the prototype is meant

This is to be whom God has created *me* to be.[2] *Outwardly* this meant that Kierkegaard's communication must be undertaken by adopting an *indirect* form, as it would be fundamentally self-defeating if given directly. And so we begin this section with an overview of "indirect communication," with a particular emphasis on Kierkegaard's use of pseudonyms.

"INDIRECT COMMUNICATION" AND THE FUNCTION OF THE PSEUDONYMS

As Anti-Climacus points out in his discussion of Pilate's question, Christ is truth.[3] If Pilate was not convinced by truth standing before him, how could an explicit explanation from the mouth of truth appeal to something greater than itself to legitimate itself to him? As has been mentioned earlier, truth is its own qualification, and it is for this reason that Kierkegaard repeatedly emphasized that *essential* truth cannot be communicated *directly* but must be communicated *indirectly*. In contrast, objective truth would be most suitable to direct communication, since the *what* is detached and is completely free of the need of a complementary *how*.[4] The learner must be free for herself to see Christ *as* truth, since a didactic communication of it would actually undermine this truth by transforming it into something else. Direct communication cannot communicate the subjective and *hidden* invitation of gospel because it takes this inwardness and instantly converts it into outwardness—into a matter of cognitive assent rather than

---

to redress the balance. Christ helps the believer, but to an end: the end of imitation. The atonement is not an end in itself, but is meant to issue in a life" (ibid., 128).

2. See, for instance, Kierkegaard's discourses on learning from "the lilies of the field and the birds of the air" collected in Kierkegaard, *Spiritual Writings*, 85–224, one of which is entitled "The Glory of Being Human" (113–33). This is what Anti-Climacus describes as being a "single individual" under God (that is, to have faith: "in relating to itself and in wanting to be itself, the self is grounded transparently in the power that established it"), rather than one who, in despair, seeks to be anything more than this, or abdicates responsibility altogether. See *Sickness*, 79ff.

3. See 1.3: "Climacus and Anti-Climacus," above.

4. "Reduplicated in the teacher through his existing in what he teaches, the communication is in manifold ways a self-differentiating art. And now when the teacher, who is inseparable from and more essential than the teaching, is a paradox, then all direct communication is impossible. But in our day everything is made abstract and everything personal is abolished: we take Christ's teaching—and abolish Christ. This is to abolish Christianity, for Christ is a person and is the teacher who is more important than the teaching" (Kierkegaard, *Practice in Christianity*, 123–24).

personal encounter—thus in the very act of communication eliminating the possibility of "the single individual."

One particular way to map this situation is, again, from Climacus (below) to Anti-Climacus (above).[5] *Philosophical Fragments* outlines how Christianity requires the *capacity* of faith rather than the acquisition of knowledge. In this work, Climacus regards the incarnation as "the Absolute Paradox" which eludes being understood by human reason. But note well, Climacus is exploring this as a "thought experiment" with the aid of the best in human reasoning abilities, and is not committing himself to the vulnerable "objective uncertainty" of being in a position to accept Christianity. He is merely arguing for Christianity's logical possibility and what it means (in an *objective* sense) to have faith.

From the other side, Anti-Climacus in *Practice in Christianity* "relates indirect communication extensively to Christ."[6] From the vantage point of faith, Anti-Climacus understands Christ to be "a *sign of contradiction*"[7] which must be *either* rejected in the self-sufficiency of "offense" *or* clung to in absolute dependency as "the object of faith."[8] Both moves are utterly subjective since "the sign of contradiction"—that this one particular human being is, in fact, God—transcends reason: *either* Christ is God, in which case the individual suspends their self-sufficient reasoning capacities, *or* he is not, in which case the individual's illusion of self-sufficiency is retained. Because this encounter questions the limits of human reason, reason itself is suspended and the individual must make an "uninformed" decision. But again note well, Anti-Climacus is speaking from the perspective that Christ is God, and is outlining the task of the individual in this light. So for Anti-Climacus, what is being discussed is not (primarily) an interesting intellectual phenomenon, but is rather a matter of fact.[9]

"Indirect communication" is the communication of a capability.[10] In regard to Christianity, this communication concerns the capacity of an individual to recognize Christ as God. Both Climacus and Anti-Climacus

---

5. Climacus being one who sympathizes with Christianity only intellectually, and does not himself have faith; Anti-Climacus being one who has extraordinary faith and is thus a kind of super-Christian. See Kierkegaard, *Journals and Papers*, 6/6349, X6 B 48, n.d., 1849.

6. Gouwens, *Kierkegaard as Religious Thinker*, 15.

7. Kierkegaard, *Practice in Christianity*, 124, emphasis author's own.

8. "The sign of offense and the object of faith . . ." (ibid., 35 etc.).

9. That is, a *theological* fact.

10. Gouwens, *Kierkegaard as Religious Thinker*, 14–15.

note that this is beyond the reach of human reason: the incarnation is the "Absolute Paradox" (Climacus), the "sign of contradiction" (Anti-Climacus) that cannot be understood by resolving this confrontation logically but must be allowed to stand, and thereby must *either* be understood by faith *or* rejected. And in order for the reader to recognize the God-man, she cannot be led one way or the other but must be given free rein in the matter to make her own decision: either to dismiss the sign as ludicrous, or to accept it in faith—the point is the individual's own ability to see this choice. "Authorial tyranny" is a direct communication that seeks to skew the presentation of such matters to the author's viewpoint.[11] This then transfers the matter into the realm of the objective, where the gospel stands or falls according to rhetoric or human reason, and the fundamental necessity of the choice is undermined. According to Anti-Climacus, a person becomes a Christian not by being won over by the communicator, but by seeing "the sign of contradiction" in faith.[12]

Now we see the important function of the pseudonyms. Through these "nonperson[s],"[13] the reader is deprived of the false security of resorting to the author as an anchor for knowing what to believe. Instead, the reader is forced to reflect on her own understanding. It is in this way that Kierkegaard provides the chance for his reader to embody subjectivity and to practice it *in the very act of reading*. Kierkegaard utilized pseudonyms to distance himself from his works for the purposes of encouraging his reader to reflect on her own subjective position as a "single individual." This distancing of himself from "his" work[14] functions to provide space for the reader to decide *for herself* whether Christianity is true or not.[15]

11. Ibid., 14.

12. "A contradiction placed squarely in front of a person—if one can get him to look at it—is a mirror; as he is forming a judgement, what dwells within him must be disclosed. It is a riddle, but as he is guessing the riddle, what dwells within him is disclosed by the way he guesses. The contradiction confronts him with a choice, and as he is choosing, together with what he chooses, he himself is disclosed" (Kierkegaard, *Practice in Christianity*, 127).

13. Ibid., 133.

14. Attempting to keep in mind Kierkegaard's (veronymous) warning at the end of *Concluding Unscientific Postscript*: ". . . in the pseudonymous books there is not a single word by me" (Kierkegaard, *Concluding Unscientific Postscript*, 626), also Climacus' assessment of the authorship of *Either/Or*: "The absence of an author is a means of distancing" (ibid., 252).

15. This also freed Kierkegaard to say what needed to be said (conveying information along with demonstrating different possible perspectives) without being personally

2.1 "The Single Individual" as Authorial Form

It is thus in the very *form* of his authorship that Kierkegaard accomplishes his task. Kierkegaard operated under the belief that subjectivity was absolutely vital for his reader to accept the communication of Christianity (essential truth). In this way, the *how* (this condition of receptivity) was just as important as the communication itself (the *what*), and they can be understood to be one-and-the-same: "The *how* of the truth is precisely the truth."[16]

This can be illustrated by looking at the following statement by Climacus as an example.

"Subjectivity is Truth"[17]

For Kierkegaard, this was a necessary point to make, since subjectivity was central to being a "single individual." But the problem was in *communicating* this fact. To avoid an untruth which would mislead both his readers and himself into the realm of objectivity, he employed "indirect communication" through the use of pseudonyms (namely Johannes Climacus) in order to make this point.

This is because if Kierkegaard was to make such a claim *directly* in his *own name* it would be unhelpful on two fronts: Firstly, it would be self-contradictory, for it is incongruous to make an *objective* claim about *subjectivity*. To *directly* advocate for subjectivity is a contradiction in terms because, as we have seen, direct communication is suitable only in communicating objective truth. An objective claim about subjectivity only hinders the reader from discovering this personal and *hidden* truth for herself, and this act of discovery is at the very heart of the point attempting to be made. In putting this claim in the mouth of Climacus, Kierkegaard acknowledges that he understands and is aware of this contradiction, and so uses a "nonperson"[18] to say what cannot be said "in truth" (i.e., congruently).

Secondly, such a direct claim would undermine the very subjectivity it sought to encourage in the reader. In order to challenge what Kierkegaard saw as the Hegelian tendency to neglect existence and the need for personal decision-making in his society, Kierkegaard could not resort to didacticism

---

implicated in having such views. This was an outworking of Kierkegaard attempting to write "in the truth," as we will explore in Part III.

16. Kierkegaard, *Concluding Unscientific Postscript*, 323.
17. Ibid., 189ff.
18. Kierkegaard, *Practice in Christianity*, 133.

PART II: THE FORM

to simply win others to his own point of view. This would, of course, defeat the very point that he wished to make. For the reader of Kierkegaard's works, there is no hiding behind the genius of the author by seeing him as an "authority": Kierkegaard deliberately removed this temptation from his readership by distancing himself from his work. Instead he sought to establish an opportunity for his reader to exercise her hermeneutical responsibility and thereby realize herself as a "single individual."

HIDDEN BENEFACTION

As we will explore below, *Works of Love* can be understood to be the heart of Kierkegaard's ethics, and is therefore important in understanding his own view of his authorship.[19] In this work, Kierkegaard outlined his understanding that, for the Christian, relational exchanges between persons are always mediated by God, who is the "middle term."[20] Because God is love, he is thereby the only foundation for true love. Therefore the greatest act of love one person can do for another is to point this person to God.[21] Given this to be the case, how did Kierkegaard himself, as one attempting to communicate Christianity, go about helping his reader toward God? How did he love his reader?

In a passage key to understanding his authorship, Kierkegaard stated: "the lover knows how to make himself unnoticed, so that the recipient does not become dependent on him—by crediting him with the greatest benefaction . . . the greatest benefaction, to help another to stand on his own, cannot be done directly."[22] Here we have a clear ethical and theological basis for Kierkegaard's authorial form of *hiddenness*, which is the attempt to *indirectly* help the reader to meet God for herself. Kierkegaard had to hide himself to avoid the reader deceiving herself by looking to him as her benefactor, which would hinder the gospel's requirement for complete dependence on God alone as a "single individual."

In contrast, to use *direct* communication (didacticism, rhetoric, romantic pathos, and the like) in communicating the secret invitation of God in Christ lends itself to the belief that such a communication can be

---

19. See below: 2.22, "The Look of Love."

20. Kierkegaard, *Works of Love*, 112–13, 282–83.

21. "Therefore to love another person means to help him to love God and to be loved means to be helped" (ibid., 124).

22. Ibid., 255–56.

2.1 "The Single Individual" as Authorial Form

enough to bring someone into the "truth" of the gospel. But as we have seen repeatedly, it is the subjective passion of *faith* and not reason or emotion that gives an individual the capacity to recognize Christ as truth.[23] As we have discussed above, this is not to dismiss reason (or emotion), but to reappropriate it under the religious:[24] Christ cannot be known objectively, but only through passionate subjectivity, i.e., in faith. Therefore reason, which is autonomous and objective, is out of place when it comes to the subjective invitation of God in Christ, and to employ such reason by communicating this invitation *directly* is to take matters out of God's hands and to place confidence in human capacity, which Kierkegaard understood to be antithetical to the gospel.[25] Such visible benefaction is dangerous for both speaker and listener, since it ignores God as the "middle term." Instead, as "one without authority" (i.e., without apostolic authority from God to speak faith into another),[26] Kierkegaard sought to bring his reader into the awareness of the choice that the gospel requires of her as a "single individual."[27]

---

23. Lee Barrett explains that the reason why Kierkegaard comes across as ambiguous regarding the origin of faith is that he is not communicating in abstract, systematic doctrine, but is rather concerned with what will be helpful for his reader in living faithfully. For him, faith is both "act" and "gift." See *Kierkegaard*, 60–66. Faith, for Kierkegaard, is first and foremost a gift from God, and then is something to be developed. It is by no means a human capacity, but is in fact the opposite: it is a complete dependence on God. Although Barrett is helpful, I myself order Kierkegaard's understanding of faith in this way because our discussion here is concerning conversion, which texts like *Philosophical Fragments* focus on, whereas for the unbeliever, faith is understood to be a gift. For the Christian, i.e., *Works of Love* or *Practice in Christianity*, faith is something already obtained and must be outworked and grown into, so faith here is an act. By favoring one reading of Kierkegaard here, I am simply doing what Kierkegaard did—presenting an existential argument rather than a systematic one.

24. Sylvia Walsh points out that Kierkegaard's three stages of existence are not mutually exclusive, as if the religious cancels out the aesthetic or the ethical, but rather that all ways of knowing are reconfigured and redirected under the religious. See her *Living Poetically*.

25. For even to assert that the gospel or some such element of Christianity is true is to undermine its truth and instead treats such an assertion as being more fundamental than the truth of what is asserted.

26. This phrase can then also be interpreted as a veiled criticism of the practice of ordinancy in the Danish established church. For a more thorough exploration of this concept, see Whittaker, "Kierkegaard on the Concept of Authority."

27. See Kierkegaard, *Point of View*, 7, 50–53; "Kierkegaard contrived his literature to make it possible only for individuals to respond to it" (Holmer, *On Kierkegaard and the Truth*, 47).

In order to do this, Kierkegaard *hid himself* through the use of pseudonyms and by deflecting his reader away from himself and toward God.[28] This *authorship of hiddenness* is indirect communication, and *inwardly* was an outworking of Kierkegaard's Christian discipleship. Likewise, it is his *outward* attempt to "reintroduce Christianity into Christendom" by stirring up room in the reader's own subjectivity in order for her to be made "aware" of the confrontation between herself and the gospel.[29] This authorship was thus Kierkegaard's way of imitating Christ (rather than simply admiring him from a distance): the one who himself was "the incognito."[30]

THE PSEUDONYMS AS PATHOS-FILLED DEMONSTRATIONS

The reason why Climacus and Anti-Climacus (and even Kierkegaard himself) can say such similar things demonstrates that it is not the *what* but the *how* of Christianity that matters.[31] The outward contents of many different issues (subjectivity, Christ as truth, "indirect communication," "the single individual," and so on) have remarkable parallels throughout the pseudonymous and veronymous works, and it is easy to expound these themes as outward, intellectual concepts without paying attention to the names of the authors that accompany these works. This is the case with Niels Thulstrup, who argues that *Philosophical Fragments* is not "genuinely pseudonymous" because the *content* of the material echoes Kierkegaard's

---

28. "However, it must be said that many who praise him most misunderstand him. He did not want readers who would become Christian in virtue of his authorship. In fact, the burden of the explanatory work, *The Point of View*, is just this, namely, that he cannot in virtue of his own understanding of himself, of the Christian faith, and of his authorship, constitute himself as a direct agent for the production of religiosity in another. The kind of publicity he gets nowadays, however, suggests that he failed. The public advocates are mistaken. Many of them, at worst, are fawning before a genius, or, at best, are overly anxious to give honor where their debt is great. There is, though another misunderstanding and this is rooted in the failure to read and to understand the man's authorship as the kind of work he wished it to be" (Holmer, *On Kierkegaard and the Truth*, 15).

29. Kierkegaard, *Point of View*, 7 n.

30. See chapter 6 in Kierkegaard, *Practice in Christianity*, 233–57 no. III; it is significant that Kierkegaard calls his own aesthetic, pseudonymous work "the incognito," the very title Anti-Climacus gives to Christ: Kierkegaard, *Point of View*, 58.

31. "Even when Climacus says something that Kierkegaard would personally agree with, there is still very often an important difference in *how* he says it" (Evans, *Kierkegaard's Fragments and Postscript*, 52).

own signed views.[32] But along with what has already been said so far in this chapter regarding the function of the pseudonyms, it is important to argue that these various voices are *demonstrations* of the *use* of these concepts, rather than the communication of various concepts *per se*.

Regarding our discussion in the previous section on *pathos*, it is vital to keep in mind (or heart, rather) that concepts relating to essential truth must be taken up in a life and used.[33] So although it may appear as problematic to Murray Rae that an outsider such as Johannes Climacus can have such insightful knowledge of the main concepts of Christianity,[34] this difficulty dissolves when we notice that this character reduces Christianity to the level of an intellectual game in the way he *uses* it.[35] Anti-Climacus, for instance, does not speak hypothetically *about* the gospel, but speaks *from* it with absolute faith since it is not merely a matter of knowledge but a matter of life. It is perfectly plausible for an outsider to have *knowledge* about the Christian understanding of truth and conversion, but it is impossible for such an outsider to live according to that knowledge: to truly *know* God is to *love* him,[36] and this is impossible from the standpoint of unbelief.[37] Such a person may have knowledge of Christianity, but it is in the heartfelt *use* of such knowledge that a person is judged.[38]

32. According to Evans, "The Role of Irony," 76.

33. As Paul Holmer helpfully articulates: "To be aware of the concepts of faith and love is not the same as the ability to use them . . . But it would have been a mistake for Kierkegaard only to contribute a few more paragraphs to compound the confusion. Therefore, he again breaks with the pattern altogether. He chooses to teach, by a kind of indirection, what it means to be a responsible person, and, thereby, he also hopes to provide the clue even to the ordering of one's concepts. His pseudonyms are living subjects who show us the uses of the 'I' with which we are already familiar" (Holmer, *On Kierkegaard and the Truth*, 139).

34. Rae, *Kierkegaard's Vision of the Incarnation*, 23–5.

35. The fact that this use of Christianity is ironic will be discussed in the following chapter, and does not impinge on my argument here.

36. Holmer, *The Grammar of Faith*, 25.

37. "Climacus affirms quite clearly that it is possible to know what Christianity is without being a Christian. But he affirms just as clearly that there is a difference between knowing what Christianity is and knowing what it is to be a Christian . . ." (Evans, *Kierkegaard's Fragments and Postscript*, 52).

38. This is a theme throughout *Works of Love*. See, for instance: ". . . mistrust, on the *basis* of the disbelief which is in mistrust, concludes, assumes, and believes what it concludes, assumes and believes; whereas from the same knowledge, on the *basis* of belief, one can conclude, suppose, and believe the very opposite. . . . one forgets that judgment lies much closer, that it takes place every moment, because existence judges you every

PART II: THE FORM

We have in the pseudonyms existence-communications which are confined to the literary realm, where we see demonstrations of the relation between concepts and their use—both exemplary (as in the case of Anti-Climacus) and otherwise (e.g., Climacus).

CONCLUSION

As we have seen in this chapter, Kierkegaard employed the use of "indirect communication" in order, by the very act of reading, to give opportunity to essential concepts being taken up and used in the reader's own life: namely, the concept of "the single individual." Kierkegaard attempted to be faithful to the form of Christian truth by *hiding* himself from the reader through employing pseudonyms. These various characters were not employed so much to present varying points of view, but were rather utilized to demonstrate the proper and improper use of Christian concepts.

---

moment you live, inasmuch as to live is to judge oneself, to become open" (Kierkegaard, *Works of Love*, 214–15).

2.2 An Overview of Kierkegaard's Authorship

INTRODUCTION

It is here that we come to an appropriate understanding of Kierkegaard's authorship as a whole—at least in terms of its outward function. According to Kierkegaard's own *direct* take on his authorial task in *Point of View*, these works are divided between the "aesthetic" and the "religious" literature. We will discuss how both of these "hands" lead the true reader into engaging with what we shall call "the hidden middle"—the *telos* of Kierkegaard's task, where the reader was deceived or directed into meeting God for herself in the hiddenness of her own heart. There is no substantial reason for not following Kierkegaard's own explanation of his authorship in *Point of View*, where he claims that the majority of his works serve to create a unified picture. Even many issues that are claimed to be later developments by some can be explained as reiterations of what was said earlier in the authorship. As Paul Holmer comments: "it seems plausible that his volumes do not describe a fundamental development in the thought of their author; instead, they can be best understood as a single work in many chapters."[1] Here we will seek to explore this division between the aesthetic and the religious works, giving special attention to how this diverse unity was designed to interact with the reader.

---

1. Holmer, *On Kierkegaard and the Truth*, 21.

Part II: The Form

THE MAIEUTIC FUNCTION OF THE AESTHETIC WORKS

> *When a man has filled his mouth so full of food that for this reason he cannot eat and it must end with his dying of hunger, does giving food to him consist in stuffing his mouth even more or, instead, in taking a little away so that he can eat?*[2]

The first step in reintroducing Christianity to Christendom was for Kierkegaard to *indirectly* communicate to his reader that she needed to realize herself as a "single individual." In order to counteract the "enormous illusion" of Christendom which he saw as preventing his reader from realizing herself as a "single individual,"[3] Kierkegaard, in his early pseudonymous work,[4] employed the Socratic method of the maieutic. This attempt at eliciting an inward realization was to be the occasion, it was hoped, for receiving faith as a gift from God in order to come into Christian truth, but until this took place, Kierkegaard understood a person to be in "untruth." After a reader had come to a realization of herself as a "single individual," she was still in the fundamental error of being apart from God,[5] and had to move *from* there to make a subjective decision for God in faith.

As we have seen in our discussion of Climacus' *Philosophical Fragments*,[6] Socrates claimed that the truth must lie innate in the human learner and the teacher of the truth was insignificant, since he or she merely helped the learner to give birth to what she already knew, hence the Greek "maieutics" meaning "that which pertains to midwifery." Through the pseudonyms, Kierkegaard saw himself following in the line of Socrates by rolling "out the carpet of the discourse"[7] and exposing his reader to what she herself *really* knew. But Socrates used this method ironically, to show

---

2. Kierkegaard, *Concluding Unscientific Postscript*, 275.

3. Kierkegaard, *Point of View*, 23.

4. This is purposely not including the religious works of the super-Christian Anti-Climacus, which did not exist at the time that Kierkegaard wrote *Point of View*. Hereafter I refer to this group of work as "the aesthetic works," following Kierkegaard's own term for them. This term is linked to Kierkegaard using these works as "crowd-pullers": providing the public with interesting works that would appeal to a general readership. See ibid., 7–9.

5. See our discussion regarding the single individual and the sins of weakness and defiance in *Sickness Unto Death* above in 1.2: "'The Single Individual': A Dialectic of Being."

6. See 1.3: "The Socratic and Christianity: Philosophical Fragments" above.

7. A phrase from Themistocles. See Kierkegaard, "Philosophical Crumbs," 102.

that his interlocutor was under the *illusion* of knowing, and in reality did not know anything!

Kierkegaard saw himself as the Christian Socrates in Christendom,[8] and therefore applied the maieutic in an attempt to help his reader to remove from her the illusion of the security of Christendom (along with accompanying fashionable intellectual errors such as German Romanticism and Hegelianism). In order for this to happen it was imperative that his reader's problems were not diagnosed from the outside, since this would in all likelihood cause the reader to be defensive of her own position. The social illusions surrounding Christendom were so pervasive and all-encompassing that to question these myths of society would be to question society itself and the reader's place within it, which is a very delicate matter. Instead, Kierkegaard sought to help the reader diagnose her *own* deluded condition, in the hope that she would willingly part with these illusions.[9]

Another way to explain this is to understand that the truth Kierkegaard sought to communicate was *essential* truth: truth relating to existence. As we have discussed above, such truth could not be merely acquired nor brushed aside, but carried existential implications in regard to whether the individual accepted them or not. For this reason, direct communication or prescription was impossible: such truth had to be discovered by the learner herself.

So his aesthetic works largely constituted the *negative* part of Søren Kierkegaard's authorship, where he sought to *remove* what was hindering his reader's ability to recognize truth. He did this by causing his reader to reflect inwardly on what she herself believed, thus promoting the reader's individuality as apart from "the crowd." This happened chiefly through the use of pseudonyms, where the "authorial tyranny" was diffused by Kierkegaard's distancing (*hiding*) himself from his works,[10] thus cutting such literary demonstrations free from any appeal to authority. The issue could no longer be "What does the author think," but rather "What do *I* think?"[11]

---

8. See Kierkegaard, *Point of View*, 24, 54–55.

9. Ibid., 42–3.

10. Gouwens, *Kierkegaard as Religious Thinker*, 14.

11. Poole, "The Unknown Kierkegaard," as quoted in Evans, "The Role of Irony in Kierkegaard's *Philosophical Fragments*," 65.

Part II: The Form

The Hiddenness of Grace

By way of example, one of the many characteristics which constituted the illusion of Christendom was the belief in human self-sufficiency. To solve this, the aesthetic works were intended to make Christianity infinitely more difficult to obtain. This occurs, for instance, in *Concluding Unscientific Postscript* where Climacus seeks to go against the grain of his contemporaries by seeking to become an author who will "make difficulties everywhere."[12] This pseudonym derides the intellectual simplification of thinkers in his society,[13] claiming that such abstract approaches are monstrous distortions of actuality. He advocates instead for the unsettling complication of *subjectivity* as the basis for knowing. More attempts at complication and disruption are carried out by Johannes De Silentio in his treatment of Abraham being willing to sacrifice his son: Abraham's Christian faith cannot be simplified to conform or sit under under such systems as humanistic ethics or rationality, but rather exists as existential anguish for him as a "single individual" (hence the title *Fear and Trembling*).

Such disruption was designed to elicit despair and a sense of the impossibility of Christianity in his reader.[14] This is the case both in the works which focus on the role of speculative thought (such as *Philosophical Fragments*), but also those works which discuss the role of the ethical (such as *Fear and Trembling*). In the latter, the infinite ethical demand of Christianity on the reader was intended to overwhelm and to throw her into despair that would lead her ultimately to abandon hope centered on her own self's performance, thus creating a crisis of decision that would make the realization of the religious possible: an existential dependence on the grace of God.

The positive element of this is most clearly seen in the concluding sermon in *Either/Or*: "The Edifying in The Thought That Against God We

---

12. Kierkegaard, *Concluding Unscientific Postscript*, 187.

13. Like Hegel, of course.

14. This is certainly the case for readers like Louis Mackey and Paul Ricoeur: the former dismisses Kierkegaard's pseudonymous presentation of Christianity as having "degenerated to contradiction and nonsense. Christianity has become not difficult to believe, but completely incredible" (Mackey, *Kierkegaard*, 242). Ricoeur states: "Surely the Christianity he described is so extreme that no one could possibly practise it. The subjective thinker before God, the pure contemporary with Christ, suffering crucifixion with Him, without church, without tradition, and without ritual, can only exist outside of history" ("Philosophy After Kierkegaard," 13).

Are Always in The Wrong."[15] This is a sermon that radically relativizes the cases of both A (an aesthetic view of living well) and Judge William (an ethical view of living well) in the earlier sections of the book by introducing the religious sphere of existence, claiming that it is not the self-sufficiency of a person's ability to attain beauty or truth, but a dependency on God through the other-affirming nature of love that is the best way to live.[16] This of course is the ultimate complication since it is the ultimate subjectivity, that a person fundamentally lacks the capacity to live *rightly* altogether. Entertaining this take on life strips the reader of any claim to autonomy and propels her into an utter dependency on God's grace.[17]

Irony

Kierkegaard based a great deal of his understanding of irony on Socrates, who was the main subject for his university thesis, *The Concept of Irony* (hence the subtitle: *With Continual Reference to Socrates*). Socratic irony was that which sought to reveal to the other (in Socrates' case, an interlocutor; in Kierkegaard's, the intended reader) the truth within them, in continuity with Socrates' theory of *anamnesis*.[18] Ironically, what Socrates always found was that those he spoke with never seemed to know with any certainty what exactly they *thought* they knew, and that Socrates himself was wise *precisely because* he was the only one who appeared to know how little he knew. So Socratic irony was always negative and did not serve any positive role in an interaction with another person: Socrates only helped his interlocutors realize that they lived under an illusion of having true knowledge and were in fact fundamentally ignorant. As a way of teaching between persons, both Socrates and Kierkegaard believed that the maieutic was the highest relation that a person could be in with another.[19]

---

15. Kierkegaard, *Either/Or*, 595–609.

16. See Rae, *Kierkegaard and Theology*, 90, 112, 179; Gouwens, *Kierkegaard as Religious Thinker*, 109.

17. The function of this sermon as being pseudonymous is again to avoid the "authorial tyranny" discussed above—to free the reader to compare and contrast the three main life-views presented before her in *Either/Or* and to make a subjective decision.

18. See 1.3: "The Socratic and Christianity: Philosophical Fragments" above.

19. See Kierkegaard, *Works of Love*, 257 cf. "For to love God is to love oneself in truth; to help another human being to love God is to love another man; to be helped by another human being to love God is to be loved" (ibid., 113).

Along with Socrates, Jesus was also a central figure in Kierkegaard's development of his use of irony, but in the opposite way.[20] Instead of being a midwife who had "no authority" and nothing to offer the learner except an awareness of herself, Jesus was, for Kierkegaard, *the truth*. Jesus was the "content" that could only be recognized by faith and not through direct communication,[21] since the truth cannot legitimate itself and since God desired an un-coerced response of love. Jesus, as the truth, had authority but refused to use it, for the sake of being "the incognito." Instead, he employed *questions* in order to stir his listeners.

In Kierkegaard's aesthetic works, irony was employed as a maieutic tool, where the reader was *herself* to recognize the incongruency between form and content: between the *how* and the *what* of the communication. Irony is to say something in such a way that means the opposite from what is actually said. Kierkegaard outlined two major forms of irony: that where a person says something in earnestness that they are really jesting about (the common type); the other, rarer type (the kind Kierkegaard typically employed) is when a person says something in jest that they are actually serious about.[22] Throughout the aesthetic works, irony functions as a way to challenge the reader to remove illusions that prevent her from encountering the Christian gospel in subjectivity. This tool is maieutic because it does not claim any authority: it is employed in the hope that the reader recognizes the incongruency and will judge the matter for herself.[23]

To take *Philosophical Fragments* as an example, after Climacus contrasts Christianity with the Socratic in regard to learning the truth, he jests with his interlocutor that he has invented the Christian gospel—the clear implication for the reader being that this claim is, of course, absurd. Every child in nineteenth-century Denmark knew the Christian story, and it was ridiculous for Climacus to claim it as his own. Along with this, Climacus

---

20. As Kierkegaard's first thesis states: "The similarity between Christ and Socrates consists essentially in their dissimilarity" (Kierkegaard, *Concept of Irony*, 6).

21. As we have seen in the discussion of Pilate's question in 1.3: "Climacus and Anti-Climacus" above.

22. Kierkegaard, *Concept of Irony*, 248, pointed out in Evans, "The Role of Irony in Kierkegaard's *Philosophical Fragments*," 67.

23. "When I am aware as I speak that what I am saying is what I mean and that what I have said adequately expresses my meaning, and I assume that the person to whom I am talking grasps my meaning completely, then I am bound in what has been said . . . If, however, what I said is not my meaning or the opposite of my meaning, then I am free in relation to others and to myself" (Kierkegaard, *Concept of Irony*, 247–48).

himself has already demonstrated throughout this work that it is far beyond the ability of humanity to come to the idea of Christianity through reason alone. Because of this, the reader can see that "Climacus has pretended to invent something that cannot be invented; if it exists at all, it is a gift from God."[24]

So the reader is confronted with this irony: Climacus has not invented this account by means of his own reasoning, so what authority does it carry? Is it true, and therefore a creation of God? Or is it false? *Reason* cannot help the reader decide, because if it is employed "[t]hen we decide the matter before we begin,"[25] and we side with the Socratic which means that Christianity is impossible. This is because without the precondition of faith given as a divine gift, reason alone will never recognize God in Jesus, the carpenter's son. Whatever she decides, the door to the claim that Christianity is reason-*able* is firmly closed to her. It is in this way that Kierkegaard is effectively pointing out Christianity's incompatibility with Enlightenment rationalism, which had mistakenly been employed (by Hegel and the like) to defend Christianity.[26] What emerges, then, in Climacus' own words, "is old-fashioned orthodoxy in its rightful severity . . ."[27]

Kierkegaard's irony was not "unstable"[28] and subject to an eternity of self-reflexivity, but halted at the point where his reader needed to make a decision. It did not promote uncertainty and a kind of pre-Derridean "deconstruction" for its own sake, but employed irony in the hope that the reader would come to her own position about a particular issue.[29] Ki-

---

24. Evans, "The Role of Irony," 71. This strategy finds echoes in Jesus' own practice of answering a question with a question. This particular instance parallels the episode when Jesus is asked concerning the origin of his authority (Matt 21:23–7). Jesus replies with a question concerning John the Baptist's authority: was it divine or human? Christ did not answer this question directly, since his interrogators, by their very question, clearly did not accept whatever authority that he did have. Instead, by way of the question, Jesus sought to expose their faulty allegiance to humanity instead of to God.

25. Rae is less clear than Evans on elucidating the significance of irony here, but is still helpful nevertheless. See Rae, *Kierkegaard's Vision of the Incarnation*, 24. See also Kierkegaard, *Works of Love*, 192–93.

26. Evans, "The Role of Irony," 72–73.

27. Kierkegaard, *Concluding Unscientific Postscript*, 275.

28. See Evans on his use of this term from Wayne Booth "The Role of Irony," 77–79.

29. "He does not know the refreshment and strengthening that come with undressing when the air gets too hot and heavy and diving into the sea of irony, not in order to stay there, of course, but in order to come out healthy, happy, and buoyant and to dress again." Also, "Even though one must warn against irony as against a seducer, so must one

erkegaard did indeed have a communicative purpose in using irony:[30] he employed irony in his aesthetic works because it demanded reflection on the part of the reader. This enabled yet another layer of distancing from his work, allowing him to remain *hidden* and the reader to have the opportunity to exercise her being a "single individual" through an exposing of what Kierkegaard believed to be illusions which hindered proper knowing.

In this way, irony was employed as a "controlled element":[31] a *negative* communication tool that sought to help the reader reflect and become aware of illusions that were potentially holding her back from knowing God "in truth" for herself.

Subjective Hermeneutics

Kierkegaard's aesthetic works are often cryptic, and his use of many conflicting voices or points of view throughout a number of works or even within a single work forces his reader to make interpretive decisions regarding the meaning of the text, since many are open to her. As we have discussed above, the gospel's requirement for every person to be a "single individual" demands a *form* of communication that goes beyond the conventions of linear literature and didacticism. Kierkegaard's goal was not merely to inform or convince his reader of the merits of a particular point of view, but instead was about the *transformation* of his reader.[32] We have seen this transformative function in Kierkegaard's aesthetic works via an examination of the use of irony, and here we will look at more *passional* approaches employed in these works, taking one of Kierkegaard's most famous works as an example.

Kierkegaard understood that his hearers were under the illusion of Christendom, and that the language surrounding the gospel had become overused to the point of cliché. This had destroyed Christianity's true *subjective* meaning for its hearers: the communication of Christianity lacked the complete destabilization and the offense that the gospel created. This meant that in Christendom, the Genesis story of Abraham being willing to sacrifice Isaac was too often glossed over as a "test of faith." Kierkegaard felt that the concept of faith had been trivialized and moved away from its

---

also commend it as a guide" (Kierkegaard, *Concept of Irony*, 326–27).

30. Contra Poole, *Kierkegaard*, 7–9.
31. Kierkegaard, *Concept of Irony*, 324–29.
32. Barrett, *Kierkegaard*, 3.

2.2 An Overview of Kierkegaard's Authorship

true essence as an embodied passion.[33] So Kierkegaard sought to make this particular story "strange" to his reader.[34]

Fear and Trembling is a work much debated by philosophers and theologians. Attempts among them to argue for a definitive reading of this work (especially under various ethical theories and systems)[35] are fundamentally misguided and miss the deeper function of the work. It is a work that is designed to unsettle the reader, forcing her to decide *for herself* what the story of Abraham and Isaac means.[36] The neutral and scientific terms of Hegel, Kant, and others are employed in this work, but in an impassioned way: the philosophical *language* of Kierkegaard's readers was utilized by him, but in a way that undermines its conventional use that hides under the pretense of objectivity. This commandeering of language serves to unsettle, destabilize, and redirect the reader herself toward a reconsideration of Abraham.[37] Kierkegaard, through the pseudonym Johannes De Silentio, can only hint at this underlying point in the communication, simply because it is subjective and must be found by the reader herself. De Silentio is particularly concerned about his reader reading the story of Abraham and Isaac rightly, with a deep-felt *knowing* of the agony of faith. Through this pseudonym, Kierkegaard demonstrated the proper use of the concept of faith: that is, a "knowing with" rather than a mere "knowing of." He did this by stranding his reader, devoid of mitigating explanation, in order for her to decide how she herself will interpret the story of Abraham and Isaac.

This is also the reason for a lack of conclusions in his works, especially the aesthetic works. Following the lead of Plato and the form of his dialogues, works like *Fear and Trembling* do not hand the answers to the reader on a platter but instead strand her with a number of points of view,

---

33. "Even if one were able to render the whole of the content of faith into conceptual form, it would not follow that one had grasped faith, grasped how one came to it, or how it came to one" (Kierkegaard, *Fear and Trembling*, 5).

34. Kierkegaard, *Concluding Unscientific Postscript*, 275.

35. For a brief survey of these debates, see John Davenport's work, "Faith as Eschatological Trust in Fear and Trembling," though he is also one who argues for a definitive reading (a helpful one, nonetheless).

36. "These complex preliminary sections [in *Fear and Trembling*] are intended to disconcert the reader and distinguish the reader's story from the scriptural story of Abraham and Isaac, in a way not dissimilar from Kierkegaard's attempt in *Works of Love* to make strange again the biblical command to love" (Hall, "Self-deception," 41) and ibid., 42: "From the outset . . . De Silentio forewarns that the form and the content of the ensuing text are intended to disconcert."

37. Rae, "The Risk of Obedience," 310.

leaving it up to her to wade through these in inward reflection.[38] Kierkegaard understood it to be completely misguided to treat life as some kind of school examination and to seek to learn answers "by rote," since such acquisition of knowledge does not have any necessary link to understanding when it comes to ethical and religious matters.[39] So in order to come to know faith *in truth*, the reader herself has to walk the three day journey to Mount Moriah, accompanying the silent Abraham.

In summary, the aesthetic works sought to remove the illusion of Christendom from the reader. They were therefore predominantly negative, and used maieutic tools such as irony, which encouraged self-reflection. These works also demonstrated an impassioned destabilization of popular language and concepts. In this way the pseudonymous authors were demonstrators of the *use* of ethico-religious concepts (both positive and negative), in an effort to remove the illusion of rationalism in regard to essential matters.[40] The ideal reader who engaged deeply with these works was then left in a state of receptivity, with an awareness of the limits of her own knowing as an existing individual.

THE UPBUILDING FUNCTION OF THE RELIGIOUS WORKS

Along with the *aesthetic works* which were published from 1843 through to 1846 (and also for the second edition of *Either/Or* in 1849), explicitly *religious works* in the form of short *Upbuilding Discourses* were published as veronymous companions to these pseudonymous works.[41] They were intended to be the actual "reintroduction" of the gospel to his reader, in contrast to the severely negative function of the aesthetic works. In addi-

---

38. Kierkegaard, *Journals and Papers*, 4/4266, VII 1 A 74, n.d., 1846.

39. Kierkegaard, *Concluding Unscientific Postscript*, 73–74; See also Aumann, "Kierkegaard on the Need," 31.

40. To recall Holmer's words: "His pseudonyms are living subjects who show us the uses of the 'I' with which we are already familiar" (Holmer, *On Kierkegaard and the Truth*, 139).

41. Hong and Hong, "Historical Introduction," ix, xxiii–xxvii; Kierkegaard, *Point of View*, 7–8, 23–24, 29–32 etc; on the differences between "Christian address," "upbuilding" or "edifying discourses," "reflections" and a "sermon," see Hong and Hong, "Translator's Introduction," xix–xx. The chief reason for not naming the "Upbuilding Discourses" sermons is due to Kierkegaard understanding the latter to operate only through authority, and Kierkegaard understood himself to be "without authority."

tion to these concurrent *Upbuilding Discourses* are the religious works in Kierkegaard's own name, such as *Works of Love*, along with the religious works by the pseudonym Anti-Climacus, such as *Sickness Unto Death* and *Practice in Christianity*.

As the *positive* element of his task, Kierkegaard sought to build on a foundation of true Christian faith in his reader: that is, faith taken up in a life as a passion. Kierkegaard believed that his works lacked the authority to speak *directly* into the heart of his reader and instil faith (through God's work), so these works sought rather to *build upon* and *presume* faith (hence the name "Upbuilding Discourses").[42] These works served to point the way forward to the simplistic purity of a life content with being a human under God. They therefore also refrain from taking a didactic or "preachy" rhetorical form, but instead seek to journey with the reader in order to help her discover for herself the "upbuilding" nature of Christianity.[43]

While the aesthetic works move the reader toward complication, confusion and impossibility (as can be seen explicitly in the case of Johannes Climacus and more implicitly the case of Johannes De Silentio),[44] the concurrent *Upbuilding Discourses* move her toward the simplicity of faith. There is a clarity brought about by such simplicity, as discussed in Kierkegaard's *Purity of Heart is to Will One Thing*,[45] which ultimately gives birth to "Silence, Obedience, and Joy."[46] In other words, it is an awareness of one's being *hidden in God*.

Against Autonomy

Such an emphasis on *hiddenness* and an utter dependence on God in the religious works is in radical contrast to the aesthetic works, which tend to use

---

42. See chapter 1 in Part Two: "Love Builds Up," in Kierkegaard, *Works of Love*, 199–212.

43. "Even with his profoundly religious and Christian writings, there is still a stylistic feature of them, and, in addition, a context of language and reflection that keeps the persuasiveness and propagandizing at a minimum" (Holmer, *On Kierkegaard and the Truth*, 15).

44. Kierkegaard, *Concluding Unscientific Postscript*, 185–88 for the former; Kierkegaard, *Fear and Trembling*, 29ff especially for the latter.

45. Søren Kierkegaard, *Purity of Heart*.

46. The title given by George Pattison to Kierkegaard's 1849 booklet which originally carried the title "The Lily of the Field and the Bird under Heaven," republished in Pattison's collection as chapter 10 in Kierkegaard, *Spiritual Writings*, 179–224.

PART II: THE FORM

language and concepts as poetic demonstrations of Kierkegaard's self-sufficient age.[47] For instance, in *Either/Or* both A and Judge William appear to operate under an illusion of autonomy: a presumption that their ability to weigh different life-views is a completely free activity, and that they believe they have the capacity to recognize what is right, true and beautiful. The concluding sermon by the Jutland pastor in this same book is a break from the norm of the aesthetic works as it fundamentally undermines this position. It argues that "Against God We Are Always in The Wrong," and that this is an "edifying" thought.[48] This presentation of the "religious sphere" suggests that our ability to know truth is only by virtue of God's grace.

As a further example of this particular function of the aesthetic works, Johannes Climacus, by the very means of his brilliant critiques of Kierkegaard's age, has been recognized as one who thinks very highly of himself, and employs an "imperialistic rationalism"—a kind of epistemic arrogance which is incongruent for a person with faith.[49] This is yet another reason why Kierkegaard, as a Christian, would not sign his name to such literary and philosophical brilliance: this communication is tarnished with the very self-sufficiency that Christianity opposes.

Johannes De Silentio, however, is a more complicated case. His work carries with it a sense of foreboding self-defeat, a tone that suggests existential uncertainty and a deep lack of confidence with regard to his identity. The only certainty that De Silentio appears to hold is how unlike Abraham is from the rest of humanity, and therefore how impossible faith is for De Silentio himself to obtain. But beneath this sentiment lies a clue: Abraham is presented as a lone hero, and the author completely misunderstands Abraham's greatness, which is fundamentally contingent on God and not Abraham himself.[50] De Silentio despairs because he believes Abraham to be extraordinarily unlike any other human being, but misses the point that Abraham was who he was only by virtue of God. Faith is a mark of self-*un*sufficiency and radical dependence on "the power which has established it,"[51] rather than a commodity to obtain. Like love, faith only exists *for* the

---

47. Again, see Holmer, *On Kierkegaard and the Truth*, 139.

48. Kierkegaard, *Either/Or*, 595–609.

49. Evans, *Passionate Reason*, 61 as cited in Rasmussen, *Between Irony and Witness*, 94.

50. David Conway argues a similar point here. See his "Abraham's Final Word."

51. Kierkegaard, *Sickness*, 99.

other.⁵² So we can see that De Silentio is an example of Anti-Climacus' despair of weakness: he lacks the "strength" to determine himself, but works from an understanding that this is at least a possibility.

So we see that the aesthetic works emphasize the *greatness* of being a "single individual," but they are fundamentally lacking in an awareness of their need for God in the deepest sense. They demonstrate to the reader a bankrupt optimism which operates according to a hope in the self-sufficiency of humanity. The religious works, however, communicate according to a deep awareness of the need to depend on God as the proper source of all human knowing. As Murray Rae points out, Kierkegaard understood that the gospel penetrates to the depths of humankind's erroneous epistemology.⁵³ We would do well to remember here our discussion in 2.1 above: "Hidden Benefaction," which considers how *Works of Love* describes all relations between persons (including the reader-author relation between us here) being mediated by God, who is love. Thus, the greatest act of love that one person can do for another is to point them to God.⁵⁴ This is the foundation for a knowing and communicating based not on human autonomy, but on God-dependency.

This is most clear in the religious works by the pseudonym Anti-Climacus. As a (non)person of incredible faith,⁵⁵ this pseudonym preaches with a sense of profound authority, from a sense of absolute dependency on God. His writings do not carry with them a need to justify their claims, and they therefore communicate with piercing clarity. Anti-Climacus appears humble, but only in the sense of being absolutely certain in God: in reading his words, there is no sense of doubt or a lack of faith. Kierkegaard presented him to his reader as the supreme example of the Christian use of ethico-religious concepts: a congruent disciple of Christ who speaks "in the truth." Such an ideal person is not necessarily possible, but one who is worth learning from: a contextual portrayal of a true Christian in the midst of Christendom.⁵⁶

---

52. Kierkegaard, *Works of Love*, 211.

53. ". . . because of human sin—humanity's existence in untruth—reason itself stands in need of redemption. Reason itself stands in need of reconciliation to that Truth which alone makes possible an authentic existence before God. . . . [contra Hegel] reason cannot bring us to the Truth" (Rae, *Kierkegaard's Vision of the Incarnation*, 137).

54. Kierkegaard, *Works of Love*, 112–13, 124, 247, 282–83, etc.

55. Kierkegaard, *Practice in Christianity*, 133; Kierkegaard, *Journals and Papers*, 6/6349, X6 B 48, n.d., 1849.

56. "Surely the Christianity he described is so extreme that no one could possibly

PART II: THE FORM

The religious works signed in Søren Kierkegaard's own name, however, appear more tentative. Their tone comes across as humble, with a subtle awareness of their author's own inadequacies of faith while he attempts to remain "in the truth."[57] It is perhaps here that the religious works are most helpful as we are given an example (though accordingly self-effacing)[58] of Christian communication from a peer: one who is indeed a "genius in reflection," but also one who is *striving*.[59] Kierkegaard, as an author, can be seen as an example of a Christian communicator: one who understood that discipleship is an ongoing journey of striving after the one God-man who truly married word and deed.[60] But before we explore the idea of Kierkegaard as an example in the next section (Part III), let us consider the function of the actual religious communications themselves, using *Works of Love* as a case study.

The Look of Love

Works of Love is at the heart of Kierkegaard's ethics.[61] Written under his own name, it discusses how Christians are to live "in the world," and is written as a response to his contemporary readers accusing him of advocating for a Christianity that was abstracted from sociality and outward behavior.[62] His concept of "the single individual" and its fundamental value regarding inwardness was at risk of being misused as an excuse for outward apathy regarding Christianity's confrontation with "the world."[63] In order to

---

practise it. The subjective thinker before God, the pure contemporary with Christ, suffering crucifixion with Him, without church, without tradition, and without ritual, can only exist outside of history" (Ricœur, "Philosophy After Kierkegaard," 13).

57. Cf. Kierkegaard, "Two Discourses at the Communion on Fridays," see also 1.3 above.

58. Cf. Kierkegaard, *Works of Love*, 68.

59. Kierkegaard, *Journals and Papers*, 6/6388, X1 A 266, n.d., 1849; cited in Kierkegaard, *Point of View*, 189–90.

60. In poetic terms, this is for the individual to let herself become "poetically composed" under God, following Christ—the only one who reconciled the distance between ideality and actuality. Rasmussen, *Between Irony and Witness*, 48, 52; see also Kierkegaard, *Concept of Irony*, 280–81.

61. Cf. George Pattison's claim that it is "the central work in Kierkegaard's entire authorship" ("Foreword," ix).

62. See ibid., ix–x.

63. This eventually came to be (satirically) articulated in Kierkegaard, *Practice in Christianity*, 216 etc.

clarify this concept and to rescue it from such a misconstrual, Kierkegaard wrote *Works of Love* to suggest how Christians are to consider their interaction with others and the world around them. But instead of focusing on explicit outward practices and running the risk of falling into a new kind of legalism,[64] Kierkegaard taught about how "the single individual" (under God) should *interpret* their world in love, and thereby live accordingly as a Christian in the world.

For instance, mercy cannot be reduced to an outward action (such as how much money a widow gives as an offering to God) but is entirely a condition of the heart. A person is merciful, then, not by virtue of any outward act, but *only* in how she sees.[65] And unlike those who ask who their neighbor is, Kierkegaard argued that a Christian is one who *sees* her neighbor.[66] In this way, *Works of Love* teaches love as a hermeneutic: a way of seeing and knowing, rather than as a matter of behavior *per se*.

In regard to how this relates to the underlying *function* of this work, Kierkegaard spoke to his reader as a "single individual" in a way designed to encourage subjective reflection on the matters being discussed. The form of the work is intentionally slow and repetitive to prevent fast and "superficial" reading, and discouraging it from being the subject of mere outward and scholarly interaction. Kierkegaard wanted to encourage deep and subjective reflection in his reader, which could not be realized through skim-reading.[67] Again, Kierkegaard was demonstrating the appropriate passional, interested *use* of Christian ethico-religious concepts—most notably love—but he did it here in his own name rather than through a pseudonym.

---

64. Keeping in mind the link between what is inward and what is outward is never necessary but always contingent. E.g., Kierkegaard, *Concluding Unscientific Postscript*, 93.

65. Chapter 7: "Mercifulness, a Work of Love, Even if It Can Give Nothing and Is Capable of Doing Nothing" in Kierkegaard, *Works of Love*, 292–305.

66. Chapter 2 B: "You Shall Love Your *Neighbour*" in ibid., 58–72; and chapter 2 C: "*You* Shall Love Your Neighbour" in ibid., 73–98, cf. Luke 10:25–37.

67. As Howard and Edna Hong explain, "The reader comes to understand the reason for the length of the work and does not complain, 'Why doesn't he say it and be done with it?'— because he realises that the work is directed to the individual who is to work his own conscious way with the help of the reading and that it is not primarily a presentation of a writer's neatly bundled opinions . . . Kierkegaard carefully developed both thought and form to prevent easy and superficial reading, requiring the either/or of thoughtful reading or no illusion of having really read at all" (Hong and Hong, "Translator's Introduction," xxii).

But although this work was written for subjective engagement by the reader, it is not correct to call it "maieutic" as David Gouwens and Paul Müller have done.[68] "Maieutic" is inappropriate here because this work is not negative, but positive: "[X] is very upbuilding to consider."[69] This work *introduces* a thought to the reader, and leads her to discover its function upon reflection. The Socratic function of the aesthetic works sought to *remove* illusions and were thereby negative and maieutic.[70] There, positions or thoughts which were established within the reader were put forward for her consideration, and then demonstrated to be found wanting.[71] So whereas the aesthetic works worked *backwards* to remove illusions (negative);[72] the religious works worked *forwards*, by considering the gospel of Christianity as a basis for living well (positive). Likewise, whereas the Socratic could only examine what existed in the mind of the reader and work from there, the Christian *introduces* newness to consider: the divine interruption of the gospel, which Climacus has shown is no invention of humanity.

So Kierkegaard's religious works *build upon* Christian concepts after the ground has been cleared of the clutter of Christendom by the aesthetic works. The form of *Works of Love* is no mere *reflection* on love and its works, but has the function of eliciting in its reader the very love that it considers. This is because to examine love as an abstract concept is monstrously self-defeating since it is a matter of existence, and can only be known by being taken up and embodied in a life.[73] And since "Love Believes [rather than mistrusts] All Things"[74] and "Love Hides the Multiplicity of Sins,"[75] it does

68. See Gouwens, *Kierkegaard as Religious Thinker*, 206–7; who works from Müller, *Kristendom*, 2. It should be warning enough that Kierkegaard himself calls his aesthetic works "maieutic," but does not extend this title to his religious works. See Kierkegaard, *Point of View*, 7, 9.

69. Kierkegaard, *Works of Love*, 206, etc.

70. We would do well to remember that this term means "midwifery": giving birth to what is *within* the learner.

71. See Walsh, *Living Poetically*, 49.

72. Again, the Socratic concept of "anamnesis" (eternal recollection) is entirely backwards-oriented.

73. We will do well to remember our discussion in 1.3: "Pathos: The Heart of the Matter," which considers essential truths of existence as needing the accompaniment of complementary passions in the knower, and cannot be known from the outside; the difference between "knowing of" and "knowing with" etc.

74. Chapter 2 of Part Two, "Love Believes All Things and Yet Is Never Deceived," in Kierkegaard, *Works of Love*, 213–39.

75. Chapter 5 of Part Two in ibid., 261–78.

not seek to point out faults in others but instead strives to change *itself*.⁷⁶ This work *of love* encourages the reader to reflect on how she sees, rather than judging what is or is not loving behavior. Again, the form complements the content.⁷⁷

By way of contrast, Anti-Climacus' work *Practice in Christianity* functioned as a mirror (typically of judgment) regarding "the spirit of [Kierkegaard's] age." This work presents necessary and helpful teachings for the Christian, but was unable to be directly communicated by Kierkegaard since he lacked the faith to speak with such authority as was necessary for this work. Anti-Climacus, a pseudonym with incredible faith,⁷⁸ is able to explain the function of the offense of the gospel, is able to explain what it means to have faith and to recognize Jesus as God and is able to teach the necessity of suffering for the true Christian. Kierkegaard could communicate these high ideals of Christian striving *poetically* rather than "in truth," since he himself understood that he lacked the faith to be able to "practice what was preached."⁷⁹ In this way, as we will explore in the next section, Kierkegaard revealed himself as one who was "barely Christian" and struggled in his striving toward the gospel. As much as *Works of Love* speaks from alongside his reader in an encouraging and humble way, *Practice in Christianity* speaks from above the reader as one who embodies the ideal of Christian faith.

THE HIDDEN MIDDLE

What is particularly interesting throughout the span of his authorship is what Kierkegaard did not *quite* say. As Wittgenstein's cryptic conclusion to his *Tractatus Logico-Philosophicus* says: "Whereof one cannot speak, thereof one must be silent."⁸⁰

---

76. "Therefore the discourse [for upbuilding] cannot be about what the lover who desires to build up should do to transform the other person or to constrain love to come forth in him; it is rather about how the lover constrains himself." ibid., 206; cf. "love does not alter the beloved, rather it alters itself" (Kierkegaard, "Philosophical Crumbs," 108).

77. This point is taken from Gouwen's otherwise masterly section in his *Kierkegaard as Religious Thinker*, 206–7 despite referring to *Works of Love* as "maieutic."

78. Kierkegaard, *Journals and Papers*, 6/6349, X6 B 48, n.d., 1849.

79. See 1.3, "Christomorphic Poetics" above. Throughout this work, the use of this colloquial phrase does not intend to convey that Kierkegaard's authorship was wholly didactic.

80. Wittgenstein, *Tractatus*, 82, §7.

Part II: The Form

Through the aesthetic works, Kierkegaard was able to exhaust the notion of objective truth by applying its own tools against itself.[81] Through Johannes Climacus, rationalism was demonstrated to be at odds with Christianity, but even more than this, it was exposed as an untenable way of life. Through *Philosophical Crumbs* and *Concluding Unscientific Postscript*, he maieutically draws the reader out of the unhelpful notion of an objective stance toward essential truth, and strands her with the understanding that it is faith *before* reason that is paramount for the Christian.[82] But because Climacus cannot provide this essential passion for his reader, she is left with the reality that she either does or does not have the precondition to encounter the truth of Christianity. This assessment of the situation can only be discerned retrospectively by the one who *has* faith and thereby accepts Christ as truth. The unbeliever dismisses this as false.[83]

This polarizes Kierkegaard's readership as can be seen in the roughly two "camps" of scholars: those who sympathize with Kierkegaard's presentation of Christianity, and those who do not. The giving of faith is the realm of mystery and of God's work, of which we cannot *in truth* speak, and it is for this reason that Kierkegaard did not *truly* speak of it. *Before* the reader can move to the religious works which presuppose and "build upon" Christian passions such as faith and love,[84] the reader herself must have the capacity (the precondition of faith) to understand them. Just like Jesus' parable of the sower and the episode of his encounter with Nicodemus, only those on the inside will *truly* know.[85] Wittgenstein once mysteriously claimed that "[i]f a lion could talk, we wouldn't be able to understand it":[86] Christianity is a language, and therefore "a form of life."[87] Like love, Chris-

---

81. According to Paul Ricoeur, *Concluding Unscientific Postscript* was "Kierkegaard's most extraordinary work." Ricoeur describes its relation to philosophy as follows: "this is not non-philosophy: it is hyper-philosophy, even to the point of caricature and ridicule. It is in connection with these categories of the existing individual that the crucial problem arises—that of the logic of Kierkegaardian discourse" ("Philosophy After Kierkegaard," 15).

82. Cf. Kierkegaard, *Point of View*, 7 n.

83. Anti-Climacus is therefore the ideal Christian perspective, who frees Kierkegaard from giving this necessary perspective in his own name. See, for instance, "The Categories of *Offense*, That Is, of Essential Offense," in his *Practice in Christianity*, 123–44.

84. Kierkegaard, *Works of Love*, 199–212.

85. Kierkegaard, "Philosophical Crumbs," 97, cf. John 3.

86. Wittgenstein, *Investigations*, 235e, §327.

87. Ibid., 11e, §19; see also McCabe, *Law, Love and Language*, 71–76, etc.

tianity must be entered into in order to be known, and this entering comes through participating in God.[88] The gap between the "left and the right hand"[89] of Kierkegaard's authorship is therefore faith.

Kierkegaard understood that a person cannot be *argued* or *reasoned into* faith; she is or is not a Christian only by virtue of her inward relationship with God, and this gives rise to the appropriate impassioned use of Christian concepts. Kierkegaard recognized this, and therefore did not attempt to tread on God's toes by *directly* discussing or suggesting how an individual might go about obtaining faith; he could only point to God and encourage the reader in her striving after him. Because God alone can give faith, and only gives it in the silence of an individual's heart, Kierkegaard *hid* himself at this crucial juncture.[90] The aesthetic works (being maieutic) pointed forward, away from backward-gazing anamnesis and toward a receptivity of faith, while the signed works reflected backward to the establishment of faith which these works presupposed and "built upon." There is, then, a chasm between the aesthetic and religious works that can be filled only with "the single individual" meeting God for herself. This is where Climacus employed Lessing's term "the leap,"[91] where Victor Eremita employed the term "either/or," where Anti-Climacus saw Christ as "the sign of offense and the object of faith,"[92] and what I choose to call "The Hidden Middle."[93]

Hiddenness

As we have repeatedly emphasized, in order to enable the possibility of subjectivity in his reader, Kierkegaard had to *hide* himself. The point was for

---

88. Kierkegaard, *Works of Love*, 282–83.

89. Kierkegaard, *Journals and Papers*, 6/6407, X1 A 351, n.d., 1849; as found in Kierkegaard, *Point of View*, 193–94.

90. As Holmer points out, Kierkegaard "did not want readers who would become Christian in virtue of his authorship. In fact, the burden of the explanatory work, *The Point of View*, is just this, namely, that he cannot in virtue of his own understanding of himself, of the Christian faith, and of his authorship, constitute himself as a direct agent for the production of religiosity in another" (Holmer, *On Kierkegaard and the Truth*, 15).

91. Kierkegaard, *Concluding Unscientific Postscript*, 93–106.

92. Kierkegaard, *Practice in Christianity*, 35.

93. My phrase here could be self-defeating, since it carries with it a sense of objective neutrality. However, I believe it to be helpful in learning the function of this dimension of Kierkegaard's authorship.

the reader to meet God in the *hiddenness* of her own heart, and therefore Kierkegaard could not obstruct this by employing didacticism or pointing toward himself. For instance, in *Works of Love* we can see how important it was for Kierkegaard that his reader have the opportunity to encounter her true self through the way she sees, even at the level of how she reads that very work.[94]

Kierkegaard did not preach to his reader, but only sought to give opportunity for the gospel to woo her instead, by letting a gentle demonstration of Christian concepts in life reveal themselves as upbuilding.[95] Here was a *use* of the content for the Christian life: after the illusory fell away, the religious works demonstrated what it meant to live as a Christian.[96] They were not direct communications of the gospel, but, as Kierkegaard explained in regard to the *telos* of his use of pseudonyms, instead served to point the reader back "once again to read through solo, if possible in a more inward way, the original text of individual human existence-relationships, the old familiar text handed down from the fathers."[97]

CONCLUSION

Kierkegaard's entire authorship (the "authorship proper") serves, on one hand, to remove what hindered his reader's own subjective engagement with God, and on the other hand, to build upon God's work in the believer. It was between these two "hands" that Kierkegaard hoped his reader would meet with God in the "hidden inwardness" of her own heart. These works serve as mirrors which employ a number of literary and rhetorical techniques designed to prompt the reader to engage with the text subjectively, and ultimately serve as judgments for the reader as to how she uses these texts. Such an elaborate strategy in Kierkegaard's authorship drew its

---

94. cf. Kierkegaard, *Practice in Christianity*, 126–27. We will explore this reflective aspect of Kierkegaard's work in the following chapter.

95. Kierkegaard, *Point of View*, 16.

96. "But, there is still the strange neutrality and dispassionateness about the man's writings that goes a-begging. Even with his profoundly religious and Christian writings, there is still a stylistic feature of them, and, in addition, a context of language and reflection that keeps the persuasiveness and propagandizing at a minimum. Kierkegaard supposes a nexus between his books and the reader, that he nowhere chooses to describe at great length. That he was aware of it, there can be no doubt" (Holmer, *On Kierkegaard and the Truth*, 14–15).

97. Kierkegaard, *Concluding Unscientific Postscript*, 629–30.

reflective power from Kierkegaard *hiding himself* in his authorship. Thus we can see that not only was such *hiding* a way of being in the truth, it was also essential in communicating it.

2.3 KIERKEGAARD'S RECEPTION TODAY

INTRODUCTION

Here we will engage with a few of Kierkegaard's interpreters, and will assess them according to the Christian hermeneutics which can be derived from the veronymous *Works of Love* and selected *Upbuilding Discourses*. These interpreters will be used as case studies for examining the outward function of Kierkegaard's authorship, and will be found to be witnesses to the ongoing dynamism and effectiveness of Kierkegaard's authorial task (and are thereby also a testament to his genius as a communicator). But first we will consider Kierkegaard's relation to philosophy, and the way this informs how he is being (mis)read today.

KIERKEGAARD AND PHILOSOPHY

> *Just as Christianity came into history as something absolutely new, so the life with Christ marks a wholly new beginning for each individual. Thus the new stands in complete and irreconcilable contrast with the old, Christianity with all philosophy.*[1]

Kierkegaard understood that the philosophers of his time, unlike the Ancient Greeks, had forgotten what it meant to exist.[2] As one completely concerned with "the single individual" *in existence*, Kierkegaard understood that philosophy had no *positive* place for his project, which was "for

---

1. Smit, *Kierkegaard's Pilgrimage of Man*, 99; as cited in Rae, *Kierkegaard's Vision of the Incarnation*, 143.
2. Kierkegaard, *Concluding Unscientific Postscript*, 331, etc.

people to become Christians."³ All Kierkegaardian philosophical discourse carried a *negative* function in his authorship: to maieutically remove the illusion of Christendom and its prostituting of Christianity to "worldly" ways of thinking and knowing.⁴ This is why Kierkegaard's religious works do not focus on philosophical matters or attempt to justify their positions using contemporary philosophy. They are instead grounded demonstrations of the Christian grammar of *faith*.⁵

Kierkegaard was not interested in existence as his peculiar and original contribution to the history of philosophy; it was his conviction that one could never get "beyond" existence (just as one never can get "beyond" faith) because it is absolutely fundamental to the human condition.⁶ Kierkegaard sought to remind his reader that a philosopher, for his philosophizing to be *true*, can never escape his own reality as an existing individual. The prevailing Hegelian thought, which believes that "thinking and being are one," misses the fact that "existence [*Existents*] separates thinking and being."⁷ That is, "to philosophize [is] an act; therefore the one philosophizing [is] an existing person."⁸ Therefore, such philosophizing which neglects existence is not just in disagreement with Kierkegaard's particular philosophical emphasis, it is completely incompatible with reality and is therefore an absurd untruth. Even if such absolute and universal objectivity were possible (by "the fantastical I-I"),⁹ it would be completely removed from human existence and therefore of absolutely no help to humanity. Such objectivity is "untruth" in the mouth of humanity, and only belongs to God.¹⁰

Because Kierkegaard attempted to commit his whole life to Christianity, his criterion for essential truth was Jesus Christ, the God-Man.¹¹

---

3. Kierkegaard, *Point of View*, 41.

4. See above, 2.2: "The Maieutic Function of the Aesthetic Works."

5. See Holmer, *The Grammar of Faith*. As I have claimed above in 1.3, this is not to advocate for an irrationalist view which has faith as opposed to reason. Instead, Kierkegaard is arguing for faith that God's revelation is the fundamental grounds for reason, and therefore cannot be critiqued by such reason. For a good summary of a similar reading of Kierkegaard, see Rae, *Kierkegaard's Vision of the Incarnation*, 53–54, 69–70, 214 etc.

6. See Kierkegaard, *Journals and Papers*, 5/5100, I A 75, August 1, 1835; Kierkegaard, *Fear and Trembling*, 9 etc.

7. Kierkegaard, *Concluding Unscientific Postscript*, 332.

8. Ibid., 331.

9. Ibid., 193.

10. Ibid., 202.

11. See 1.3 above.

PART II: THE FORM

This truth was embodied—form and content as an inseparable unity—and therefore attempts to "put asunder what God has joined together" was to be in untruth. A human being can only know as an existing individual, and thereby lives properly not on her own terms, but on God's.[12] This commitment manifested itself in Kierkegaard's task as an author. He understood that he had to practice what he preached as a matter of simple obedience to God, and was therefore absolutely opposed to abstract philosophizing which universalized, objectified (and therefore annulled) subjective existence in order to comment on issues concerning ethics and religion.[13] It is on this basis Kierkegaard has been frequently misunderstood by scholars.[14] Attempts to relegate the thinker "to a paragraph in the system" both in encyclopedias of thought and in the history of philosophy are ill-conceived[15] and testify to the incompetence of such commentators with regard to their own subjectivity. Kierkegaard was therefore an "anti-philosopher"[16] who sought to turn philosophy against itself for the sake of highlighting the forgotten importance of subjectivity.[17]

Contemporary commentators like Paul Ricoeur in his article "Philosophy after Kierkegaard" are most helpful in discussing Søren Kierkegaard's philosophical genealogy and placing his pseudonymous texts in their intellectual context (especially in relation to Hegel). However, such attempts to locate a "new" Kierkegaard are based on a Socratic (mis)understanding of truth, and are at risk of pursuing cognitive abstraction over lived life.[18] Such

---

12. In other words, Kierkegaard understood that a person lives well by being poeticised by the divine poet. See "Christomorphic Poetics" in 1.3 above.

13. This is a theme which pervades Kierkegaard's *Concluding Unscientific Postscript*. For an excellent summary as to how Kierkegaard reintroduced subjectivity into philosophy in order to comment on ethical and existential matters, see Holmer, *On Kierkegaard and the Truth*, 6–13, e.g., "His own literature is a criticism of all objectivity, whatever its kind, that becomes of culminating importance, and with this he writes out a description in great detail of the subjectivity, the concerns, passions, interests, and enthusiasms which he believes are the essential expressions for personality" (ibid., 11).

14. I am attempting to keep in mind Paul Holmer's claim about Kierkegaard and using it as a warning to myself: that "many who praise him most misunderstand him" (Holmer, *On Kierkegaard and the Truth*, 15).

15. Gouwens, *Kierkegaard as Religious Thinker*, 2.

16. Ricœur, "Philosophy After Kierkegaard."

17. For a more detailed discussion of Kierkegaard's relation to philosophy, see Aumann, "Kierkegaard's Case."

18. "[Søren Kierkegaard] was the creator of a new intellectual epoch, following on from German idealism: the era of post-philosophy" (Ricœur, "Philosophy After

scholarship can easily collapse into merely a more focused objectivity—the truth according to Kierkegaard—and can therefore still abstract the scholar from the existential challenges to which Kierkegaard points.[19] For instance, although Ricoeur states that philosophy is concerned with "truth and reality," his following claim that it remains "theoretical and reflective" does not appear to embrace Kierkegaard's understanding of the philosopher needing to live poetically.[20]

Alongside this fact, works which attempt such relegation and systematization are often unable to understand the function of Kierkegaard's religious works, and therefore are severely diminished in their ability to comment on Kierkegaard's authorship as a whole.[21] Kierkegaard's simplistic yet idealized Christian teachings elude being relegated to "a paragraph in the system." Their unphilosophical tone baffles scholars who seek to understand Kierkegaard exclusively in terms of his contribution to Western philosophy.[22]

Kierkegaard's authorship was ultimately about the communication of the gospel, and all his works—whether they carry his own name or not—serve that end.[23] Kierkegaard understood "[the] gospel, which is wise in the matter of a good upbringing, does not let itself get involved with us in a

---

Kierkegaard," 10).

19. Again, it is appropriate to cite Murray Rae here: "To take refuge in critical distance from the existential and theological challenges of the Bible or indeed from *Fear and Trembling* itself, is already to have misunderstood both texts" (Rae, "The Risk of Obedience," 310). I would extend this warning to any of Kierkegaard's writings.

20. Ricœur, "Philosophy After Kierkegaard," 14; cf. Kierkegaard, *Concept of Irony*, 280; and Kierkegaard, *Concluding Unscientific Postscript*, 303, 309, etc.

21. For instance, Ricoeur correctly points out that "Kierkegaard thrust himself into both philosophy and Christian dogmatics, and this somewhat upsets and destabilizes our relationship to him." But Ricoeur doesn't seem to give any credence to Kierkegaard himself discussing how such destabilisation is intended to thrust the reader onto God. "Philosophy After Kierkegaard," 15; cf. Kierkegaard, *Point of View*, 41–53, etc. Ricoeur also seems to struggle to place the religious works in terms of their function in Kierkegaard's authorship as a whole. See Ricœur, "Philosophy After Kierkegaard," 13. As a further example of how the religious works are neglected, see Barrett, Review of *Søren Kierkegaard*, 153.

22. Mackey calls Kierkegaard's Christianity "imbalanced and excessive" (Mackey, *Kierkegaard*, 243); see also Kierkegaard, *Spiritual Writings*, 212; and the first half of Kierkegaard, *Works of Love* especially.

23. As Murray Rae reminds us, even Kierkegaard's most famous aesthetic work "The Seducer's Diary" must be understood as carrying some function toward this *telos* (Rae, *Kierkegaard and Theology*, 2).

quarrel about ideas or words, so as to *prove* to us that it is right."[24] Kierkegaard is at pains throughout his authorship to communicate one thing: that the gospel is truth, and this truth confronts every "single individual" with an *either/or*—it is not "true to a certain degree," but is a matter of a binary choice.[25] It is for this reason that philosophy and philosophical approaches to Kierkegaard are helpful in understanding Kierkegaard's pseudonymous work, but they are very limited in helping us understand Kierkegaard's authorship as a whole. Instead, we see that a theological reading of Kierkegaard's entire authorship is the most faithful and true to these works, despite the fact that this may appear "boring" to many scholars.[26]

KIERKEGAARD'S WORKS AS MIRRORS

Kierkegaard's *entire* authorship was designed to cast the reader into reflection of what she herself believes.[27] In a manner of speaking, both "hands" of his authorship function as mirrors, attempting to relay faithfully the subjective confrontation of the gospel.[28] As already discussed, Kierkegaard understood that it would not be helpful for his task to *directly* administer his understanding of the truth, but he instead sought, through his work, to lead the reader as a "single individual" toward meeting truth for herself within her own inwardness. Both the aesthetic *and* the religious works had this function—the former draws the reader *forward toward* the challenge of faith; the latter *backwards to* the establishment of faith.[29]

The aesthetic works serve as *maieutic* mirrors—mimicking the views of common Danish intellectual positions but pushing them to their

---

24. Kierkegaard, *Spiritual Writings*, 212, emphasis author's own.

25. Regarding those who are confronted by Christianity: "Let him be offended; even so, he is a human being. Let him despair of ever becoming a Christian himself; even so, he may be closer than he thinks. Let him to his very last drop of blood work to root out Christianity; even so, he is a human being—but if here he also has it in him to say, 'It is true to a certain degree,' then he is obtuse" (Kierkegaard, *Concluding Unscientific Postscript*, 229); see also "II" in the 1849 booklet, *The Lily of the Field and the Bird Under Heaven*, published as chapter 10: "Silence, Obedience and Joy," in Kierkegaard, *Spiritual Writings*, 200–13.

26. Kierkegaard, *Point of View*, 91–93.

27. Ibid., 7–11, etc.

28. See "Mirrors of Judgement of Joy," in 1.3 above.

29. See 2.2 above.

self-defeating extremes.[30] Thus the works were designed to invoke in the reader a realization of their own foolishness, in the hope that they themselves might deconstruct and reevaluate their own positions, and look for a new way forward.[31] In particular, it is through such inward questioning that the bankruptcy and precariousness of the reader's ability to know God *by herself* (that is, apart from faith) is revealed to her. Such use of "indirect communication" for the purpose of "answering a fool according to his folly" can also be seen to linked to Christ's practice of exposing the inhumanity of those who opposed him and his followers. Just as Christ taught the strategy of "turning the other cheek" and to "walk two miles instead of one," Kierkegaard carried his neighbor's life-views to their logically absurd conclusions, in the hope that they themselves might reflect and change as a result of inward realization.[32]

The religious works serve as the corrective. But not in the sense of *directly* offering an answer; instead they *presume* the answer of faith. These works are written for the reader already in the truth, who seeks God out of her own condition as a "single individual." In this way these works also function as mirrors, and the reader can either welcome and respond to these discourses recognizing their applicability to her *or* she can dismiss them as irrelevant. Ultimately, Kierkegaard saw that this response of an *either/or* was a response concerning faith: *either* the reader chooses out of her own self-delusion, *or* she chooses in humble abdication to God. It is in this way that Kierkegaard's work helps to expose and reflect to the reader what she herself believes, and it was intended by Kierkegaard for his reader to meet God for themselves in between the two hands of his works. But how have some of his commentators today used his works? What have they seen in the Kierkegaardian mirror?

Paul Holmer claims that Kierkegaard sought to oppose the universalism common to those entrapped in the "intellectualist-myth" that consisted

---

30. E.g., Ricoeur on *Concluding Unscientific Postscript* "Philosophy After Kierkegaard," 15; and Rasmussen on "The Seducer's Diary," in *Between Irony and Witness*, 43. This demonstration in the aesthetic works is what Holmer points out as a *reductio ad absurdum* argument: Holmer, *On Kierkegaard and the Truth*, 39–40.

31. Roger Poole is, in my view, right to link Derrida's work to Kierkegaard's, but Poole goes to far. Kierkegaard's irony is a "controlled element," and is not infinitely deconstructive. See Poole's *Kierkegaard*, 5–8, etc.; Evans, "The Role of Irony," 64–7; Kierkegaard, *Concept of Irony*, 324–29.

32. Referencing *Practice in Christianity*, Rasmussen states: "Thus, the celebrated indirection for which Kierkegaard the author has become infamous is attributed by Anti-Climacus to Christ" (*Between Irony and Witness*, 99 cf. Matt 5:38–41).

of applying a kind of rigorous objectivity to any and all subjects of knowing. Kierkegaard saw this as transgressing proper epistemic limits. "Like is known only by like" he was often fond of quoting,[33] and this could be claimed as a key component of Kierkegaard's epistemology.[34] Likewise, to love is to know,[35] and love changes itself according to the subject matter, rather than the other way around.[36] So, true knowing is loving, and is contextual: it is willing to bend in order to accommodate what it attempts to know.

However, the trend among some scholars of Kierkegaard today is to impose a different type of objectivity across all Kierkegaard's work, failing to bend according to the inherent difficulties of the nature of his texts. This is particularly the case regarding the difference in the function of the aesthetic and religious works and how a reader is to derive meaning from them. Appropriate critique has been leveled at those who adopt the stance in which *all* of Kierkegaard's works (both those carrying his name and those which do not) reflect exactly what Kierkegaard himself meant,[37] but not enough critique has been given to those who import a blanketing objectivity to *all* the works in the opposite way. For instance, Roger Poole claims that, against such Hegelian "objectivity," Kierkegaard ran in the *complete opposite direction* by creating "literary machines that, like those of the Dadaists, actually work but carry out no function at all."[38] Both "blunt" readings and those of the "deconstructive turn" actually fall into the same trap: that of adopting an objective, distanced, and universal disposition toward Kierkegaard, where their advocates attempt to universalize their

33. E.g., Kierkegaard, *Works of Love*, 33.

34. A kind of Christian Aristotelianism.

35. Kierkegaard, *Journals and Papers*, 2/2299, IX A 438, n.d., 1848, quoted in Nelson, "Revelation and the Revealed," 89–90.

36. "... love does not alter the beloved, rather it alters itself..." (Kierkegaard, "Philosophical Crumbs," 108); and "We usually think that the recipient is inactive and that the object manifesting itself communicates itself to the recipient, but the relationship is this: the recipient is the lover, and the beloved becomes manifest to him, for he himself is transformed in the likeness of the beloved; the only fundamental basis for understanding is that one himself becomes what he understands and one understands only in proportion to becoming himself that which he understands" (Kierkegaard, *Journals and Papers*, 2/2299, IX A 438, n.d., 1848).

37. See Rasmussen's critique of Poole in *Between Irony and Witness*, 5–8; regarding Poole, "The Unknown Kierkegaard."

38. Poole, *Kierkegaard*, 7; for a list of such scholars and a brief critique of them, see Gouwens, *Kierkegaard as Religious Thinker*, 6–7.

own subjective encounters with his work. What they see is what *you* get. So ironically, Poole himself falls into the trap of "the bad old tradition of seeking univocal meaning."[39]

"Like is known by like." If a reader intends to criticize Kierkegaard, there is more than enough "knowledge" to use to that end, both intentional and unintentional.[40] But there is also a great deal from which to learn: it depends on how the reader *sees*. Subjective reflection is essential to engaging with Kierkegaard in truth. His writings are far too polemical to allow us a kind of objective comfort regarding the subject of which he speaks. However, he can be evaluated according to the integrity of his communication, but the problem is *how*, and what that means for us as interpreters.

It is clear that making Kierkegaard a hero—either of orthodox Christianity or postmodern literary theory—is to misuse and therefore misunderstand him. What Kierkegaard was advocating was *subjectivity*: for his reader to *personally* engage with both "hands" of his authorship, and to judge for herself the picture that it painted.[41] Hence, Kierkegaardian scholarship, if it is to read Kierkegaard in love, must only serve to help the reader read Kierkegaard well *for herself*, since this is the only way its subject can be *truly* understood.[42] Many scholars are apt helpers in this regard.[43]

It is interesting to note that Roger Poole and Joakim Garff (advocates somewhat of "the deconstructive turn" in Kierkegaard) both reference Kierkegaard's fondness of the following quote: "Such works are like mirrors, when a monkey peers into them, no Apostle can be seen looking out."[44] But, like our discussion of "the single individual," Kierkegaard's point in utilizing this quote is *not* an arbitrary seeing which gives free license to any

---

39. Poole, *Kierkegaard*, 7.

40. See Kierkegaard, *Works of Love*, 216. We are not those to pretend to know the mind of the author, but we assume there are lots of unintentional faults to be found in Kierkegaard's work, for instance those which Joakim Garff has uncovered in his discussion of *Point of View*: see Garff, "Eyes of Argus." But there are of course also intentional "faults" like how he seemed to will his own social martyrdom in the Corsair affair.

41. See Aumann, "Kierkegaard's Case."; see also Gouwens, *Kierkegaard as Religious Thinker*, 2.

42. Kierkegaard, *Works of Love*, 61.

43. See for instance Evans, *Kierkegaard's Fragments and Postscript*, xiii–xiv; Gouwens, *Kierkegaard as Religious Thinker*, 1–3; Barrett, *Kierkegaard*, xii; Rae, *Kierkegaard and Theology*, 1–3.

44. Poole, *Kierkegaard*, 7; Garff, "Eyes of Argus," 89 n. 46; Kierkegaard, *Point of View*, 92 n.

and all hermeneutical activity.⁴⁵ It is not a matter regarding the reader's creative and conscious will, but is rather a matter of cultivated passion: the reader who loves will attempt to accommodate herself to what Kierkegaard's many voices are saying, and *subjectively* come to a point of "at least being made *aware*" of the need to encounter God for herself. However, Roger Poole seeks to objectify and play in Kierkegaard texts, bending them to his own ends, encouraging others to do the same. He appears to understand and read well the "deconstructive" function of the aesthetic works, but then mistrusts Kierkegaard's own application of these works, preferring instead to play in these texts as "an endless succession of signifiers."⁴⁶

Joakim Garff

Joakim Garff in his article "The Eyes of Argus: The Point of View and Points of View on Kierkegaard's Work as an Author"⁴⁷ also mistrusts Kierkegaard's "Point of View,"⁴⁸ rather preferring to treat the text as a sort of objective "commodity."⁴⁹ Garff seeks to destabilize "Point of View"'s hermeneutical authority, and thus could be seen to attempt to establish *his own* authority over this work. Such irony is unlikely to be lost on Garff and others who form similar arguments, but they would appear to see no need to "control" such irony. Both Poole and Garff seem to avoid encountering Kierkegaard's texts as they stand, particularly "Point of View." They instead seek to "pre-scribe" an objective (anti-)reading for others through their respective works. Therefore, in recognizing their views as arising out of mistrust, Poole and Garff are revealed in the very way they judge.⁵⁰ C.

---

45. Holmer, *On Kierkegaard and the Truth*, 135.

46. Poole, *Kierkegaard*, 9; cf. Evans, "The Role of Irony," 78.

47. Garff, "Eyes of Argus."

48. NB: "Point of View," is used here as a reference to the work "The Point of View for My Work as an Author" found in the Hong's collection of Kierkegaard's works on his authorship: *Point of View*, 21–97.

49. Garff, "Eyes of Argus," 93, etc. In reference to the concept of Derrida treating text like "commodities," see Jacobs, *A Theology Of Reading*.

50. See chapter 3: "Love and the Suspicious Spirit," in Jacobs, *A Theology Of Reading*, 77–90 where the author suggests that Derrida et al. treat texts as commodities that "divide," and work out of "a Platonic view of selfhood." Instead, Jacobs suggests seeing texts as "relational goods," where reading with love is both appropriate and necessary for reading well. He establishes this understanding in Christianity. I unfortunately lack the space here to engage with this work, but Jacobs would be very helpful in creating a

2.3 Kierkegaard's Reception Today

Stephen Evans appeals to what he perceives to be their "aesthetic" life-view by summarizing why he rejects such views:

> If everything in the Climacus readings is "nonsense," and the point that I am supposed to gain from the books is that they are saying what cannot be said, then the specifics of the discussions of contemporaneity, history, suffering, guilt, subjectivity, and truth all become less interesting. If it is all nonsense, then why waste time making sense of the distinctions and arguments?[51]

What is said here of Climacus can be said of all Kierkegaard's works: if Kierkegaard is really communicating nonsense (i.e., nothing), and that even Kierkegaard's writing in his own name is to be mistrusted, what is there to engage with? In his article on *Philosophical Fragments*, Evans points out that simply because Climacus employs irony does not mean he has nothing to say. In fact, he points out that in order to recognize *Philosophical Fragments as* irony (that is, the kind that jests when the author is in fact in earnest), the reader needs to recognize the underlying *truth* of what has been said to make such irony possible.[52] To disregard Kierkegaard *a priori* as a communicator of truth says more about the reader than Kierkegaard's works.

Joakim Garff seeks to subvert Kierkegaard's own take on his authorship by using the deconstructive tools of Kierkegaard's aesthetic works (namely the work by Johannes Climacus) to pull apart the veronymous "Point of View." As Garff cleverly comments on his subversive task, "this will make it possible to read Kierkegaard with Kierkegaard against Kierkegaard. And Kierkegaard could hardly hope for a more Kierkegaardian reading."[53] As a result, Garff points out a number of inconsistencies in "Point of View," including Kierkegaard's apparent exclusion of a number of his own works, Kierkegaard's tendency to contradict his use of explanations and assurances, and the unrepentant seduction of his reader which resembles "his" own perverse "Seducer's Diary."[54] Among other things, Garff also points

---

Christian general hermeneutic, in closer dialogue with Kierkegaard.

51. Evans, "The Role of Irony," 78.

52. "Climacus' irony does not undermine but presupposes the claims of Christian revelation" (ibid., 79).

53. Garff, "Eyes of Argus," 77.

54. Ibid., 80, 84, 85. Garff's strongest critique, in my view, is that related to the "assurances" given throughout *Point of View*. I have no space here to explore this in detail, except that I believe these references to be ironic on Kierkegaard's part: intentional

out the uncertainty of whether to believe in Kierkegaard's account of his real-life pious practices around the writing of *Either/Or* or whether this is merely another (self)deception.[55]

Although these critiques are indeed plausible and seem helpful on the surface of the matter, they ultimately serve no constructive purpose for understanding Kierkegaard's work. "Point of View" is alleged by Kierkegaard himself to be his own understanding of his entire authorship. This *allegedness* is precisely what Garff is commenting on. He points out that Kierkegaard was deceptive in his use of pseudonyms, and even in his public performance as a citizen of Copenhagen, so how could we trust his own direct "report to history"? What good are his "explanations" and "assurances" if he himself has disclosed that he cannot be trusted? Supposing that "Point of View" to be ironic, Garff is reading this work as Kierkegaard communicating: "Trust me: I am not to be trusted!"[56] But this work can rather be understood to be Kierkegaard communicating: "Trust me: the *pseudonyms* are not to be taken at face value!" Thus Garff is merely negating the difference between works that carry Kierkegaard's name and works that do not, collapsing into an objectivity which seeks to "uncover" Kierkegaard's *real* "point of view" instead of engaging with these works as they reveal themselves to be.

Garff contends that Kierkegaard depends heavily on "the excessive goodwill of the reader" and that such a reader resembles the naive simplicity of the young girl who was seduced by Johannes the Seducer in *Either/Or*.[57] But if this is the case, a more prominent scholar could label Garff as one of a number of "clever" persons who resemble Lewis' dwarfs: they are "not to be taken in" by what they believe to be another deception, when the facts of the matter are laid before them.[58] Garff therefore can be understood

---

opportunities for those who want to discredit him. Such a forgiving view requires substantiation, which I will give indirectly in the next chapter when we consider Kierkegaard's life as a substantiation of his authorship ("existence-communication"). Perhaps this then is another reason why Kierkegaard did not publish *Point of View* in his lifetime.

55. Ibid., 87–88.

56. Cf. Aumann on the irony in fragments: "Here is a bit of philosophical knowledge that is important in the sphere of religion: 'Philosophical knowledge is not important in the sphere of religion'" ("Kierkegaard's Case," 222).

57. Garff, "Eyes of Argus," 81, 85.

58. See Lewis, *The Last Battle*, 135–40 especially. On "cleverness," see Kierkegaard, *Spiritual Writings*, 238.

to reveal himself to be one who is living and seeing out of an aesthetic or ethical life-view, rather than one who strives to look in love.

Michael Watts

Michael Watts in his book *Kierkegaard* attempts to give an analysis of the different approaches of interpreting Kierkegaard, critiquing the approach of the school of thought led by Walter Lowrie as "blatantly contraven[ing] Kierkegaard's wishes."[59] Watts critiques Lowrie and his followers by claiming that Lowrie neglects the distinctive importance of Kierkegaard's pseudonyms. Lowrie is accused of squeezing and twisting these works into a straightforward "expression of Søren Kierkegaard's personal, philosophical and religious views." Watts is absolutely right to critique such a view, if this is indeed the case for this school. But upon what does he base this critique? Watts claims to follow Kierkegaard's own wishes in having the pseudonyms read as voices distinct from Kierkegaard, by drawing on his "postscript" to *Concluding Unscientific Postscript.*[60] Thus, Watts gives hermeneutical priority to Kierkegaard's veronymous works, and this appears to be his basis for critiquing the Lowrie school.

The other school of thought which Watts critiques is that of the poststructuralists, who "treat the entire authorship, even his private journals and signed works, as though it were *all* the product of pseudonyms," and deny any "conclusive meaning."[61] This school claims that *all* of Kierkegaard's works serve to prompt the reader to reflect upon what she herself thinks, without any positive communicative function. Watts suggests that this is more faithful to "Kierkegaard's request to acknowledge pseudonymous material" but, as opposed to scholars like Poole, he suggests this view is potentially too open in its interpretation to be able to link "viewpoints to Kierkegaard."[62] This second approach may respect Kierkegaard's wishes in terms of the pseudonyms, but, as we have argued above, it blatantly undermines the veronymous works by seeking to *demote* them (hermeneutically at least) to the status of maieutic pseudonymity. But more importantly, Watts' critique of the poststructuralists is based on the assumption that it

---

59. Watts, *Kierkegaard*, 60–62.
60. Kierkegaard, *Concluding Unscientific Postscript*, 625ff; Watts, *Kierkegaard*, 60.
61. Watts, *Kierkegaard*, 60.
62. Ibid., 61.

is essential to be able to uncover what Kierkegaard *really* thought.[63] This is problematic, because it is again a kind of focused objectivity, seeking to distance the reader from the subjective demand of Kierkegaard's writings.

If we follow Watts in giving hermeneutical priority to Kierkegaard's veronymous works, we see that the Lowrie school (aka "Blunt Reading"[64]) neglects the *form* but attempts to respect the *content* of Kierkegaard's authorial task, whilst the poststructuralists respect its *form* but not its *content*. There is a significant problem with both approaches. By the Lowrie school neglecting the function of the pseudonyms as prescribed by Kierkegaard, they are ignoring his teaching on the significance of subjectivity. This leaves Lowrie with the same error as Hegel: that of believing that being an author exempts him from the necessities of existence.[65] By reducing *all* of Kierkegaard's works to the level of being solely deconstructive and devoid of controlled irony, the content of the veronymous works lack any positive communicative element. Therefore, even Kierkegaard's own theory of "indirect communication" for which he has been praised, is emptied of meaning. Such an approach also restricts Kierkegaard to a privatistic and even solipsistic reading, and falls into what Anti-Climacus attacked as the triumphant illusion and improper use of the concept *hidden-inwardness*.[66]

So the misconception of the Lowrie school, the poststructuralists, *and* Michael Watts is that they reduce these works to the level of objectivity, ignoring the depth to which Kierkegaard embodied his teaching and enabled his reader to do likewise.

Murray Rae, C. Stephen Evans, Paul Holmer

Murray Rae, C. Stephen Evans, and Paul Holmer have attempted to write in such a way that takes Kierkegaard seriously in *both* content *and* form: by attempting to read him in love. But this has not been a straightforward task,

---

63. Poole is helpful in this regard, since he sees "the search for 'Kierkegaard's view of X'" as misguided. But Poole mistakenly sees this as "[the] theological tradition of reading" when the true theological reading of Kierkegaard is to read *past* Kierkegaard to encounter God in subjectivity. See Poole, *Kierkegaard*, 12.

64. Poole, "The Unknown Kierkegaard," as referenced in Rasmussen, *Between Irony and Witness*, 5.

65. See Evans' comments on Niels Thulstrup, for instance Evans, "The Role of Irony," 66.

66. See Kierkegaard, *Practice in Christianity*, 214, etc.; see also Gouwens, *Kierkegaard as Religious Thinker*, 213.

and all three have had to blur the conventionally understood boundaries between their roles as scholars and as people, a blurring that is faithful to Kierkegaard's work, but difficult to communicate.

For instance, Murray Rae points out that the incarnation is no mere idea, and that Louis Pojman, although helpful, is "nevertheless wrong in suggesting that 'the idea of the incarnation' is put at the foundation of one's noetic structure. It is not an idea (a doctrine?) but the *relationship of faith in Christ* which constitutes the new foundation for thought."[67] By using the concept of the incarnation appropriately—that is, subjectively—Rae cannot remain on the fence of objective observation. Instead, he enters into "scholarly" conversation by carrying with him and then using his own Christian convictions. Throughout his works, he encourages others to do the same.[68] In communicating in this way, he embraces his own position as a "single individual," thus communicating in a form which complements the content.[69]

C. Stephen Evans also outlines his understanding that Kierkegaard must be encountered by the reader as a "single individual." By attempting to "make the reader's task easier" through an elucidation and clarification of Climacus' terms and ideas, Evans in his *Kierkegaard's "Fragments" and "Postscript"* mimics Kierkegaard's own *hiddenness*. Evans helps the reader to hear what Kierkegaard is saying through Climacus, while attempting to *hide* his own scholarship by using it as a way to point to the value of interacting with Kierkegaard directly. Also, in his article, "The Role of Irony in Kierkegaard's *Philosophical Fragments*,"[70] Evans argues in a tone which seeks to make Kierkegaard's work clear. He argues against overly simplistic and objective readings of *Philosophical Fragments*, clearing the air for a true engagement with Kierkegaard to occur. Through this work, he presents his own humble reading, which inevitably reveals himself as one who can be read as being sympathetic to Kierkegaard's Christian convictions since he appears to take Climacus' irony "seriously."[71]

---

67. Rae, *Kierkegaard's Vision of the Incarnation*, 164, citing Pojman, "Kierkegaard on Faith and History," 65.

68. Rae, "The Risk of Obedience," 310; Rae, *Kierkegaard and Theology*, 1–4; Rae, *Kierkegaard's Vision of the Incarnation*, viii.

69. See the favorable review of Rae's work from Simon D. Podmore, who praises him for openly speaking from his own perspective of Kierkegaard: Podmore, Review of *Kierkegaard and Theology*, 370–73.

70. Evans, "The Role of Irony."

71. Ibid., 78–79 especially.

PART II: THE FORM

Paul Holmer in his book *The Grammar of Faith*[72] is exemplary in the way he has embraced the teaching of Kierkegaard by seeking to direct his readers not primarily to the genius of Kierkegaard himself, but by *using* Kierkegaard (and especially Ludwig Wittgenstein) to redirect his readers to redefining theology by emphasizing the irreducible subjectivity of Christianity. His grasp of the distinction between "language about" and "language of" faith is clearly derived from Kierkegaard's distinction between the "what" and the "how" of Christianity, a differentiation which he uses to get beyond the distractions of historical-critical analysis.[73] But it is precisely because of his emphasis on the "how" that Holmer *uses* this Kierkegaardian distinction to call his readers to a theology that *knows* God and not merely *knows about* him.[74] Holmer is therefore faithfully Kierkegaardian in that he moves beyond him whilst remaining *in* and advocating *for* a subjective dependence on God as a "single individual."[75]

Although Kierkegaard teaches that it is impossible for a person to perfectly marry ideality and actuality, the works of these three scholars seek to embrace the difficulties in writing "about" Kierkegaard in a form that attempts to take seriously his emphasis on the "how." Like Kierkegaard, the imperfections of these works make critical reading of them possible in terms of the "what." But their literary self-awareness is commendable, and can be used as excellent demonstrations of what it means to read—and write—about Kierkegaard in love.

---

72. Holmer, *The Grammar of Faith*.

73. See for instance chapter 7: "Scientific Language and the Language of Religion," ibid., 54–80.

74. "But to use [theology] supposes that we translate from the third-person mood of being their knowledge and language 'about' God to becoming my language 'of' faith . . . theology is not done best in scholarly forms and artifices of the learned . . . Theology, to the extent that it becomes knowledge of God, has to have the form of personal appropriation built in. Otherwise, it is not about God at all but is only a history of someone's thoughts. For to have knowledge of God you must fear him and you must also love him" (ibid., 25).

75. See especially ibid., 16, and chapter 2: "What Theology Is and Does—Again," 17–36.

2.3 Kierkegaard's Reception Today

READING SØREN KIERKEGAARD

Kierkegaard, in his veronymous sermons entitled "The Look of Love" and "Love and Sin,"[76] focuses on the claim of the Scriptures that "love hides a multitude of sins" (1 Pet 4:8). It is the judgment of the world that discovers sin, while love *hides* a multitude of sins.[77] Although the ability of an individual to discover sin would ordinarily seem like something to be praised, Kierkegaard suggests that such discovery seeks "worldly" praise rather than the superior praise of love. Again, there is here the undergirding matter of the problem of truth and its relation to existence. The claim that there is some objective reality of sin behind and irrespective of our perception of it, would seem (according to conventional wisdom) to be wise and sensible, and therefore one who can *uncover* such things is normally considered "clever."[78] But for Kierkegaard, such "objectivity" is irrelevant for the existing individual, since she can only interact with reality subjectively. In this way, he claims that "an understanding of evil (however much one tries to make himself and *others* think that one can keep himself entirely pure, that there is a pure understanding of evil) nevertheless *involves* an *understanding with* evil."[79]

In applying such a hermeneutic, we are *not* saying that Kierkegaard is beyond critique, that his works are flawless and consistent (such as the view regarding "Point of View," highlighted by Garff from 1926),[80] or that his words carry divine "authority"; rather, we have been attempting to demonstrate *how* Kierkegaard's works function as mirrors by looking at their contemporary interpreters.

A *loving* reading of Kierkegaard attempts to take his works seriously both in form and content. Kierkegaard understood that the communication of essential truth cannot be done objectively, so Kierkegaard's writing itself must be considered in this light: does he fall into his own critique? If not, how does he embody what he seeks to teach? Such questions remove the possibility of reading and using Kierkegaard as a disseminator of objective content, but, as we have seen, many scholars still fall into the comfortable trap of using him in this way. By reading Kierkegaard in love, however, we

---

76. From 1843–44's *Eighteen Upbuilding Discourses*, published as chapters 11 and 12 of Part III in Kierkegaard, *Spiritual Writings*, 227–42 and 243–53 respectively.

77. Ibid., 252.

78. Ibid., 235–36.

79. Kierkegaard, *Works of Love*, 266, emphasis author's own.

80. Garff, "Eyes of Argus," 101–2 n. 46 from page 89.

are given eyes to see how Kierkegaard used his *outward communicative* task to meet his reader where she was, and to give her opportunities to outwork faith, hope and love in the very interpretation of his works.

Reading Kierkegaard in love is not simply a tautology. *Works of Love* is not simply a work of original ethical teaching which focuses on hermeneutics. Instead, it is simply a reiteration of "boring" old Christianity, namely the teaching of Christ.[81] Christ both taught and embodied the concepts regarding "do not judge, and you will not be judged" and so on. Therefore, Kierkegaard's hermeneutic which we are attempting to consider him by is really the hermeneutic of Christ, the one who perfectly married form and content, ideality with actuality. It can be understood, therefore, that a theological reading of Kierkegaard is not only the most faithful to him, but also—and most importantly—the most upbuilding to *us* and our interaction in the world.[82]

As "single individuals" who seek to understand Kierkegaard, we have attempted to read Kierkegaard with "goodwill"[83] in an attempt to be the reader he has written for.[84] Love gives Kierkegaard the benefit of the doubt, and endeavors to bend accordingly to the intrinsic *logos* of his work.[85] It is indeed upbuilding for us to consider Kierkegaard in this way, since it is upbuilding to recognize love.[86]

---

81. Kierkegaard, *Point of View*, 91–93; and also Kierkegaard, *Concluding Unscientific Postscript*, 629–30: Kierkegaard's description of the function of his pseudonyms, which I believe he would have said equally of his religious works.

82. Remember the section "'Hidden Inwardness As Individualism?'" in 1.2 above.

83. Cf. Garff, "Eyes of Argus," 81.

84. That is, the reader next to Regine. See Kierkegaard, *Christian Discourses*, 359; McDonald, "Kierkegaard, Søren"; Hong and Hong, "Historical Introduction," xix.

85. Torrance, *Mediation*, 13.

86. Part One, chapter 1, "Love's Hidden Life and Its Recognisability by Its Fruits," in Kierkegaard, *Works of Love*, 23–33. In regard to the tone of this paragraph and its attempt to mirror that of Kierkegaard's veronymous religious works, Sylvia Walsh's elucidation of Climacus' position on subjective communication is informative: ". . . instead of giving a direct account of personal actions so as to become an object of admiration by others, the subjective thinker should present that which constitutes what is admirable in the universally human ideal to which the thinker is related and present that as an ethical requirement, as a challenge to the recipient to exist in it (CUP, 1:358–59). In presenting the universal human ideal as a possibility, the subjective thinker's communication conforms to the traditional concept of poetry as concerning itself with ideality, but there is an important difference here too, in that the ideal is set forth as an ethical requirement, not merely as an imaginative possibility" (Walsh, *Living Poetically*, 207–8).

CONCLUSION

What these various readings point to is how Kierkegaard's works still function as mirrors today, revealing to the reader the subjective *how* of her existence. What we are reading in Kierkegaard's detractors is typically closer to what the commentators themselves believe, whereas those who attempt to read the works in the generosity of love appear (in our view) to give more constructive readings. We have critically considered these commentators in light of Kierkegaard's emphasis on a hermeneutics from the heart, thereby learning the importance of reading Kierkegaard in *love*. All of this is, again, made possible through Kierkegaard's *hidden authorship*, where he removes himself from the equation, giving the reader the space to reveal herself, in the hope of her meeting God in her own "hidden inwardness."

Part III: Kierkegaard as an Example of a Christian Communicator

So far in this book we have outlined the key concepts in Kierkegaard's authorship ("the single individual" and truth) in terms of their explicit content (Part I). These concepts form the overall emphasis and first layer of Kierkegaard's task: the understanding that a person meets God, who is *hidden* in Christ, only in "hidden inwardness." Our discussion of this *content* led us to look into the second, deeper layer, where we sought to show that these concepts shaped the *form* of Kierkegaard's authorship, and this is the central concern of this book. The form complements the content to provide a deep, *hidden* communication which carries both an outward and an inward dimension.

The second layer is the *outward* dimension, and this has been discussed in Part II. There we argued that the form of Kierkegaard's writing served not only to complement the existential material, but also to existentially involve the *reader* in the midst of her reading. We have argued that it is as the reader meets God for herself in what we have termed "the hidden middle" that Kierkegaard's authorial task of "reintroducing Christianity into Christendom" is fulfilled for "the single individual."

Now we come to the deepest layer, the *inward* dimension: that is, how does Kierkegaard's authorship impinge on his own life? Does Kierkegaard practice what is preached in his very authorship, or does his own existence serve to undermine his entire project? Given his impassioned critique of Hegel, that he was writing himself out of existence and thus fundamentally negating his own work, how does Kierkegaard overcome this possible critique of his own writing? In particular, how does his use of pseudonyms serve as an embodiment of Christian truth? This is the task before us for this section.

3.1 The Inward Dimension of Kierkegaard's Authorship

INTRODUCTION

Kierkegaard can be recognized as having been no mere outsider who communicated Christian truth superficially but can be seen as a "reduplication" of that love he sought to communicate. That is, out of his attempt at other-centeredness he can be understood to have become one who embodied the truth in love. In this section we will explore the concepts of "existence-communication" and "reduplication" in an attempt to make sense of some of the ethical practices behind Kierkegaard's authorship, as well as attempting to understand how we should interpret Kierkegaard's life in relation to his authorship. *Works of Love* will act as our point of departure as it illustrates the kind of ethics which Kierkegaard sought to employ in his own life as an author. This veronymous work outlines Kierkegaard's understanding of the threefold relation of love—that love (that is, God) mediates the relation between two human persons.[1] Thus, by pursuing an authorship of *hiddenness*, Kierkegaard can be understood to have been striving to remain in love while simultaneously striving to point his reader to God, which he understood to be the highest act of love.[2]

It is important for us to note that the once-fashionable psychological-biographical readings have come under heavy criticism in recent years.[3] Such scholarship has been critiqued from a number of angles, the most

---

1. Kierkegaard, *Works of Love*, 112–13, 282–83.
2. Ibid., 124, 256–60.
3. For such a critique of a "psychological diagnosis" approach and the tendency to objectivise Kierkegaard's work, see Gouwens, *Kierkegaard as Religious Thinker*, 1–4.

important criticism being that it blatantly ignores the end to which Kierkegaard's writings were employed, and can actually be seen to objectivise Kierkegaard, relegating him to "a paragraph in the system." Such readings also serve to excuse readers from engaging with the writings for themselves, instead reducing the writings to the out-workings of Kierkegaard's personal issues.[4] Such historical knowledge is valuable and has its place, but should not replace the greater and fundamental existential claims which these works seek to make on the reader.[5] So we must tread lightly in discussing Kierkegaard's work in relation to his lived life. We will do this by looking at Kierkegaard as an *example*, though not an ideal one, of what it looks like to be a Christian: in particular, a Christian *writer*. In this we will not seek to elicit admiration for him, but rather to find encouragement in learning from him and possibly to attempt to pick up where he left off—as a "witness to the truth."[6]

THE ETHICS OF KIERKEGAARD'S AUTHORSHIP

As Murray Rae points out, Johannes Climacus' *Philosophical Fragments* focuses on the epistemological and ontological aspects of Christian conversion, but does not explore the *ethical* implications of "the moment." Rae claims that we find these instead in Kierkegaard's veronymous works such

---

4. See, for instance, Lee Barrett's critique on Joakim Garff's influential biography of Kierkegaard: Barrett, "Review of *Søren Kierkegaard*."

5. Regarding *Fear and Trembling*'s relation to Kierkegaard's own broken engagement to Regine Olsen, Murray Rae states: ". . . Kierkegaard is reading the Bible so as to find light for his own path, rather than imposing the pattern of his own life upon his reading of the Bible . . . we need to read *Fear and Trembling*, not as revealing the idiosyncrasies of Kierkegaard's own person, but as a wrestling with those difficulties in the Abraham story that confront problematically whoever counts scripture as in some way authoritative for Christian faith" (Rae, "The Risk of Obedience," 309–10). See also Aumann, "Kierkegaard's Case."

6. Again, Gouwens is helpful here: ". . . 'helper' is apt if it means that the solution to scholarly misunderstanding of Kierkegaard is not hagiography—indeed, Kierkegaard would himself see hagiography as yet another misreading. The solution to both scholarly misunderstanding and hero-worship is, rather, engagement with his writing. What Kierkegaard desired—and deserves—above all is readers (and writers) who attempt to 'think with' (and 'against') him, to enter into the concerns and issues he raises with philosophical *eros* and passion" (Gouwens, *Kierkegaard as Religious Thinker*, 2); see also Rae, *Kierkegaard and Theology*, 3. We will discuss Bishop Mynster in relation to this phrase further below.

as *Works of Love* and the various religious discourses.⁷ This is significant for our discussion here because as we know, Climacus was an outsider to the Christian faith and could not give any kind of positive *existential* detail to Christianity because he himself did not live from within it.⁸ Instead, the best that he could do was to describe it negatively in contrast to the Socratic cognitive-exclusive forms of knowing, as in his Hegelian description: "an objective uncertainty."⁹ However, for the insider Kierkegaard, his outworking of the ethics of the gospel is *primarily* about living his life as an author, in a way that is faithful to Christ. In this light, these veronymous works are primary for understanding the ethics of Kierkegaard's authorship, since they carry the insider's knowledge and a life-embedded teaching of what Paul Holmer calls "the grammar of faith."¹⁰

As George Pattison points out in his foreword to *Works of Love*,

> Socrates played a key role [in Kierkegaard's lectures on ethical and religious communication as well as in *Works of Love*] as the exemplar of how to teach ethics—not as a theory or academic discipline but as life. Insisting on what he called the "indirect method," in which (like Socrates) the teacher refrains from giving direct instruction but lets the pupils work the question out for themselves, Kierkegaard regarded this as integral to Christian communication also.¹¹

So how did Kierkegaard's authorship embody these ethics?

The point here is that *the presence of an author is a means of indwelling* (to say what Climacus did not and Kierkegaard *could* not).¹² The veronymous works carry Kierkegaard's name because he desired to be credited with the views they expressed. That is, Kierkegaard's *life*—even that manifested in his literary works (the emphasis for our research) can be understood as an attempt to live out these ethics. But ultimately, God is the only teacher:¹³

---

7. Rae, *Kierkegaard's Vision of the Incarnation*, 109 n. 3.

8. See Evans, *Kierkegaard's Fragments and Postscript*, 52–53.

9. Kierkegaard, *Concluding Unscientific Postscript*, 203–4.

10. ". . . this is how one becomes a true theologian, one who actually knows God" (Holmer, *The Grammar of Faith*, 212). Holmer accredits Wittgenstein with the claim that "theology is the grammar of faith" (ibid., 17). See also ibid., 190 n. 15.

11. Pattison, "Foreword," xv.

12. Cf. Kierkegaard, *Concluding Unscientific Postscript*, 252; see also 1.3: "Climacus and Anti-Climacus," and "Christ the Truth" above, along with Kierkegaard, *Works of Love*, 108. In short, truth is its own justification and cannot be justified by anything else.

13. See Part Two, chapter 4: "Love Seeks Not Its Own," in Kierkegaard, *Works of*

it is only from the revelation of God that one can come to know what it means to live as a Christian, since faith is not a matter of objective intellectual assent, but rather one of *metanoia*—a deeply subjective conversion which redefines how the believer relates herself to God and the world. Such a perspective cannot be known from the outside, and therefore the communication of Christian ethics must be undertaken by a Christian.[14]

By way of contrast, David J. Gouwens suggests that it is a "lie" to claim that "only practitioners of a faith can understand it."[15] This is the case only if such an understanding is merely *poetic* (a knowing "of"), but this is not the case for embodied knowing (knowing "with"). Only those inside the Christian faith can communicate what it means to be a Christian *in truth*—it is a passional communication, which requires the work of God in the communicator.

"EXISTENCE-COMMUNICATION"

Kierkegaard sought to embody his task in his life. Joakim Garff is correct to an extent, that Kierkegaard "wrote himself into existence,"[16] that his journals were self-constructions or self-narrations on his own peculiar life.[17] This can easily be seen, for instance, in how *Fear and Trembling* is suggestive of Kierkegaard's own actions regarding Regine.[18] Although we will critique this view below, Kierkegaard's authorial project was indeed one that embodied his entire life. He despised perpetual abstraction in essential

---

Love, 247–60; cf. Kierkegaard, "Philosophical Crumbs."

14. "Christianity is not the kind of teaching that is the same whoever proclaims it but is as the one who proclaims it and is true according to the truth of the life of the one who proclaims it . . ." (Kierkegaard, *Spiritual Writings*, 267). Since Christ is the only one who could make such a proclamation, the issue of authority becomes important here, but is beyond the scope of this work. Suffice it to say, Kierkegaard acted as a "witness to the truth," rather than one who proclaimed Christ with divine authority.

15. Gouwens, *Kierkegaard as Religious Thinker*, 216 n. 26.

16. The phrase is Lee Barrett's summary of Garff's view regarding Kierkegaard's authorship. See Barrett, "Review of *Søren Kierkegaard*," 154; For a brief critique of this view, see Barrett's *Kierkegaard*, 3, who pushes us back toward reading Kierkegaard existentially.

17. ". . . I came to understand myself by writing" (Kierkegaard, *Journals and Papers*, 6/6227, IX A 213, n.d., 1848); ". . . Kierkegaard saw his entire authorship as being instrumental in his own essential education" (Hong and Hong, "Translator's Introduction," xxi).

18. Rae, "The Risk of Obedience," 309.

3.1 The Inward Dimension of Kierkegaard's Authorship

matters, and instead sought for a lived continuity and an embodied Christianity in his attempt to be a "single individual" under God.

Of course, this is not to say that Kierkegaard disregarded abstraction altogether; his writings are, of course, embedded in the fundamental abstraction of language. But he refused to *remain* in abstraction, because he was a religious poet rather than a Romantic one.[19] In terms of ethico-religious matters, abstraction (like language itself) was only utilized by Kierkegaard for the sake of being embodied.[20] He endeavored to ground his communication in real life, first of all his own. This is what he understood to constitute an "existence-communication." That is, in order to lend credibility to what he taught, Kierkegaard did what he could to be one who could be recognized as attempting to carry out his own teaching.[21] As a religious poet who communicated the infinitely high ideal of Christianity, he knew he could not perfectly live up to what he communicated, but lent credibility to his communication by being one who strove toward this truth.[22] This was not to point to himself, but rather to protect his readers from being distracted by any potential personal hypocrisy.

The claim that Kierkegaard was against perpetual abstraction in his language (and its poetic counterpart "unstable irony")[23] is most obvious in this statement regarding the key point for his authorial task:

> My thesis . . . is not that the substance of what is proclaimed in Christendom as Christianity is not Christianity. No, my thesis is that the proclamation is not Christianity. I am fighting about a

---

19. "I cannot express reality in language, because I use ideality to characterize it, which is a contradiction, an untruth" (Kierkegaard, *Journals and Papers*, 3/2320, IV B 14:6, n.d., 1842–3, cited in Walsh, *Living Poetically*, 48). See also 1.3, "Christomorphic Poetics" above.

20. Unlike romantic irony, religious poetics has a telos for personal existence. See Walsh, *Living Poetically*, 57.

21. See Whittaker, "Kierkegaard on the Concept of Authority," 98.

22. ". . . I understood myself to be what I must call a poet of the religious, not however that my personal life should express the opposite—no, I strive continually, but that I am a 'poet' expresses that I do not confuse myself with the ideal . . . I am not that, but I strive. If the latter does not prove correct and is not true about me, then everything is cast in intellectual form and falls short" (Kierkegaard, *Journals and Papers*, 6/6511, X2 A 106, n.d., 1849).

23. See Evans' discussion on this term by Wayne Booth, used also by John Lippitt: "The Role of Irony," 77–79.

how, a reduplication. It is self-evident that without reduplication Christianity is not Christianity.[24]

Kierkegaard understood Christianity, like all matters concerning essential truth (i.e., ethical and religious matters) to require an embodied, passional use of its concepts. Therefore, he could not himself write in such a way that was confined to abstract, disembodied analysis. He instead sought to involve himself subjectively in his communication, since, in a manner of speaking, his communication *was* subjectivity.[25] In this way, Kierkegaard's life was vital to his work, but should not be used "in the too frequent improper sense of a historico-psychological approach to [his] works in order to dig out clues to Kierkegaard's life, but in order to become aware of clues to one's own life, its shape and direction."[26]

This subjective embodiment was not merely for the sake of his outward "existence-communication," but was also an outworking of his own being in the truth. Through his writings it can be understood that he himself carried the communicated ideal as a subjective conviction, and wanted to be recognized by God as one who strove after an ever deepening Christianity.

Such an embodiment was not intended to be an outward demonstration of his own faith as a follower of Christ; on the contrary, he sought to protect his "hidden inwardness" from worldly admiration ("the bestial flattery of the crowd").[27] He can be understood to have valued his subjective relation with God to be so intimate and so precious that he did not dare to disclose the depth of this to anyone else, for fear that the temptation of admiration would rob both his reader and himself of the prize of the gospel.[28] His authorship was rather one that pointed *away* from himself and toward

---

24. Kierkegaard, *Journals and Papers*, 3/3684, X3 A 431, n.d., 1850, quoted in Rae, *Kierkegaard and Theology*, 3. We will explore the concept reduplication below.

25. Holmer, *On Kierkegaard and the Truth*, 112.

26. Hong and Hong, "Translator's Introduction," xxi; Also, "the literature is not the resolution of Kierkegaard's problems and should not be interpreted simply autobiographically . . ." (Holmer, *On Kierkegaard and the Truth*, 39).

27. Kierkegaard, *Point of View*, 59.

28. Kierkegaard understood this, but could not say such a thing directly, so he put a similar sentiment in the pen of the super-Christian Anti-Climacus: "I say, in fact, that I am an extraordinary Christian such as there has never been, but, please note, I am that in hidden inwardness. I shall see to it that no one, not one, detects anything, even the slightest, but profess I can, and I can profess (but I cannot *really* profess, for then, after all, I would violate the secret's hiding place) that in hidden inwardness I am, as I said, an extraordinary Christian such as there has never been" (Kierkegaard, *Journals and Papers*, 6/6349, X6 B 48, n.d., 1849).

God. But again, this is not the incongruence of a "triumphant" pointing, in which he would be praised for his humility and such "pointing" would be a farce, but rather a "pointing" characterized by the witness of martyrdom. For Kierkegaard, this meant ensuring his own exclusion from the "worldly" triumph of being a "successful" author-thinker.[29]

To be in the truth was to strive toward Christ, which was characterized by "hidden inwardness." Therefore, if we are to believe that Kierkegaard was indeed one who sought to embody the subjectivity that he attempted to communicate, then we will be unable to observe Kierkegaard's Christianity *directly*. But we are able to observe *how* he went about his authorship, in an attempt to see if this can be recognized as being congruent with the Christianity he expounded.

LOVE AS "REDUPLICATION"

In *Works of Love*, Kierkegaard distinguished between two main forms of love. The Danish word *Kaerlighed* is one, and is used for the eternal love of God which is unconditional and non-preferential toward all people. This is contrasted with the human-based, temporal, spontaneous, and preferential love of *Elskov*.[30] The latter we will focus our attention on here in this section, in an effort to understand Kierkegaard's term "reduplication."[31]

Many of Kierkegaard's *Upbuilding Discourses* focus on the importance of choice, and it is this characteristic of reflection and eternity which distinguishes humankind from the rest of creation. He sees that many who live in the immediate (the aesthetic sphere in particular) are not proper human selves, and so he encourages such persons to learn from the bird and the lily who depend on God for their everyday existence. The difference for the individual human person is that she has the power of choice: she can will to

---

29. Cf. Kierkegaard, *Practice in Christianity*, 221–24, etc. This is what I understand the reason to be behind Kierkegaard inciting his own suffering at the hand of the editors of the *Corsair*. See also Barrett, "Review of *Søren Kierkegaard*," 14.

30. Pattison, "Foreword," xi.

31. Roger Poole makes the mistake of claiming that this term wasn't used in *Postscript*, but came later, especially in *Practice in Christianity* in his *Kierkegaard*, 13. However, Arnold Come clarifies that it first appeared in *Concluding Unscientific Postscript*, then in a number of Kierkegaard's veronymous religious works, and then *Practice in Christianity*. See Come, *Kierkegaard as Humanist*, 364. Perhaps this was to do with the translators use of "redoubling" instead. Come cites the following in support: McKinnon, *Fundamental Polyglot Konkordans Til Kierkegaards Samlede Vaerker*.

live out of her own efforts and thoughts of being self-sufficient, but worship occurs when a person embraces her responsibility to choose God, which is also her joy.[32] Kierkegaard points out that God wants to be freely chosen by each and every "single individual."

When this happens, the possibility of faith is taken up by the person, and she makes this possibility a reality for herself. This is a *reduplication*, or *redoubling*: to indwell a possibility.[33] It is akin to "living poetically" because, rather than simply thinking or communicating an ideal like a poet does, a person who takes up the appropriate passions to exist *in* this possibility—to *embody* this truth—is the one who *reduplicates* herself.[34]

So we come to the possibility of love. As opposed to understanding love as a self-contained virtue akin to wisdom in Aristotelian fashion, Kierkegaard claims that love exists *for* others.[35] While virtues carry the connotation of a badge of superiority for those who "possess" them, love, for Kierkegaard, is fundamentally self-effacing, or *hidden*.[36] This is because *God* is love, and Kierkegaard understands him to be the middle term who mediates all human relations.[37] The ultimate act of love is to freely choose to point a person to God, who is himself eternal love. Therefore, for a person to be love toward another is actually for her to *hide* herself in the hope of the other knowing the love of God.[38] When we love, we participate in the eternal, and we are to that person who God is to us.[39] And because love is something which grows and multiplies, it is in this way that the one who loves comes to know in truth, that God is also this way toward her.

32. ". . . when that which is to be drawn is in itself a self, then truly to draw to itself means first to help it truly become itself in order then to draw it to itself, or in means in and through drawing it to itself to help it become itself . . . And what, then, is to be a self? It is to be a redoubling . . ." (Kierkegaard, *Practice in Christianity*, 159); also the opening paragraph in Kierkegaard, *Sickness*; see also "The Lily of the Field and the Bird under Heaven," from 1849, published as chapter 10: "Silence, Obedience, and Joy," in Kierkegaard, *Spiritual Writings*, 179–224.

33. Evans, *Kierkegaard's Fragments and Postscript*, 57–58.

34. Ibid., 58 see also 1.3 above: "Christomorphic Poetics."

35. "Love is not an exclusive characteristic, but it is a characteristic by which or in virtue of which you exist for others" (Kierkegaard, *Works of Love*, 211); see also ibid., 177.

36. See Alan Jacobs considering John Milbank in *A Theology Of Reading*, 49; see Part Two, chapter 4: "Love Seeks Not Its Own," in Kierkegaard, *Works of Love*, 247–59.

37. Kierkegaard, *Works of Love*, 112–13, 282–83.

38. Ibid., 124, 256–60.

39. This can simply be understood to be an elucidation on Jesus' words, for instance those in Matt 25:40.

3.1 The Inward Dimension of Kierkegaard's Authorship

In choosing to be love to others, she therefore comes to a proper self-love, since she sees herself through God's eyes.[40] This is love's "reduplication":

> What love does, it is; what it is, it does—at one and the same moment; simultaneously as it goes beyond itself (in an outward direction) it is in itself (in an inward direction) . . .[41]

An "existence-communication" regarding eternal love occurs when the communicator seeks to lend existential credibility to her communication with others by striving after this ideal of love which she expresses. And in seeking to embody love, she becomes *for* others—she loves. This is how speaking about such love is "upbuilding": it produces what it is witness to. So when we talk about love, such love reduplicates itself in us, and we participate in the eternal love of God.

It is in this way that we can consider how the form matches the content in Kierkegaard's communication of Christianity: it was in *hiding* himself and pointing to God throughout his entire authorship that Kierkegaard can be recognized as one who embodied inwardly the very love of which he was a witness.[42] This can be understood to be a key element in Kierkegaard's own Christian development, being one who lived in the categories of his own thought.[43] It is our belief, then, that Kierkegaard's authorship was contingent on his *hiding* himself in the eternal.

Humor

While irony was employed to transition between the aesthetic and ethical spheres of life, humor was used as Kierkegaard's own "incognito." Irony functioned to point out the shortcomings of a person's ability to live out her own ideals, while humor functioned in a similarly outward way, but to protect her own "hidden inwardness."[44] Although Kierkegaard and his

---

40. See Part One, chapter 2 A: "*You Shall Love,*" in Kierkegaard, *Works of Love,* 34–57. This paragraph has been helped by the clear summary of this concept found in Come, *Kierkegaard as Humanist,* 366–70.

41. Kierkegaard, *Works of Love,* 270.

42. Even to the extent of being a social martyr, as we shall see in the section "Kierkegaard: The Hidden Author," below.

43. LeFevre, "Part II. An Interpretation," 188.

44. "Humor is in fact defined by Climacus as always involving a 'revocation.' The communication that is a 'unity of jest and seriousness' becomes a riddle to the recipient, which the recipient must solve for himself . . . The ironical and humorous form once

pseudonyms could poetically describe the ideal, his own striving toward this ideal was between himself and God alone. Humor was employed as a way for the author to admit that he believed in what was being written, and was himself being judged by it. Such humor is particularly strong in *Concluding Unscientific Postscript* and Kierkegaard's signed works, where it is employed to highlight the author's own awareness of his secret shortcomings. This was yet another way in which Kierkegaard hid and protected his own "hidden inwardness."[45]

KIERKEGAARD: THE HIDDEN AUTHOR

Kierkegaard's message was not original. Many have emphasized the importance of existence in relation to thought and language pertaining to moral and ethical knowing. But what we have discovered here is more unique to Kierkegaard: that he can be understood as one who "reduplicated" this knowing in his life, even in his life as an author. The very *form* of Kierkegaard's authorship attempts to embody the very hiddenness that he was communicating.[46] How are we then to interpret Kierkegaard's life in relation to his works?

Although history may have relegated Kierkegaard to a sound byte, his reputation as a "melancholy Dane" is somewhat accurate, even if emasculating. Raised in a strictly religious household under a father who was convinced of his being cursed by God, churched under the ubiquitous image of the crucified Christ, for a time the suicidal hedonist, then the lone "witness to truth," Kierkegaard described his life as one of immense suffering.[47] Three episodes of his life in particular have elicited both mockery and silent fascination in many: his breaking off of an engagement with his lifelong love Regine Olsen; his social crucifixion by the magazine *Corsair*; and his ferocious attack on the Danish state church at the end of his life. A historico-biographical reading of Kierkegaard beyond what we have ex-

---

more is a way of securing the author's distance from the reader and thereby the reader's independence and responsibility" (Evans, *Kierkegaard's Fragments and Postscript*, 107).

45. My treatment of this concept is severely limited, and possibly reveals (somewhat accurately) a lack of understanding. However, space restricts remedying such a shortcoming. For an attempt at an explanation of this concept, see chapter 10: "Irony and Humor: Some Boundary Situations," in ibid., 185–205.

46. Evans also makes this point. See his ibid., 10.

47. Garff, *Søren Kierkegaard*, 16.

3.1 The Inward Dimension of Kierkegaard's Authorship

plored in the introduction is beyond the scope of this work, but here we can attempt to give the briefest of readings regarding these key events in Kierkegaard's life, considering what we have explored so far.

In the episode with Regine we can recognize outward hints of the "hidden inwardness" of which Kierkegaard speaks. He did not give any substantial explanation or justification for breaking the engagement: he simply appears to have regarded it as a command from God. Just as Abraham did not pause to make himself understood by others, so also was Kierkegaard utterly alone in this act.[48] Even our attempt here to understand is heavily speculative, so we are left only with the assurance that he was, indeed, alone.

Kierkegaard believed that voluntary suffering was an inevitable characteristic of a Christian life. His repeated emphases regarding "hidden inwardness," which was in contradistinction to "the world," "the single individual" against "the crowd," and how God's "incognito" was a suffering servant, all led him to construct his own "incognito" for the sake of embodying his message while rejecting any kind of popularity or success as an author. Seeing these as temptations and risks to both his own Christianity and his outward task, he instead pursued situations where he could be scorned by society as a fanatic.[49] This is how his social "martyrdom" by the *Corsair* can be understood, since it appears that he encouraged the magazine to make him a figure of public ridicule.[50] As an author who advocated for such hiddenness, he did not believe any form of worldly success to be helpful to his task or himself. He seemed desperate to depend on God totally, and so, later in life especially, determinedly sought to provide society no opportunity to praise his genius.[51] Perhaps he expected his faith to wane in the face of temptation, so he distanced himself the best he could from any form of self-sufficiency.[52]

---

48. See Kierkegaard, *Fear and Trembling*.

49. "My incognito was to be a sort of nobody, peculiar, odd-looking, with thin legs, an idler, and all that. All this was my own free will. Now the rabble have been trained to stare at me . . ." (Kierkegaard, *Journals and Papers*, 6/6327, X1 A 78, n.d., 1849). This statement was in regard to him being tempted out of his "incognito" by wanting to make himself understood to the public, after being an object of scorn in Danish society for so long.

50. See Hannay, "Introduction," 19.

51. "The Point of View for My Work as an Author" will be discussed further below in 3.3.

52. This can also be seen in how he handled his considerable inheritance—he died

Lastly we consider his final, all-out attack on the Danish state church. This was initiated in response to the Hegelian H. L. Martensen (the subject of many of Kierkegaard's critiques aimed at Hegelians) who labeled Bishop Jakob Mynster "a witness to the truth," at a church service after Mynster's death in 1854. Mynster was Kierkegaard's family pastor who later became Bishop of Zealand in the Danish state church, and was one with whom Kierkegaard was on friendly terms. But he refused to take Kierkegaard's advice to publicly admit that his preaching of Christianity was at odds with his comfortable ("triumphant") personal existence, which Kierkegaard hoped would protect an understanding of true Christianity in Denmark.[53] Kierkegaard was convinced that being a Christian was to be at odds with the established order, since the truth was Christ's triumph through abasement. That is, Kierkegaard understood that the Christian was not to be concerned with conquering the world or winning admiration from "the numerical," because he was convinced that only those who recognize Christ in his abasement will be drawn to him.[54] This is the basis for Kierkegaard's emphasis on the voluntary suffering for the Christian, in which Kierkegaard himself seemed to participate heavily.

But with Martensen's eulogy Mynster, as the figurehead of Christendom, was established as the epitome of what it meant to be a Christian: "a witness to the truth." Mynster's teaching may have been true poetically (i.e., portrayed the ideal of Christianity), but Kierkegaard lamented such a disembodied "witness." Kierkegaard's entire authorial task of reintroducing Christianity to Christendom took a heavy blow. Whereas during his life Mynster could have repented and vindicated Kierkegaard's critiques of Denmark's pseudo-Christianity, his beatification by Martensen cemented exactly what Kierkegaard had dedicated his life to oppose.[55] It prompted

---

with almost no money left, having poured all his savings into achieving his task, funding his own (typically unsuccessful, bar *Either/Or*) publishing. See Rae, *Kierkegaard and Theology*, 22–23.

53. See the collection of journal entries in the supplement of Kierkegaard, *Practice in Christianity*, 352–71 including journal entry X 4 A 365 n.d., 1851 on p. 364–66; see especially Kierkegaard, *Journals and Papers*, 6/6938, XI 2 A 252, n.d., 1854; 6/6723, X 4 A 9, n.d., 1851; 6/6795, X 4 A 511, n.d., 1852.

54. This is the emphasis of the last sections of *Practice in Christianity*. For instance, see 160–61.

55. See especially the journal entries in Kierkegaard, *Practice in Christianity*, 364–66, especially X 4 A 365 n.d., 1851.

3.1 The Inward Dimension of Kierkegaard's Authorship

Kierkegaard to give an extended *direct* attack on the state church and Danish Christianity, less than two years before his death.[56]

These acts can be understood as a "reduplication" of love: having known love, Kierkegaard would not risk losing it by being distracted with immediacy. He also appears very weary of causing others to lose or miss this love, preferring instead to stand outside society in order to speak into it. In this way, we see that Kierkegaard's life was *hidden* for the sake of "hidden inwardness": both inwardly and outwardly.

Kierkegaard, as a thinker, was one who attempted to live in the categories of his thought: to "reduplicate" or "live poetically" in the world in which he found himself. As a thinker, he appeared to work out of the understanding that he was first of all a human being and a creature under God, and so therefore his life (the totality of thought, language, writing, eating, conversing, publishing, etc.) was implicated in his ideas.[57] As a poet who grasped an understanding of the ideal, he was painfully aware of his own shortcomings in existence, but, as we will explore in our next chapter, he can be recognized as one who strove after the ideal he communicated, thus giving concrete plausibility to his words.

In this way, his works *are indeed* independent communications *per se*, but only to a limited degree.[58] We can only recognize the existential weight and credibility of Kierkegaard's communications (be they written in

56. It is here that Kierkegaard might possibly be critiqued as having abandoned his practice of "indirect communication" by seeking to condemn the established order directly. Perhaps Kierkegaard could no longer bear to be misunderstood in his tireless attempts to be a "witness to the truth" *in truth*: thinking that his "reduplication" was falling on deaf ears. But this should be left for the biographers to discuss. The interpretations here are suggestions of a possible interpretation of these three episodes of Kierkegaard's life, and are intended as examples to illustrate this thesis.

57. See especially Kierkegaard, *Concluding Unscientific Postscript*, 303, 331–33, 351; and also the following quote: "Kierkegaard clearly wants his reader to think with him, but philosophizing does not require another 'what' as much as it does the 'how.' Part of the 'how' is simply remembering that one is an existing individual, and that requires that one think with the customary 'I,' not as an universalized 'ego' or a general disembodied spirit, and not *sub specie aeternitas* either" (Holmer, *On Kierkegaard and the Truth*, 138).

58. "[Kierkegaard's] works themselves have a high degree of autonomy apart from the intricacies of episodes in Kierkegaard's life" (Holmer, *On Kierkegaard and the Truth*, 42–43); "I shall therefore ignore as irrelevant the relationship between Kierkegaard's personal life and the content of the books, rejecting (by ignoring them) attempts to explain away the content of the books through psychoanalytic interpretations (which are plenteous here)" (Evans, *Kierkegaard's Fragments and Postscript*, 4). These are two examples of how otherwise exceptional scholars are at risk of treating Kierkegaard himself as a disembodied thinker.

his own name or in the name of a "nonperson") by paying attention to how they affected his own lived life. As Kierkegaard once remarked of Luther:

> ... the error from which Luther turned was an exaggeration with regard to works. And he was entirely right; he did not make a mistake—a person is justified solely and only by faith. That is the way he talked and taught—and believed. And that this was not taking grace in vain—to that his life witnessed. Splendid![59]

CONCLUSION

Understanding the importance of the interrelated concepts "existence-communication" and "reduplication" in particular lead us to take seriously the life that Kierkegaard led. We have given a brief suggestion of how episodes in his life might serve these concepts, but the greatest and most concrete evidence of Kierkegaard's "reduplication" is in the very *form* of his authorship. In the concluding sections of this book, we will explore further how Kierkegaard *as an author* lived in the categories of his own thought.

---

59. Kierkegaard, *For Self-Examination and Judge for Yourself!*, cited in Rae, *Kierkegaard and Theology*, 144–45.

3.2 Pseudonymous Authorship as Reduplication

INTRODUCTION

We have so far explored how the form of Kierkegaard's authorial task was derived from the gospel of Christianity. In the previous chapter, we suggested how Kierkegaard understood his entire life to be a "reduplication" of his own works; he attempted to live and write as one *hidden* in Christ. In this chapter, we will test these claims by giving particular attention to how his employment of pseudonyms related to his own inwardness: how was his employment of these voices congruent with his communication of Christianity? How do they feature in Kierkegaard's own discipleship? We will see in this chapter that the pseudonyms enabled Kierkegaard to "reintroduce Christianity" by first demonstrating untruth, yet all the while remaining *in* the truth.

PSEUDONYMS AS HYPOCRISY?

Kierkegaard is famous for opposing Hegel and his followers.[1] As we have seen above, Kierkegaard's main critique of the philosopher was that he did not consider existence: in particular, the ongoing existence of himself as a thinker. Thus Kierkegaard accused him of being a "phantasm," and

---

1. We must also keep in mind that Hegel wasn't merely a negative influence for Kierkegaard. For instance, Malantschuk points out that Kierkegaard was heavily dependent on Hegel in the formation of his doctoral dissertation, though he moved "beyond" these views later. See Malantschuk, *Kierkegaard's Thought*, 64–66.

a "fantastical I-I," whose thoughts had no real purchase in actuality.[2] In short, Kierkegaard accused Hegel of writing himself out of existence. But, of course, Kierkegaard wrote these critiques largely in pseudonyms![3] This situation seems at least somewhat hypocritical, because accusing Hegel of acting as a non-existent "phantasm" by using such a phantasm seems to be the pot calling the kettle black. The way out of this problem then, is to consider this form of communication as ironical, which we will come to in due course.

To summarize this issue in relation to Kierkegaard's understanding of his task as a Christian author, we begin with how he understood that existence was what separates thinking and being, ideality and actuality, and that this existence was tainted by sin. Because of this (theological) fact, there was no shortcut to simply be an ideal self. Kierkegaard understood that Christ was the only one who truly married ideality and actuality; he was the only one who spoke and acted in the truth, since he *was* truth. As a Christian who was saved into the truth from the condition of sin by Christ the savior, he was then called to strive to be like Christ the prototype. This striving was a "becoming" (rather than Hegel's static "being"): a lifelong process, where a Christian was one who *attempted* to marry ideality and actuality in every facet of life, but in the knowledge that this could only come about by God's work. Such striving was through a dependence on the sanctifying work of God through faith, and living in the reality of knowing that "against God we are always in the wrong."[4]

To be an author who was in the truth meant that he must strive to say only what he himself believed and lived out. But this was, strangely enough, only realized through a lived dependence on God and an embracing of the author's own inevitable sin of incongruence.[5] He understood his task as an author to be concerned with communicating Christianity to his "neighbor."[6]

---

2. E.g., Kierkegaard, *Concluding Unscientific Postscript*, 193.

3. Particularly in the name of Johannes Climacus and in *Concluding Unscientific Postscript*.

4. Kierkegaard, *Either/Or*, 591–609.

5. Cf. 1 Pet 1:5–10. See also Rae, *Kierkegaard's Vision of the Incarnation*, 27 n. 3: "It was not the *failure* of Kierkegaard's own generation to exist in the Truth which raised his ire so much as their refusal to recognize the incongruity of their situation." See also Rae, *Kierkegaard and Theology*, 13–14.

6. Cf. Part One, chapter 2, A, B, C in Kierkegaard, *Works of Love*, 34–98.

3.2 Pseudonymous Authorship as Reduplication

But Kierkegaard understood his society to be gripped by an illusion in which they believed themselves to be Christian, and thus in no need of Kierkegaard's communication. Direct communication would have his words fall on deaf ears, and regardless, an encounter with Christian truth could not be brought about by conventional linear argument.[7] So indirect communication was necessary to first of all remove the illusion of Christendom. But as an author, and by communicating *en masse*, Socratic questioning was not an option.[8] He instead employed irony in a form in which he would demonstrate the error of a (popular but misguided) position which would hopefully resonate with the reader, and such a mirror would give her the opportunity to confront her own mistaken belief.[9]

The problem was that in giving these demonstrations, Kierkegaard could not commit his own name to these views, since this would constitute a falling away from a striving in, and toward, the truth. His own Christian understanding carried the conviction that "one may not communicate more than what one's own life conforms to . . ."[10] Therefore, Kierkegaard overcame this incongruence by distancing himself from these demonstrations by employing the use of pseudonyms. Therefore, his pseudonymity was not hypocrisy, but irony: it was out of his very own understanding of the importance of *existing* as an author that he employed them.

What particularly irked and disturbed Kierkegaard was how thinkers like Hegel, Martensen and Mynster could not see the incongruence of their own positions.[11] Kierkegaard understood them to often contradict

---

7. See Walsh, *Living Poetically*, 206–7.

8. While Socrates, Christ, and P. M. Møller communicated through public demonstration and personal conversation, Kierkegaard sought to apply such a method to his own field of literature.

9. "Though Kierkegaard was a religious author from first to last as he repeatedly says, he refused to use his talents for a forthright apologetic for religious faith. To do so would have involved him in the same tissue of difficulties he had noted in the classical metaphysicians and theologians" (Holmer, *On Kierkegaard and the Truth*, 13–14); and ". . . the thrust of the literature is a kind of reductio ad absurdum of a whole group of traditional philosophical problems like 'truth,' 'reality,' 'the good,' 'objective,' and others. The result is an entirely new notion of what philosophy is and does" (ibid., 39–40).

10. "From an ethical-religious standpoint, one may not communicate more than what one's own life conforms to . . ." (Walsh, *Living Poetically*, 240, citing Kierkegaard, *Journals and Papers*, 6/6528, X2 A 184, n.d., 1849); and Kierkegaard, *Armed Neutrality*, 92.

11. Rae, *Kierkegaard and Theology*, 13–14; Rae, *Kierkegaard's Vision of the Incarnation*, 27 n. 3.

their communications by their own existence. And although Kierkegaard can still be understood to have formulated the arguments and perspectives voiced by the pseudonyms, and was therefore thinking and writing in such ways that were problematic for his own faith, *the simple fact that he used pseudonyms is an ironic acknowledgment of this incongruence.* In this way, he managed to stay a step ahead of Mynster and others by at least *acknowledging* his own sin: his inability to perfectly live up to the Christian ideal that he communicated.

It was therefore precisely *because* he valued the embodiment of truth that pseudonyms were necessary in his authorship. He believed that "material works of art have, or should have, an existential relation to the life of the artist as well as an existential significance for those who view, read, or hear them."[12] Kierkegaard took responsibility for the *existence* of these works—he did not pretend that anyone else had written them—but he distanced himself from being *associated* with them and their views.[13] He vigorously requested that these works stand alone and apart from him, and that readers treat them as communications in their own right.[14]

PSEUDONYMS AND "HIDDEN INWARDNESS"

Kierkegaard used pseudonyms as a way for him to inwardly distance himself from the viewpoints expressed in these works. Because Kierkegaard understood that philosophical and theological concepts required appropriate passional use, he could not in good conscience be a witness to this need if he published works in his own name which were at odds with what he believed.[15] So in contrast to Climacus, Kierkegaard *had* faith; in con-

---

12. Walsh, *Living Poetically*, 6.

13. Louis Mackey points out that in regard to Kierkegaard's pseudonyms, " . . . no one in the gossipy little world of Danish letters had any doubt about their origin. Nor did he mean they should; his purpose was not mystification but distance. By refusing to answer for his writings he detached them from his personality so as to let their form protect the freedom that was their theme" (*Kierkegaard*, 247). *Concluding Unscientific Postscript* and *Practice in Christianity* are interesting cases, since Kierkegaard included his own name as editor of these works, thereby suggesting a closer accountability to these communications.

14. See "A First and Last Explanation," in Kierkegaard, *Concluding Unscientific Postscript*, 625–30.

15. "Kierkegaard continues to write about the big issue of philosophy. But the mode in which he does it still puts enormous distance between himself and his readers. Kierkegaard secures his critical and detached vantage point by contriving pseudonymous

trast to Johannes De Silentio, Kierkegaard probably could understand (at least to some extent) Abraham's faith due to his experience with Regine; in contrast to both A and Judge William, Kierkegaard believed that a complete dependence on God was the only true way to live well; and in contrast to Anti-Climacus, Kierkegaard did not have enough faith to be able to be published as one who could truly communicate what it meant to live as an ideal Christian.[16] Kierkegaard saw that for the sake of his own subjectivity or inward relation with God, there must be a coherence between his message (both in passional form and content) and his own life with God.

Along with hypothesizing about Kierkegaard's passional dis-relations with the pseudonyms, there is also the further inward matter for Kierkegaard. Because of his understanding of "hidden inwardness" and deep subjectivity being the place of his own relation with God, the pseudonyms also enabled Kierkegaard to speak about faith while hiding his own inwardness. As much as he did not wish to be seen as a shining example of a Christian for the sake of his reader (whether this actually was the case or not cannot be known, and is actually irrelevant), it also appears to have been for his sake: that is, to keep his own Christianity a secret, and to strive to be a "single individual" under God alone.[17]

PSEUDONYMS AND JUDGMENT

There is more to explore here in relation to how Kierkegaard's use of pseudonyms could be understood to affect his own discipleship—the issue of judgment. We have established how *Works of Love*, the most concise work of Kierkegaard's ethics, explores the concept of judging others and the dangers of being complicit with evil when an individual attempts to *see* such

---

authors to do the asserting for him. This very device both credits the passions as the source of the affirmations and philosophy as the formal study of such affirmations and their reasons and causes" (Holmer, *On Kierkegaard and the Truth*, 10).

16. "Kierkegaard does not wish to impute as much religious perfection to himself as the lofty ideality of these works presupposes. He says specifically that his 'anti-Climacus' pseudonym is so high that 'he' stands condemned by his own creation 'because my life does not correspond to so lofty a claim'" (ibid., 36, quoting Kierkegaard, *The Point of View for My Work as an Author: A Report to History*, 146). See also Kierkegaard, *Journals and Papers*, 6/6349, X6 B 48, n.d., 1849; and ibid., 6/6528, X2 A 184, n.d., 1849.

17. Again, this is not to suggest that Kierkegaard's Christianity was privatistic: a "single individual's" hidden relationship with God outworked itself in a life. See 1.1: "'Hidden Inwardness As Individualism?" above.

evil. A person is revealed in the way she sees and to judge is to be judged in turn—the Christian "like-for-like."[18] Kierkegaard, in his *own* name, claims that he has "passed judgment on no one."[19] But how does this stand up with the fact that his pseudonyms heavily critique the likes of Hegel, for instance? Hegel is named *directly*, especially in *Concluding Unscientific Postscript*. Such confrontations could be dismissed as mere scholarly critique, but given the ridiculing nature of such critiques, this does not seem accurate. So assuming that these criticisms are in fact judgments, how does Kierkegaard avoid revealing himself as one who does not look with love?

As we have considered above, Kierkegaard understood that his form of utilizing various demonstrative voices for "indirect communication" was necessary. In order to remove the illusion of Christendom and other related intellectual errors, such voices needed to be heard and considered in order for the reader to realize the incongruence and untenable nature of such views. So one way of redeeming Kierkegaard here would be to admit, *but only to a limited extent*, that he was indeed a hypocrite. Given his stance on art,[20] Kierkegaard knew and expected that he would be implicated in giving such judgments, and could be judged as not practicing what he preached.[21] This is especially the case in regard to *Concluding Unscientific Postscript* where he attached his own name to this work as editor.[22] But because Kierkegaard believed these demonstrations to be necessary, he can be understood to be sacrificing his own striving and discipleship for the sake of his reader, resembling St. Paul in being willing to give up his salvation for the sake of the Jews (Rom 9:3).

But such a high view of Kierkegaard is perhaps not necessary, as long as we emphasize the fact that Kierkegaard acknowledged this incongruence

---

18. Kierkegaard, *Works of Love*, 345ff.

19. Kierkegaard, *Point of View*, 15.

20. As Walsh helpfully articulates: "In Kierkegaard's estimation even material works of art have, or should have, an existential relation to the life of the artist as well as an existential significance for those who view, read, or hear them" (Walsh, *Living Poetically*, 6).

21. But here, of course, we encounter one of the innumerable difficulties in writing about Kierkegaard. This is because in judging Kierkegaard, we fall into the same trap of not seeing in love.

22. See, for instance, Kierkegaard's journal entries relating to *Practice in Christianity*, which was also a pseudonymous work published with his name attached as editor: Kierkegaard, *Journals and Papers*, 6/6578, X2 A 393, n.d., 1850; 6/6506, X2 A 90, n.d., 1849; collated in Kierkegaard, *Practice in Christianity*, 333–34, 349–50.

and hypocrisy.[23] The use of pseudonyms points to the fact that Kierkegaard was *aware* of the problem of incongruence (of such a communication not being able to be placed in actuality; of the form not cohering with the content), unlike his fellow Danes, especially Mynster. Remember, "[it] was not the *failure* of Kierkegaard's own generation to exist in the Truth which raised his ire so much as their refusal to recognize the incongruity of their situation."[24]

CONCLUSION

The pseudonyms were a tool for Kierkegaard to say *indirectly* necessary truths which he could not in truth say *directly*. It is in this way that Kierkegaard could *poetically* demonstrate erroneous ways of thinking to his reader while remaining hidden in the truth that he sought to communicate. Kierkegaard understood that such a stance did not constitute a perfect congruence between actuality and ideality, but instead that this was found in acknowledging his imperfection. As we can then see, the pseudonyms were not an impossible abstraction of the author from his work as in the likes of Hegel. Instead they were a rhetorical device which sought to remove what he understood to be erroneous points of view from the inside in a *reductio ad absurdum* manner, whilst attempting to distance himself from such errors. So we conclude that Kierkegaard's use of pseudonyms, therefore, shows an *awareness* of the importance of his own relation to his works, and is ultimately evidence of Kierkegaard's own "hidden inwardness."

---

23. And also that Kierkegaard's salvation was not contingent on authorial perfection!
24. Rae, *Kierkegaard's Vision of the Incarnation*, 27 n. 3.

3.3 Kierkegaard's *Point of View*

INTRODUCTION

In this final discussion, we will look at Kierkegaard's veronymous work "Point of View,"[1] and how it relates to Kierkegaard's task. "Point of View" is a work that *directly* relays Kierkegaard's own understanding of his authorship. That it was written veronymously is an indication that the work is intended as a "direct communication," representative of Kierkegaard's own views of the matter rather than a maieutic work intended for removing illusions in the reader. It was a work to orient his reader: an explanation of his authorship and the strategies he employed.

Much of our discussion in this book is sympathetic to "Point of View," and we have used this work as the hermeneutical key for understanding Kierkegaard's authorship as a whole, which has been contingent on reading this work with excessive "goodwill."[2] But how does "Point of View" fit with Kierkegaard's own attempt at Christian communication: does he remain in the truth throughout his writing and publishing "Point of View"? We have seen how his use of pseudonyms can be understood to be in line with his attempt to be "poetically composed" as an author in a negative sense,

---

1. I am using "Point of View" as a reference to *The Point of View for My Work as an Author*. This needs to be differentiated from *On My Work as an Author*, which was also published in the Princeton compilation of Kierkegaard's main direct accounts of his own authorship which was translated and edited by Howard and Edna Hong. Notably, *On My Work as an Author* was published in 1849, while *The Point of View for My Work as an Author*, though finished in 1848, was only published posthumously. This is significant, as I will seek to explain.

2. See Garff, "Eyes of Argus," 81.

but what about this particular work? Do we have here the exception, an incongruence between what is said and how it is said?

HOW "POINT OF VIEW" RELATES TO KIERKEGAARD'S "AUTHORSHIP PROPER"

In light of our emphasis on the relation between form and content and how this was derived from the gospel, what we are particularly concerned with here is what "Point of View" means for Kierkegaard's authorship. To begin with, should this be considered part of Kierkegaard's "authorial task"? Kierkegaard himself in this work declared his task to consist of two "hands," with *Concluding Unscientific Postscript* serving as the bridge between the aesthetic writings and the religious ones.[3] The translator notes here that the works not included in this scheme are left out due to Kierkegaard considering *Either/Or* "as the beginning of his authorship proper," and the translator claims further that Kierkegaard also excluded his masters thesis along with various reviews that he wrote for the reason that these were peripheral works not intended to form coherent components of his authorial task. "Point of View" was written in 1848, and so subsequent works (such as those by Anti-Climacus) are not included in this list.[4] But should "Point of View" itself be included? There are at least two good reasons why not: for one, it resembles Kierkegaard's master's thesis *Concept of Irony* in its meta-function, and for another there is the significant fact that it was left unpublished at the time of Kierkegaard's death. It is therefore a work that lies *outside* his "authorship proper." It is outside his task, instead functioning as a way to make the authorial task clearer.

So in regard to the matter in question, "Point of View" relates to Kierkegaard's "authorship proper" by standing outside it and standing as a thankful witness to God's work in Kierkegaard's life. Kierkegaard also appears to have been convinced that this work would be beneficial to his reader, enabling her to understand his authorial project. By explaining the communicative strategies he employed, Kierkegaard hoped that his works would have the appropriate and lasting influence beyond his lifetime. That is, one that was linked (poetically) to his person, time, context, and most importantly to their *telos* in God.[5]

3. Kierkegaard, *Point of View*, 29 n.
4. Ibid., 315 n. 9.
5. This was not for Kierkegaard to prescribe a strict "authorial intent" on the works

PART III: KIERKEGAARD AS AN EXAMPLE OF A CHRISTIAN COMMUNICATOR

A REVELATION OF KIERKEGAARD'S OWN "HIDDEN INWARDNESS"?

Kierkegaard recorded in his journals that he oscillated between whether or not to publish this work and even contemplated making it pseudonymous, giving it to Johannes De Silentio.[6] It cannot be that Kierkegaard disagreed with the explicit *content* of what was written, since it was written in his own name and was "a direct report to history" (if we are to trust his words). But neither can it be that he disagreed that it was *said* in this particular way. It was a personal "witness" to what he perceived to be God's work through his life, and, unlike Abraham perhaps, he wrote in order to make himself understood.[7] But understood by whom?

The temptation to be understood by others was of course in tension with his desire to "live poetically" by embodying truth—that is, by being one who strives after Christ *alone* through attempting to unify actuality and ideality.[8] This meant communicating what was possible for the communicator to communicate "in truth"—i.e., speaking out of the individual's own lived life, preaching what was practiced, even *in the midst* of such preaching.[9] To speak what was not lived by the speaker was to nullify such communication by virtue of its being an "existence-communication." This is seen most clearly in a journal entry concerning "Point of View" from 1849:

> ... I understood myself to be what I must call a poet of the religious, not however that my personal life should express the opposite—no, I strive continually, but that I am a "poet" expresses that I do not confuse myself with the ideal ... I am not that, but I strive. If the latter does not prove correct and is not true about me, then everything is cast in intellectual form and falls short.[10]

---

themselves, but rather an "authorial function" on how the works were to be used as subjective engagements with the reader. See for instance, Kierkegaard's complaint regarding how *Either/Or* was received: Hannay, "Introduction," 3–5.

6. Garff, "Eyes of Argus," 97, citing Kierkegaard, *Journals and Papers*, 6/6327, X1 A 78, n.d., 1849; 6/6511, X2 A 106, n.d., 1849.

7. See Kierkegaard, *Fear and Trembling*, 98–148, esp. 106–7.

8. See Rasmussen, *Between Irony and Witness*, 53–55 esp.

9. Cf. "It is also conceit to believe in one's own forgiveness when one will not forgive, for how in truth should one believe in forgiveness if his own life is a refutation of the existence of forgiveness!" (Kierkegaard, *Works of Love*, 349).

10. Kierkegaard, *Journals and Papers*, 6/6511, X2 A 106, n.d., 1849.

3.3 Kierkegaard's *Point of View*

Kierkegaard, as a "poet of the religious," understood his task to be the communication of Christianity to his fellow Danes. He understood and explained what constituted this ideal, but did not want to present himself as one who had grasped it—such outward fame would be problematic to an essentially *inward* relationship—so he dubbed himself a "poet." But in saying this, he did not want to be understood as being the kind of poet who communicated that which was removed from actuality (for instance, the kind of poet he accuses Schlegel of being in *Concept of Irony*), but the kind of poet that strove after the ideal of which he spoke. Kierkegaard's poetic communication was not some irrelevant impossibility of imagination, but was made possible at every moment by virtue of being *hidden* in Christ.

But if Kierkegaard believed his own "poetic" descriptions of the Christian life—namely, that it is primarily a matter of "hidden inwardness," how is "Point of View" congruent with such *hiddenness*? Is it not an outright contradiction of this concept? By *unhiding* himself in his writing of "Point of View," Kierkegaard could be seen to have destroyed his own safeguard from the temptation of outward fame. So, first of all, was this primarily an *outward* communication?

Kierkegaard's writing is not merely outward but also inward. His journals, for instance, can be understood to be outworkings of his own development as a "single individual" before God: an attempt to come to understand himself.[11] Like "Point of View," the journals were left unpublished during his lifetime, but unlike "Point of View" appear to have never been written *for* such an end.[12] So it is clear that he used his own process of writing to come to understand himself, and God's work in his life.

Secondly, although Kierkegaard felt that he understood *himself* correctly, he was wary of being misunderstood by making such reflections public. Nevertheless, he did not destroy this work because he understood that it was a necessary, outward communication: *not* for vindicating himself, nor making himself understood *per se*, but to leave a witness to God's grace in his life. In the work he is quick to point toward "providence" and incessantly repeats that his work was not his own but was led by God: "throughout all my work as an author I have incessantly needed God's

---

11. Kierkegaard, *Point of View*, 87.

12. Garff appears to disagree with me here, arguing that the journals were primarily for posterity. But Garff does agree that writing was essential to Kierkegaard's own self-development. See Barrett, "Review of *Søren Kierkegaard*," 154.

assistance . . . I have basically lived like a scribe in his office."[13] It was in this emphasis of portraying himself as a humble sinner and God as the orchestrator and source of his genius that Kierkegaard hoped to push his reader, yet again, toward contemplation of the wonder of God:

> Thus my entire work as an author revolves around: becoming a Christian in Christendom. And the expression for Governance's part in the authorship is this: that the author is himself the one who in this way has been brought up, but with a consciousness of it from the very beginning.[14]

Thus we can see that even here the point is God, not Kierkegaard. Even here Kierkegaard *hides* in the hope of pointing the reader to God. This work therefore functions like Climacus' irony in *Philosophical Fragments*: the reader's admiration for Kierkegaard is either transformed into a wonder directed to God, *or* Kierkegaard is dismissed altogether as a deluded mystic. Kierkegaard does not leave the reader with the choice of considering him a hero: his complete dependence on God's work ensures that this is the case. He presents himself as a *hidden* penitent, a lowly "spy in a higher service."[15]

THE POSTHUMOUS PUBLISHING

Kierkegaard believed he was one who understood in theory what it meant to be a Christian. He seemed to attempt to live according to this understanding, and encouraged his reader to do likewise.[16] So in the midst of his aesthetic and religious works, Kierkegaard saw himself as communicating the ideal of Christianity, an ideal which he believed himself subject to.[17] He openly admitted to falling short of this ideal but attempted to pursue it, firstly to validate his communication, but more importantly to be *hidden* in

---

13. Kierkegaard, *Point of View*, 74.

14. Ibid., 90.

15. Ibid., 87.

16. This can clearly be seen in the tone of language employed in the veronymous *Works of Love*. Kierkegaard is openly implicated in the ideas he discusses, and seeks to journey *with* the reader deeper into "the upbuilding." See 2.2: "The Upbuilding Function of the Religious Works" above.

17. "When a man puts ideals together with realities, not in cognitive endeavors but in his daily life, he becomes the subject of his own endeavor" (Holmer, *On Kierkegaard and the Truth*, 140).

Christ, as this appears to have been his goal as a Christian. But why was this work left unpublished during Kierkegaard's lifetime?

Because the work inevitably presented Kierkegaard as a Christian who gave all credit to God, he chose not to publish "Point of View" in his own lifetime for fear of being admired as "an extraordinary Christian."[18] This was, as we have said, a temptation where his *inward* relation with God would be uprooted and placed in the *outward*, open to the gaze of "the crowd." The risk of admiration was a serious threat for Kierkegaard, since he believed himself to have unusual gifts of genius in regard to understanding and articulating Christianity. But of course, knowing "about" is not nearly the same as knowing "with."[19]

In order to protect *himself* from winning the blind admiration of others, Kierkegaard did not publish "Point of View" during his lifetime. He did not give any substantial clarification of his authorship or himself,[20] and was left alone with God, while being misunderstood by many. By refraining from publishing this work, he was free to point to God in it without any *inward* risk pertaining to winning the admiration of "the crowd" as it would only be seen after his death. "Point of View" explained Kierkegaard's genius as an author, but then directed the reader to its source being Providence. If a living author was to say such a thing, it is clear that he would be subject to admiration from others for his humility, and that this humility would be in danger of becoming false under the influence of such admiration.[21] So by postponing the publishing until after his death, Kierkegaard pointed to God freely.[22]

To stay *hidden* during his life was for Kierkegaard to remain misunderstood. This was taken by him to be a suffering that was a necessary part of a true Christian life, where he saw himself as suffering as a witness for

---

18. Kierkegaard, *Journals and Papers*, 6/6511, X2 A 106, n.d., 1849.

19. See 1.3: "Pathos: The Heart of the Matter," above.

20. That is, apart from 1849's "On My Work As An Author," in Kierkegaard, *Point of View*, 1–20.

21. "Despite all the disclaimers in the writings, it would not have been possible to prevent my being regarded as an extraordinary Christian, instead of being only a genius; eventually I perhaps would have made the error of regarding myself as an extraordinary Christian. The truth of the matter, however, which I have learned by the very writing of these books, is that I am far, far from being an extraordinary Christian . . ." (Kierkegaard, *Journals and Papers*, 6/6511, X2 A 106, n.d., 1849).

22. See Part two, chapter 8: "The Victory of Reconciliation in Love Which Wins the Vanquished," in Kierkegaard, *Works of Love*, 306–16.

the sake of the truth.[23] Ultimately, Kierkegaard hid himself in his death by being hidden in Christ, leaving us alone with his works which point to God.

CONCLUSION

In this section we have suggested that even in Kierkegaard's direct accounts of his own authorial task he can be understood to have been communicating the truth while remaining in it. Although Kierkegaard, in "Point of View," reveals (un-*hides*) himself, he only does so in regard to his communication strategy and not in regard to his own "hidden inwardness." He pointed to the providential grace of God, and refrained from publishing this work in his lifetime. Therefore, "Point of View" can be seen to be another example of Kierkegaard's own "reduplication" as a Christian author: how he *hid himself in Christ*.

---

23. See, for instance, Kierkegaard, *Practice in Christianity*, 173.

Conclusion

In this work I have sought to demonstrate how understanding Kierkegaard's authorial task through the concept of "hiddenness" is helpful in making sense of the form that his authorship took. I have argued that his understanding of the gospel led Kierkegaard to adopt a hidden form of authorship.

We began with a brief outline of Kierkegaard's life and times, and how Kierkegaard understood his life's task to be about reintroducing Christianity into his context of Christendom. We then divided the rest of our investigation into three parts: the first being concerned with the content of his task, the second with the outward form his authorship took, and the third discussing how this form related to Kierkegaard himself.

Firstly, the content of Kierkegaard's task was his understanding that the truth of Christianity could only be apprehended subjectively. Because of this, direct communication along with other forms of outwardness were seen to be incompatible and contradictory to his task. Christian truth was contrasted with the Socratic understanding of truth, and found to emphasize an embodied, passional knowing, which therefore required the knower herself to be a "single individual" under God and not lost in "the crowd." Both elements—the truth, along with the way it was to be received—were crucial dimensions of what Kierkegaard sought to communicate. His message was this: that *the hidden truth of the gospel can only be known in truth in "hidden inwardness."*

In the second part, we explored how the form of Kierkegaard's work was oriented to bring about this subjective encounter within his reader. Kierkegaard's task was not merely one of explicit or direct transmission, but the very form of the communication itself was put to use to bring about what was spoken in the heart of reader. By employing the strategy of "indirect communication," we suggested that Kierkegaard enabled his reader to encounter Christian truth within her own "hidden inwardness." This strategy consisted of two "hands": the aesthetic works served to remove the illusion of Christendom in his reader, while the religious works served as a corrective and as a demonstration of Kierkegaard's understanding of true Christianity. These two groups of works were separated by what we called "The Hidden Middle": the former cleared the way for faith, the latter built upon it, but in between these works Kierkegaard left the reader to come to faith herself through her own encounter with God in "hidden inwardness." We saw here that *Kierkegaard hid himself for the sake of his reader*: behind pseudonyms and ultimately behind God himself, in order to point the reader away from himself and toward her own subjective encounter with God in the "hidden inwardness" of her own heart.

In the third part, we suggested how *Kierkegaard can be understood to have adopted a hidden authorship for the sake of his own self before God*. Using *Works of Love* as a hermeneutical lens, we saw that Kierkegaard's communication was not only outward, but also involved Kierkegaard's own inwardness. The concepts of "existence-communication" and "reduplication," along with a closer look at the pseudonyms and "Point of View," led us to hypothesize regarding the implications of Kierkegaard's authorship for his own hidden relationship with God. Such suggestions were seen not as definitive proofs of the depth of Kierkegaard's own discipleship, but were put forth as tentative ways of reading Kierkegaard in love.

So we see that Kierkegaard's concept of "hidden inwardness" can be applied to the entire spread of his authorial task. By understanding Kierkegaard's authorship as adopting the form of the very hiddenness that he taught, we have come to a deep understanding of how Kierkegaard is exemplary as a Christian communicator. As one who strove to be in the truth, Kierkegaard can be seen to have attempted to only speak what his own life could uphold, and to communicate deeply in a form which complemented what he spoke. In other words, *Kierkegaard embodied the very message that he sought to communicate, and we have seen this through his concept of "hiddenness."*

FURTHER STUDY

Due to the colossal scope of this work where I have attempted to analyze Kierkegaard's prolific authorship with its multiple layers of communication, there have inevitably been casualties. I regret that I have not had more

Conclusion

time to investigate the roles of irony and humor in this work. What is also missing here is a substantial reflection on Kierkegaard's influences, especially Johann Georg Hamann but also Møller, Hegel, and Luther, as well as an overview of Kierkegaard's reception which would have also been helpful in setting the scene for my investigation.

Despite these limits, there are still a few areas identified by this study that could be of interest to scholarship. For instance, we have discovered that Kierkegaard's work confronts the use of language on a number of levels. To begin with, at least in regard to essential truth, words require appropriate passional use: an appropriate *form* in which these words are used. Not only does this relate to literary context, but also to lived context: an embodiment of language. Because of this, the speaker is somewhat responsible for what is spoken.[1] This is a powerful challenge for those who would follow the unstable irony of Roland Barthes' "Death of the Author."[2] Much of this movement can be traced back to an individual's understanding of the truth that is spoken: is it Socratic or is it Christian? Is it fundamentally individualistic, or is it relational? It appears that the conversation on either side of modernity is taken up with the possibility or impossibility of Socratic truth, whereas Kierkegaard redirects us to another perspective altogether.[3] Despite a common misconception, Kierkegaard's understanding of essential truth is not private but relational: the fact that God communicated himself in the incarnation of Jesus Christ enables the possibility of true communication and thereby true sociality.[4]

In this way, those who would attribute autonomy to Kierkegaard's written works—in sum or in part—are actually (despite many having good intentions) in danger of missing the deeper demonstrative communication of his entire task as a Christian: *what it means to be a person and author*. We have here a helpful starting point for understanding the vital link between Kierkegaard's life and his work.

---

1. This has been discussed most clearly in Kierkegaard's demonstration of the use or nonuse of pseudonyms. See especially 3.2 above.

2. Barthes, "The Death of the Author," 142–48.

3. As a starting point for hermeneutics, see Jacobs, *A Theology Of Reading*.

4. For an argument of Kierkegaard's epistemology being relational, see Rae, *Kierkegaard and Theology*, 144–48. It is in this way that I understand Kierkegaard to be related, or at the very least helpful, to the projects of Ludwig Wittgenstein, Bernard Lonergan, Michael Polanyi, Herbert McCabe, and others.

WITTGENSTEIN'S LADDER: A REFLECTION ON METHODOLOGY

Due to the layered and self-reflexive demands of studying Kierkegaard "in truth," I have struggled repeatedly with how I myself as a writer and academic should be writing this work. I have wrestled over whether to make this book pseudonymous, but was concerned with how I myself would then have to write some "direct report to history" in order to make myself (and my writing) more fully understood. Although it should be apparent that there are intrinsic incongruencies between the *form* and *content* of this book, and that therefore my attempt to *demonstrate* my understanding of Kierkegaard falls short, I hope that I have at least conveyed a surface-level, cognitive understanding of Kierkegaard's task, enough to satisfy my academic reader.

These incongruencies, if I have done my job well, should now be obvious. If we are to take Kierkegaard and his teaching and demonstrations concerning subjectivity seriously, there is indeed a problem with how I have led us in considering his work in such an objective way. I have attempted to overcome this by involving you, reader, in a proposal that seeks to read Kierkegaard in love, but what is ultimately important is my and your own engagement with his work. As someone trying to outwardly justify his understanding of Kierkegaard's authorship, I am ultimately revealing that I *do not* understand it in the way that matters most: I am revealing my own "hidden inwardness," and therefore, in Kierkegaard's eyes, transforming my understanding into an untruth. I may write as a struggling poet, but I do not write *in the truth*.

In this way, the very structure of this work (not merely its objective perspective) is helpful, but ultimately false. Kierkegaard's work helps us to rethink the dichotomy of form/content, simply because he understands there to be *no* formless content, *nor* content-less form.[5] As we have now seen, Kierkegaard's authorship was largely derived from his understanding of the gospel—the incarnation of the God-man. By this ultimate unity of ideality and actuality, form and content, the Christian writes as a person who strives to embody what she speaks. This is the reality of the nature of the world and the human individual: it is one that embraces life instead

---

5. The former is the error of the Socratic or "speculative reason" (along with the Lowrie school); the latter is the error of German Romanticism (along with the "deconstructivist turn"). *Concluding Unscientific Postscript* addresses the former; *Concept of Irony* addresses the latter. See especially 2.3 above.

of attempting to escape or poeticize it. We have seen how Kierkegaard attempted to undertake this as an "existence-communication," but I, as a commentator, have sought to "deceive" the reader "into the truth" by attempting to rewrite the problems of these dichotomies from the inside. The dichotomy of form/content has been valuable for giving a clear outline of Kierkegaard's authorship, but this very dichotomy must now be realized to be a false one. Like Wittgenstein's ladder (and, indeed, the function of Johannes *Climacus*), it is only from the vantage point of having climbed that we realize we must now "throw away" our means of ascent.[6] I am merely a step below Kierkegaard in that I have written this "poetic" work under my own name.

A PERSONAL NOTE

Kierkegaard appeals to me because I have encountered here an attempt at a deep outworking of the gospel. This outworking is not restricted to the surface of prescription and argumentative correction, but permeates the very form such correction takes. And behind even this there can be discerned a sense of deep penitence—a true fear and trembling being undertaken by the author himself. There is here a depth of understanding regarding the profundity of the gospel that penetrates down to the very core of language, thinking, and being: not a kind of "folk-Christianity" which merely replaces the surface of society whilst leaving the underlying structures and cultic practices unchanged. Here is a presentation of the gospel as a *metanoia* of the very way we live.

I have presented Kierkegaard here as an excellent example of a Christian communicator because he does not, in my view, merely conform to the "worldly" ways of his society, but rather seeks to subvert its ways of thinking and speaking from the inside. Like St. Paul in his Greco-Roman context, "[the] *language* of [the empire] may have come across to [him], but the *system* did not."[7] It appears to me that much of Christian theology is superficial simply by virtue of the *way* it is spoken. It is often devoid of deep passions and convictions, making the truth of such arguments questionable. Such lifeless words can actually serve to distract or discourage people

---

6. Wittgenstein, *Tractatus*, 82, §6.54. This is also similar to how Kierkegaard understood that governance's work in his own life, as well as throughout his authorship, could only be fully seen in retrospect.

7. Strom, *Reframing Paul*, 92.

in the service of lived life. To speak even more pointedly, such thinking and speaking are often implicitly a willing part of "worldly" or cultural socio-linguistic empires which serve to maintain the *status quo* rather than transform them. Kierkegaard reminds us that the gospel demands no less than radical transformation, and his critique of society is still relevant for today. From universities that commodify knowledge to churches that produce respectable consumers, there is the ongoing danger of "the crowd," the "fantastic I-I," the hubris of anthropocentricism and self-sufficient rationalism. To address these problems by opposing these grammatical mistakes[8] directly is simply adding to this noise, even this noise of another book.[9] What is needed is nothing less than a radical overhaul of the very way we live and speak.[10]

What I encounter in Kierkegaard is a demonstration of the gospel: an example of someone attempting to "reduplicate" what he speaks, and therefore of someone to listen to and from whom to learn. In light of this, I can be confident of learning from Kierkegaard as a teacher (or "helper") of life "all the way down," as it were,[11] and am encouraged to take this up in my own living as a Christian. It is such a "knowing with" that seems most worthwhile for myself. In light of the limits of teaching in both the church and in theological education institutions (particularly in the lack of existential and self-reflexive embodiment), I have found in Kierkegaard a substantive help for my own life under God. I believe I can use what he has attempted to teach, even to the very depth of reading and writing this book. Such an example is surely rare, valuable, and worthy of imitation.

But there is one last question. Am I blinded by my own admiration of Kierkegaard? In seeking to defend him against those who I perceive to be his detractors, can I be understood to have fallen from the demand on the

---

8. I.e., mistakes pertaining to the social conventions concerning the *use* of language.

9. Stanley Hauerwas' emphasis on the church being an embodied alternative to the world could be a helpful starting point here. See his *Learning the Languages of Peace*.

10. Kierkegaard's emphasis on lived life away from rationalism also seeks to bring about the equality of the gospel—declaring its accessibility by "the simple man" and the "simple wise man" alike. By pointing away from the complexities of high-brow intellectualism and toward the simplicity of faith available to all (as a "single individual"), Kierkegaard sought to institute the radical critique of Christianity for his context. This is just one example of Kierkegaard's critique of society, and I regret not to have had the space in this book to explore this particular issue further. See Kierkegaard, *Concluding Unscientific Postscript*, 227–28; see also Holmer, *The Grammar of Faith*, 16.

11. See Kierkegaard, *Works of Love*, 61.

Christian to see in love?[12] If I believe that Kierkegaard is right, and that those who oppose him are wrong, am I not revealed in the way I judge? Am I not guilty of the "hagiography" Gouwens speaks of?[13] Perhaps this is so, and I here again display my lack of proper understanding, but I hope that my critiques are helpful in steering me and other readers of Kierkegaard away from the disengagement such detractors advocate and exemplify. Perhaps this "look of love" also stands as a critique of academia: what does a Christian academic look like? What does it mean to engage well with those with whom we disagree? This is a question for another time.

But still, am I wrong? Has my admiration of Kierkegaard blinded me to a deeper deception of his? Have I been dragged along as a gullible fool by some sort of triple or quadruple agent, who is merely out to poke fun? Is there actually no end to his deception: is it irony all the way down? Regardless, Kierkegaard's work still stands. At the risk of presenting a tautology, we have seen above that his words do not rely on his person, and they do not therefore fail on account of any personal failure of his—he wrote to ensure this to be the case.[14] And regardless, "love is never deceived": these are the words of Scripture, not Kierkegaard.

I have presented an argument for Kierkegaard to be seen as a profound Christian thinker, but more than this: a profound Christian *communicator*, who used his life to communicate the gospel with great depth. I hope that I, along with other Christians today can learn from his example, and attempt to live and speak in the truth.

---

12. See 2.3 above.

13. Gouwens, *Kierkegaard as Religious Thinker*, 2.

14. See above 3.1: "Existence-Communication." An "existence-communication" draws *credibility* from the life of the speaker, but it does not draw *truth* from him or her. Something may be poetically true without being spoken in truth.

Bibliography

Adorno, T. W. "On Kierkegaard's Doctrine of Love." *Studies in Philosophy and Social Science* 8 (1939) 413–29.
Aumann, Antony. "Kierkegaard on the Need for Indirect Communication." Indiana University, 2008. http://www.academia.edu/944013/Kierkegaard_on_the_Need_for_Indirect_Communication.
———. "Kierkegaard's Case For the Irrelevance of Philosophy." *Continental Philosophy Review* 42/2 (May 2009) 221–48.
Barrett, Lee C. *Kierkegaard*. Abingdon Pillars of Theology 5. Nashville: Abingdon, 2010.
———. "Review of *Søren Kierkegaard: A Biography*, by Joakim Garff." *Journal of the American Academy of Religion* 75/1 (March 2007) 153.
Barthes, Roland. "The Death of the Author." In *Image, Music, Text*, 142–48. Translated by Stephen Heath. London: Fontana, 1977.
Berlin, Isaiah. "The Hedgehog and the Fox." In *The Proper Study of Mankind*, edited by H. Hardy and R. Hausheer, 436–98. New York: Farrar, Straus & Giroux, 1998.
Come, Arnold B. *Kierkegaard as Humanist: Discovering My Self*. Montreal: McGill-Queen's University Press, 1995.
Conway, Daniel W. "Abraham's Final Word." In *Ethics, Love, and Faith in Kierkegaard*, edited by Edward F. Mooney, 175–95. Bloomington: Indiana University Press, 2008.
Crabtree, John A. *Kierkegaard and His Culture 1*. Mp3. Kierkegaard & Artmaking, Gutenberg College, n.d.
Creegan, Charles L. *Wittgenstein and Kierkegaard: Religion, Individuality, and Philosophical Method*. London: Routledge, 1989.
Creegan, Nicola Hoggard, and Christine D. Pohl. "Evangelical and Feminist Maps: Redefining the Theological Interior." In *Living on the Boundaries: Evangelical Women, Feminism, and the Theological Academy*, 126–51. Downers Grove, IL: InterVarsity, 2005.
Davenport, John J. "Faith as Eschatological Trust in Fear and Trembling." In *Ethics, Love, and Faith in Kierkegaard*, edited by Edward F. Mooney, 196–233. Bloomington: Indiana University Press, 2008.
Evans, C. Stephen. *Kierkegaard: An Introduction*. Cambridge: Cambridge University Press, 2009.
———. *Kierkegaard's 'Fragments' and 'Postscript': The Religious Philosophy of Johannes Climacus*. New York: Humanity, 1999.
———. *Passionate Reason: Making Sense of Kierkegaard's Philosophical Fragments*. Bloomington: Indiana University Press, 1992.

Bibliography

———. "The Role of Irony in Kierkegaard's *Philosophical Fragments*." In *Kierkegaard Studies Yearbook*, edited by Heiko Schulz et. al., 63–79. Walter de Gruyter, 2004.

———. "Who Is the Other in Sickness Unto Death? God and Human Relations in the Constitution of the Self." In *Kierkegaard on Faith And the Self: Collected Essays*, 263–75. Waco, TX: Baylor University Press, 2006.

Ferreira, M. Jamie. "Other-Worldliness in Kierkegaard's Works of Love." *Philosophical Investigations* 22/1 (1999) 65–79.

Fitzpatrick, Joseph. "Subjectivity and Objectivity: Lonergan and Polanyi." In *Philosophical Encounters: Lonergan and the Analytical Tradition*, 64–74. Toronto: University of Toronto Press, 2005.

Gadamer, Hans-Georg. *Truth and Method*. Translated by Donald G. Marshall and Joel Weinsheimer. Rev. 2nd ed. London: Continuum, 2004.

Garff, Joakim. "The Eyes of Argus: The Point of View and Points of View on Kierkegaard's Work as an Author." In *Kierkegaard: A Critical Reader*, edited by Jonathan Ree and Jane Chamberlain, 75–102. Translated by Jane Chamberlain and Belinda Ioni Rasmussen. Oxford: Blackwell, 1998.

———. *Søren Kierkegaard: A Biography*. Translated by Bruce H. Kirmmse. Princeton: Princeton University Press, 2007.

Gouwens, David Jay. *Kierkegaard as Religious Thinker*. Cambridge: Cambridge University Press, 1996.

Hall, Amy Laura. "Self-deception, Confusion, and Salvation in *Fear and Trembling* with *Works of Love*." *Journal of Religious Ethics* 28/1 (March 2000) 37–61.

Hannay, Alastair. "Introduction." In *Either/Or: A Fragment of Life*, by Soren Kierkegaard, 1–21. London: Penguin, 2004.

Hauerwas, Stanley. *Learning the Languages of Peace*. Mp3. Grenz Lectures 2009, Regent College, n.d.

Hinkson, Craig Q. "Luther and Kierkegaard: Theologians of the Cross." *International Journal of Systematic Theology* 3/1 (March 2001) 27–45.

Holmer, Paul L. *The Grammar of Faith*. New York: Harper & Row, 1978.

———. *On Kierkegaard and the Truth*. Edited by Lee C. Barrett and David J. Gouwens. Eugene, OR: Cascade, 2012.

Hong, Howard Vincent, and Edna Hatlestad Hong. "Historical Introduction." In *The Point of View*, by Søren Kierkegaard, ix–xxvii. Kierkegaard's Writings 22. Princeton: Princeton University Press, 1998.

———. "Translator's Introduction." In *Works of Love*, by Søren Kierkegaard, xix–xxvi. New York: HarperPerennial, 2009.

Jacobs, Alan. *A Theology Of Reading: The Hermeneutics Of Love*. Boulder, CO: Westview, 2001.

Jensen, Finn Gredal. "Poul Martin Møller: Kierkegaard and the Confidant of Socrates." In *Kierkegaard and His Danish Contemporaries: Tome I: Philosophy, Politics and Social Theory*, edited by Jon Bartley Stewart, 7:101–67. Kiekegaard Research: Sources, Reception and Resources. Surrey, UK: Ashgate, 2009.

Kierkegaard, Søren. *Armed Neutrality and An Open Letter*. Translated by Howard Vincent Hong and Edna Hatlestad Hong. Bloomington: Indiana University Press, 1968.

———. *Attack Upon "Christendom," 1854–1855*. Translated by Walter Lowrie. Princeton: Princeton University Press, 1968.

———. *Christian Discourses and The Lilies of the Field and the Birds of the Air and Three Discourses at the Communion on Fridays.* Translated by Walter Lowrie. Princeton: Princeton University Press, 1940.

———. *The Concept of Dread: A Simple Psychological Deliberation Oriented in the Direction of the Dogmatic Problem of Original Sin.* Translated by Walter Lowrie. Princeton: Princeton University Press, 1957.

———. *The Concept of Irony, with Continual Reference to Socrates/Notes of Schelling's Berlin Lectures.* Translated by Howard Vincent Hong and Edna Hatlestad Hong. Kierkegaard's Writings 2. Princeton: Princeton University Press, 1992.

———. *Concluding Unscientific Postscript to Philosophical Fragments.* Translated by Howard Vincent Hong and Edna Hatlestad Hong. Vol. 1. Kierkegaard's Writings 12. Princeton: Princeton University Press, 1992.

———. *Early Polemical Writings.* Translated by Julia Watkin. Kierkegaard's Writings 1. Princeton: Princeton University Press, 2009.

———. *Either/Or: A Fragment of Life.* Translated by Alastair Hannay. London: Penguin, 2004.

———. *Fear and Trembling.* Translated by Alastair Hannay. London: Penguin, 1986.

———. *For Self-Examination and Judge for Yourself!* Translated by Howard Vincent Hong and Edna Hatlestad Hong. Kierkegaard's Writings 21. Princeton: Princeton University Press, 1990.

———. "For the Dedication to 'That Single Individual.'" In *The Point of View*, 105–12. Translated by Howard Vincent Hong and Edna Hatlestad Hong. Princeton: Princeton University Press, 1998.

———. *Journals and Papers.* Translated by Howard Vincent Hong and Edna Hatlestad Hong. 7 vols. Bloomington: Indiana University Press, 1967.

———. "Philosophical Crumbs." In *Repetition And Philosophical Crumbs*, 83–173. Translated by M. G. Piety. Oxford: Oxford University Press, 2009.

———. *The Point of View.* Translated by Howard Vincent Hong and Edna Hatlestad Hong. Kierkegaard's Writings 22. Princeton: Princeton University Press, 1998.

———. "The Point of View for My Work as an Author." In *The Point of View*, 21–97. Translated by Howard Vincent Hong and Edna Hatlestad Hong. Kierkegaard's Writings 22. Princeton: Princeton University Press, 1998.

———. *The Point of View for My Work as an Author: A Report to History.* Translated by Walter Lowrie. London: Oxford University Press, 1939.

———. *Practice in Christianity.* Translated by Howard Vincent Hong and Edna Hatlestad Hong. Kierkegaard's Writings 20. Princeton: Princeton University Press, 1991.

———. *Purity of Heart Is to Will One Thing.* Translated by Douglas V. Steere. http://www.religion-online.org/showbook.asp?title=2523.

———. *The Sickness Unto Death.* Translated by Alastair Hannay. London: Penguin, 2004.

———. *Spiritual Writings: Gift, Creation, Love: Selections from the Upbuilding Discourses.* Translated by George Pattison. New York: HarperCollins, 2010.

———. *Stages on Life's Way: Studies by Various Persons.* Translated by Howard Vincent Hong and Edna Hatlestad Hong. Kierkegaard's Writings 11. Princeton: Princeton University Press, 1988.

———. "Two Discourses at the Communion on Fridays." In *A Kierkegaard Anthology*, edited by Robert Bretall, 418–26. Translated by Walter Lowrie. Princeton: Princeton University Press, 1973.

Bibliography

———. *Works of Love*. Translated by Howard Vincent Hong and Edna Hatlestad Hong. New York: HarperPerennial, 2009.

Kirmmse, Bruce H. *Kierkegaard in Golden Age Denmark*. Bloomington: Indiana University Press, 1990.

LeFevre, Perry D. "Part II. An Interpretation of Kierkegaard's Life and Thought." In *The Prayers of Kierkegaard*, 125–226. Chicago: University of Chicago Press, 1956.

Lewis, C. S. *The Last Battle*. The Chronicles of Narnia 7. New York: Macmillan, 1956.

Lippitt, John. "What Neither Abraham Nor Johannes De Silentio Could Say." *Aristotelian Society Supplementary* 82/1 (June 2008) 79–99.

Mackey, Louis. *Kierkegaard: A Kind of Poet*. Philadelphia: University of Pennsylvania Press, 1971.

Malantschuk, Gregor. *Kierkegaard's Thought*. Translated by Howard V. Hong and Edna H. Hong. Princeton: Princeton University Press, 1971.

Malesic, Jonathan. "Illusion and Offense in Philosophical Fragments: Kierkegaard's Inversion of Feuerbach's Critique of Christianity." *International Journal for Philosophy of Religion* 62 (2007) 43–55.

McCabe, Herbert. *Law, Love and Language*. London: Continuum, 2003.

McDonald, William. "Kierkegaard, Søren." *Internet Encyclopedia of Philosophy*, 2005. http://www.iep.utm.edu/kierkega/#SH3c.

McGrath, Alister E. *Luther's Theology of the Cross: Martin Luther's Theological Breakthrough*. Oxford: Wiley, 1990.

McKinnon, Alastair. *Fundamental Polyglot Konkordans Til Kierkegaards Samlede Vaerker*. Vol. 2. Leiden: Brill, 1971.

Morelli, Elizabeth A. *Anxiety: A Study of the Affectivity of Moral Conciousness*. Lanham, MD: University Press of America, 1985.

Müller, Paul. *Kristendom, etik og majeutik i Søren Kierkegaards 'Kjerlighedens gjerninger' (Skrifter udgivet af Københavns universitets Institut for religionshistorie)*. Copenhagen: Københavns universitets institut for religionshistorie, 1976.

Nelson, Christopher A. P. "Revelation and the Revealed: The Crux of the Ethical-Religious Stadium." In *The Book on Adler*, edited by Robert L. Perkins, 24:67–96. International Kierkegaard Commentary. Macon, GA: Mercer University Press, 2008.

Niebuhr, Reinhold. *The Nature and Destiny of Man: A Christian Interpretation*. Vol. 1. New York: Scribner, 1964.

Pattison, George. "Foreword to the Harper Perennial Modern Thought Edition." In *Works of Love*, by Soren Kierkegaard, vii–xvii. New York: HarperPerennial, 2009.

———. "Kierkegaard as Feuilleton Writer." *Enrahonar* 29 (1998) 125–30.

Plato. "Meno." Translated by Benjamin Jowett. Project Gutenberg, 2008. http://www.gutenberg.org/files/1643/1643-h/1643-h.htm#2H_4_0003.

Podmore, Simon D. Review of *Kierkegaard and Theology*, by Murray Rae. *International Journal of Systematic Theology* 14/3 (2012) 370–73.

Pojman, Louis P. "Kierkegaard on Faith and History." *International Journal for Philosophy of Religion* 13/2 (1982) 57–68.

Polanyi, Michael. *Personal Knowledge: Towards a Post-Critical Philosophy*. Rev. ed. New York: Harper & Row, 1962.

Poole, Roger. *Kierkegaard: The Indirect Communication*. Charlottesville: University Press of Virginia, 1993.

———. "The Unknown Kierkegaard: Twentieth-Century Receptions." In *The Cambridge Companion to Kierkegaard*, edited by Alastair Hannay and Gordon Daniel Marino, 48–75. Cambridge: Cambridge University Press, 1998.
Rae, Murray. *Kierkegaard and Theology*. London: Continuum, 2010.
———. *Kierkegaard's Vision of the Incarnation: By Faith Transformed*. Oxford: Oxford University Press, 1997.
———. "The Risk of Obedience: A Consideration of Kierkegaard's Fear and Trembling." *International Journal of Systematic Theology* 1/3 (November 1999) 308.
Rasmussen, Joel D. S. *Between Irony and Witness: Kierkegaard's Poetics of Faith, Hope, and Love*. New York: Continuum, 2005.
Ricoeur, Paul. "Philosophy After Kierkegaard." In *Kierkegaard: A Critical Reader*, edited by Jonathan Ree and Jane Chamberlain, 9–25. Translated by Jonathan Rée. Oxford: Blackwell, 1998.
Smit, Harvey Albert. *Kierkegaard's Pilgrimage of Man: The Road of Self-Positing and Self-Abdication*. Amsterdam: W. D. Meinema, 1965.
Stewart, Jon Bartley. *Kierkegaard's Relations to Hegel Reconsidered*. Cambridge: Cambridge University Press, 2003.
Storm, D. Anthony. "Kierkegaard's Authorial Method." *D. Anthony Storm's Commentary On Kierkegaard*. N.d. http://sorenkierkegaard.org/kierkegaard-authorial-method.html.
Strawser, Michael. *Both/And: Reading Kierkegaard—From Irony to Edification*. New York: Fordham University Press, 1996.
Strom, Mark. *Reframing Paul: Conversations in Grace and Community*. Downers Grove, IL: InterVarsity, 2000.
Thiselton, Anthony C. *The Two Horizons: New Testament Hermeneutics and Philosophical Description with Special Reference to Heidegger, Bultmann, Gadamer, and Wittgenstein*. Grand Rapids: Eerdmans, 1980.
Torrance, Alan J. *John MacMurray and Personhood*. Mp3. Liberating Grace, Regent College, n.d.
Torrance, Thomas Forsyth. *The Mediation of Christ*. Colorado Springs: Helmers & Howard, 1992.
Walsh, Sylvia. *Living Poetically: Kierkegaard's Existential Aesthetics*. University Park: Pennsylvania State University Press, 1994.
Watts, Michael. *Kierkegaard*. Oxford: Oneworld, 2003.
Whittaker, John H. "Kierkegaard on the Concept of Authority." *International Journal for Philosophy of Religion* 46 (1999) 83–101.
Wittgenstein, Ludwig. *Philosophical Investigations*. Rev. 4th ed. Chichester, UK: Wiley-Blackwell, 2009.
———. *Tractatus Logico-Philosophicus*. In *Major Works: Selected Philosophical Writings*, 1–82. New York: HarperCollins, 2009.

Index of Subjects

Numbers in bold indicate key passages. Titles of Kierkegaard are in italics. Only key passages are recorded for core subjects.

"The Absolute Paradox," 19, 43, 54, **57–60**, 81–82
Abstraction, xi, 6n30, 34n49, 49, 62, **66**, 71–72, **73–75**, 79, 112, 134–35, 151
Academia/Scholarship, ix-x, 6, 8, 40, 70n103, 77, 103, 106, **110–27**, 131–33, 162, **164–65**
Actuality/Ideality, 19n18, 21n30, 27, 52, 55, **69–73**, 92, 102n60, 124, 126, 135n19, 146, 149n16, 151, 154–55, 162
Admiration/Hagiography, x, 29, 63, 66, 86, 117, 126n86, 132, 136, 142, 156–57, 164–65
"The Aesthetic Works," 12–13, 43–44, 67n86, 86n30, 89, **90–98**, 99–101, 106–7, 113–19, 153, 156, 160
Aestheticism/"The Aesthetic," 2–3, 29, 47, 71, 85n24, 119–21, 137, 139
Anamnesis, 53, 93, 104n72, 107
Anxiety, 27
Authority, 6, 27, 36, 68, 84–85, 91, 94–95, 98–101, 105, 118, 125, 132n5, 134n14, 135

Being/Becoming, 4, 6, 34n49, 37n62, 40–46, **111**, **146**, 163

Bible/Scripture, 27–28, 49, 64, 58, 108, 125, 132n5, 165
"Blunt Reading," 116, 122

Capacity, 41, 53, 57, 63, 81, 85, 93, 100, 106
Christendom, 3–4, 12, 15–16, **25–27**, **36–38**, 48, 56, 90–92, 111, 142–43
Christianity, **15–22**
Choice. *See* Responsibility/Choice.
"Church Triumphant"/"Church Militant," 48, 63n66, 122, 137, 142
Concept of Irony, 13, **93–96**, 155, 162n5
Concluding Unscientific Postscript, 13, 20, 27n9, 31n34, 34, 56, 59n37, 61, 66, 92, 106, 112n13, 115n30, 121, 137n31, 140, 146n3, 148n13, 150, 153, 162n5
Contemporaneity, 20, **60–64**
Contradiction/"Sign of Contradiction," 6, 55, 63n64, 65n75, 81–82, 83, 135n19
Conversion/Metanoia, *see also* Moment/Crisis, 16n5, **52–75**, 79n1, 80, 85n23, 87, 115, 132, 134, 163–64
The Corsair, 117n40, 137n29, **140–41**
"The Crowd," 5, 6, 25, 27, 30–31, 40, 59, 66, 90–91, 136, 157

173

Index of Subjects

Culture. *See* Society/Culture.

Danish State Church (Lutheran), 3, 4, 26, 36n58, 142–43
Deconstruction/"Deconstructive Turn," ix, 95, 115–19, 162n5
Destabilize, 96–98, 113n21, 118
Demonstration, 7–12, 19–21, 34n51, 65–68, 86–88, 96–98, 100–108, 124–25, 147, 150–51, 159–64
Denmark/Copenhagen, 3–5, 25–26, 31, 39, 57, 58n33, 94, 120, 141–43
Dialectics, 5, 40–46
Didactic/Preaching, 37, 68, 80, 83–84, 96, 99, 101, 108, 142
Direct Communication. *See* "Indirect/Direct Communication."
Discipleship/Striving, 4, **6**, 22, 52, 63, **69**, 73, 75, 86, **102**, 105, 107, 121, 131, 135n22, 137, 139–40, 145–47, 149–50, **154**, 160, 162
Dispositions, 49–50, 67, 116

Either/Or, 13, 34n49, 82n14, 93n17, 98, 100, 120, 141–42n52, 153, 153–54n5
The Edifying in The Thought That Against God We Are Always in The Wrong, 44n18, 64n68, 92–93, 100
"The Seducer's Diary," 71, 113n23, 115n30, 119–20
Ethics/"The Ethical," 9, 27–32, 40–42, 71, 74–75, 79n1, 84, 85n24, 92–93, **96–98**, 102, 126, **131–37**, 149
Embodiedness/Indwelling, **52–75**, 106–7, **131–44**, 162–65
Epistemology/Knowing, 19–20, 33, 52–64, 66, **68–75**, 97–101, 104, **116**, 132–34, 157, 161n4
Evangelism, 2–3, 15–16, 19, 38, 40, 86, 155
Existence. *See* Life/Existence.
"Existence Communication," 11, 36n58, 88, 119–20n54, 134–37, 139, 154, 160, 163, 165n14
Existentialism, 4, 111

Faith, **60–64**, **80–83**, **99–102**, 105–7
Faithfulness, 7, 42, 56, 79, 88, 114, 121, 123, 126, 133
Fear and Trembling, 12, 27–30, 41, 58n33, 74n128, 92, 97, 99n44, 132n5, 134
"For the Dedication to 'That Single Individual,'" 26
Forgiveness, 64–65
Form/Content; "The How"/"The What," **15–27**, **52–88**, **122–26**, **159–63**
"From the Papers of One Still Living," 55n20

Glory, 15n2, 18–19, 44n21, 45, 59
Grace, **92–93**, 100, 144, 155, 158

Hermeneutics/Judging, **64–67**, **96–98**, 102–27
"The Hidden Middle," 89, **105–7**, 129, 160
History, 5, 19–20, 32–33, 42n11, 54, 57–58, **60–64**, 71–73, 140
"The How"/"The What." *See* Form/Content; "The How"/"The What."
Humility, 18, 43–45, 54–55, 63, 101–2, 105, 115, 156–57
Humor, 34, **139–40**
Hypocrisy, 135, **145–48**, 150–51

Ideal/Idealism, 11n51, 17n8, 21n30, 34, 45, 68, 71–72, 98, 101, 105, 106n83, 113, 126n86, 132, 135–40, 142–43, 146, 148–49, 154–56
Ideality. *See* Actuality/Ideality.
Illusion/Deception, 3, 6, 12, 16, 25, 31–32, 35–36, 40, 50, 81, 84, 89, **90–98**, 100, 104, 111, **120**, 122, 147, 150, 152, 160, 163, 165
Incarnation. *See* Jesus Christ/Incarnation.
"The Incognito," **60–64**, 75, 86, 94, 139, 141
Indirect/Direct Communication, ix, 9n44, 11, **25–38**, 44, 51, 77, 79–88, 90–91, 94, 99, 105, 107–8,

174

Index of Subjects

114–15, 122, 133, 136n28, 143, 147, 150–52, 159
Individualism, 16n5, 31n32, 39, **46–50**, 126, 149n17
Indwelling. *See* Embodiedness/Indwelling.
Intellectual Fashions, 4–6, 27, **30–35**, 54–58, 91–95, 98, 100, 106, 112–15, 150, 164
Intelligibility/Being Understood, 17–19, 25, **27–30**, 36, 42, 56–58, 63, 117, 136, 141, 143n56, **153–56**, 162
Inwardness/Outwardness, **25–38**, **46–51**, **129–58**
Irony, **71–73**, **93–96**, 98, 115n31, **118–23**, 135, 139, 146–47, 156, 165

Jesus Christ, **18–22**, **52–75**
   Incarnation, **15–22**, 42, 61, 63, 68–69, 72–73, 81–82, 123, 161–62
   As Prototype, 4, 52, 63, 69, 73, 79, 146
   As Savior, 4, 53, 59, 63, 79, 146
Journals, ix, 13, 19n17, 43, 54, 121, 134, 154–55
Judgment, *see also* Hermeneutics/Judging, **64–67**, 87, 108, 118, 125, **149–51**

Knowing. *See* Epistemology/Knowing.

Language, 23n1, 33, 71n106, **73–75**, 96–98, 99n43, 106, 124, 135, 140, 156n16, **161**, 163–65
Life/Existence, *see also* Actuality/Ideality, 2–6, 20–22, **52–75**, **131–58**
"Life-view." *See* "Spheres of Existence"/"Life-view."
Literature, 21, 40, 88, 96, 100, 116–17, 147n8, 153, 161
Love, 17–19, 32, 34n50, 36, 42n11, 46n30, **48–50**, 56, 63–65, 68n90, 70–71, 72, 75, 84, 87, 93–94, 101, **102–5**, **116–18**, **121–27**, 131, 137–40, 143, 150, 160, 162, 165

Maieutic, 53, **90–98**, 104–7, 111, 114, 121, 152
Martyrdom, *see also* Suffering, Witness, 117n40, 137, 139n42, 140–44
Mercy, 31–32, 103
Metanoia, *see* Conversion/Metanoia.
Mirrors, **64–65**, 105, 108, **114–18**, 125–27, 147
Moment/Crisis, *see also* Conversion, 34n49, 53, **64–65**, 92, 132, 139, 155
Morality, 42, 59, 70n102, 71, 140
Moravians, 3

Nihilism, 71

"Objective Uncertainty," 66, 81, 133
Objectivity. *See* Subjectivity/Objectivity.
Offense/"Sign of Offense," 54n10, 56, **60–64**, 81, 96, 105, 107
Orthodoxy, 4, 42, 69, 95, 108, 114, 117
Outwardness. *See* Inwardness/Outwardness.

Paradox, *see also* "The Absolute Paradox," 19, **42–43**, 45, 50, 54, **57–60**, 81–82
Passion/Pathos, 9, 20, **32–35**, 54, 70–71, **71–73**, **84–88**, **96–98**, 99, 101, 103–4, 106–7, 118, 129, 134, 136, 138, 148–49, 157, 159, 161, 163
Personhood/Selfhood, 4, 6, 15, **26–31**, 34, 37n62, **39–51**, 52–55, 64, 71–73, 79–80, 84, 87n33, 92, 94n23, 99–101, 108, 111–12, 114n25, 118n50, 125, 127, **136–39**, 143, 146, 150, 161–63
Philosophical Fragments, 13, 19n17, 35, **52–57**, 61, 81, 85n23, 86, 90, 92, 94–95, 106, 119, 123, 132, 156
"The King Who Loved a Humble Maiden," 17–19, 36, 55
Philosophy, 5–6, 20, 33, 40, 57, 59, 97, 106n81, **110–14**, 143n57, 147n9, 148–49n15

Index of Subjects

Poet/Poetic, 17n8, 21n30, 44–45, 71–73, 100, 102n60, 105, 112n12, 113, 126n86, 134–35, 138, 140, 142–43, **151–55**, 162–63, 165n14

Point of View/"The Point of View for My Work as an Author," 2n7, 8–10, 12–13, 16, 43n17, 77–78, 86n28, 89, 107n90, 117n40, **118–21**, 125, **152–58**, 160

Poststructuralism, **121–22**

Practice in Christianity, 13, 62, 81, 85n23, 99, **105**, 137n31, 142n54, 148n13, 150n22

Pragmatics, 23n1

Preach. *See* Didactic/Preaching.

Press-culture, *see also* The Corsair, 26–27

Privatism/Sociality, *see also* Individualism, 30–31, 39, **47–50**, 65, 93, 94n23, 102–3, 122, 138–39, 149n17, 161

Pseudonyms, 79–88, 145–51

Psychological-biographical readings, 131–32, 136n26, 140–44, 153

Purity of Heart is to Will One Thing, 99

Rationalism/"Speculative Thought," 31–33, 37n62, 54, 56–59, 68, 92, 95, 98, 100, 106, 162n5, 164

Reason, **19**, 28, 34, 54, 57, 59, 61, 73–74, **81–82**, 85, 95, 101n53, 106–7, 111n5, 162n5

Reduplication, 11, 50, 131, 136, **137–40**, 143–44, **145–51**, 158, 160

Reflection, 32, 40, 46–8, 58n34, 63, 82, 91, 96–99, 102–5, 109, **114–24**, 137

Reflexivity, 7, 57n29, 85n23, 95, 119–20, 124, 135, 150n21, **162–65**

Relationality, 4, 18, 20, 25, 31–32, 35, 37, 39, 42, **46–47**, 52–55, 59, 61–62, 65n77, 69, 75, 84, 93, **101**, 107–8, 116n36, 118n50, 131, 134, 138, 149, 161

Religion/"The Religious," 16, 25–26, 30–31, 42, 47–48, 72, 74n125, 85, 92–93, 135, 140, 147n9, 149n16, 154–55

"The Religious Works," 13, 43–44, 54n13, 89, **98–105**, 106–8, 111, 113, 114–16, 126n81, 133, 153, 156, 160

Responsibility/Choice, 4–6, 26–27, 31, 34, 40–46, 55–56, **64–65**, 67, 71, 80n2, 82, 84–85, **96–98**, 114–15, 137–39, 148, 156, 161

Romanticism, 17n8, 54, 57, **71–73**, 84, 91, 135, 162n5

Savior. *See* Jesus Christ/As Savior.

Scholarship. *See* Academia/Scholarship.

Scripture. *See* Bible/Scripture.

The Sickness Unto Death, 5, 13, 42, **45–46**, 47, 63n65, 99.

"Sign of Contradiction." *See* Contradiction/"Sign of Contradiction."

"Sign of Offense." *See* Offense/"Sign of Offense."

"The Single Individual," **39–51**

Sin/Human Autonomy, 27, 30, 41–42, 44, **53**, 59, 63, **71–73**, 75, 81, 92–93, **99–102**, 111, 115, 138, 141, **146**, 164

Sociality. *See* Privatism/Sociality.

Society/Culture, 2, 4–5, 15–16, 25–27, 29–31, 37, **39–51**, 58, 63, 70n101, 83, 91–92, 140–43, 147, 163–64

Speech-Act Theory, 23n1

"Spheres of Existence"/"Life-view," 9n44, 29–30, 44, 47, 55, 72, 85n24, 93n17, 100, 115, 119, 137, 139

Striving, *see* Discipleship/Striving

Subjectivity/Objectivity, **29–38**, **52–75**, 83–84, **112–27**, 162

Suffering, *see also* Martyrdom, 63, 105, 137n29, 140–42, 157

Teacher, 20, 44n20, 53–56, 59, 62, 80n4, 90, 133, 164

Theology, x, 4, 17, 19, 21, 33, 69, 74, 81n9, 84, 113–14, 122n63, 124, 126, 163–64

Truth, *see also* Jesus Christ, **52–75**, 83–84

176

As Relational, 53–55, 69, 116, 161
"In The Truth," 10, 21–22, 52, **69**, 73, 75, 79, 82–83n15, 101–2, 109, 115, 136–37, **145–46**, 151, 152, 160, 162, 165

Upbuilding Discourses/Upbuilding Discourses in Various Spirits/Christian Discourses, 13, 44, 56n27, 98–99, 110, 137

Virtue, 138

Witness, *see also* Martyrdom, 3, 36n58, 60, 110, 132, 134n14, 137, 139, 140, **142–44**, 148, 153–57

Works of Love, 13, 31, 46n30, 48–49, 66n82, 68n90, 71–72, 84, 85n23, 87n38, 97n36, 99, 101, **102–5**, 108, 110, 113n22, 126, **131–33**, 137, 149, 156n16, 160

Index of Names

Pseudonyms of Søren Kierkegaard:
"A," 44
 Anti-Climacus, 5, 8, 19, 42, 60–65, **65–68**, 79n1, 81, 86–88, 99, 101, 105, 106n83, 136n28, 149
 Climacus, Johannes, 5, 10n47, 17–19, 26, **34–35**, 40–41, 44, 52–65, **65–68**, 69, 73, 79n1, 81, 83–84, 86–88, 92, 94–95, 99–100, 106, 119, 126n86, 132–33, 148, 163
 Eremita, Victor, 107
 Silentio, Johannes De, **28–29**, 41, 54, 58, 92, 97, 99, **100–1**, 149, 154
 William, Judge, 44, 93, 100, 149

Abraham, 25, **27–30**, 37, 41–42, 44, 59, 92, **96–98**, 100, 141, 149, 154
Albertini, Bishop, 45
Andersen, Hans Christian, 55n20

Barrett, Lee, 85n23, 132n4, 134n16
Barthes, Roland, 161
Berlin, Isaiah, 1
Buber, Martin, 31n32, 46

Come, Arnold B., 137n31, 139n40
Conway, David, 100n50

Davenport, John J., 28n20, 29, 97n35
Derrida, Jacques, 115n31, 118n49–50

Evans, C. Stephen, 9n44, 31n32, 34n48, **46–47**, 54n7, 117n43, 119, **122–24**, 135n23, 143n58

Ferreira, M. Jamie, 49n48
Feuerbach, Ludwig, 57, 58n35

Gadamer, Hans-Georg, 23n1
Garff, Joakim, 12n59, 14, 16n7, 117, **118–21**, 125, 132n4, 134, 155n12
Gouwens, David Jay, 41n8, 50n50, 79n1, 104, 131n3, 132n6, 134, 165

Hamann, Johann Georg, 161
Hauerwas, Stanley, 164n9
Hegel, G. W. F., 5–6, 7n34, 11, 25, 31, **32–35**, 37, 58n33, 59, 74n128, 92n13, 95, 97, 111, 122, 129, 145–47, 150, 161
Hinkson, Craig, 19n17
Holmer, Paul, 1n2, 5n23, 7, 32–33, 70, 73–74, 89, 112n13, 112n14, 115–16, **122–24**, 133

Jacobs, Alan, 118n50, 138n36, 161n3
Jesus Christ, **18–22**, **52–75**

Kant, Immanuel, 28, 58, 74n128, 97
Kierkegaard, Michael, 2, 140

Lessing, G.E., 61n51, 107
Lewis, C.S., 120
Lonergan, Bernard, 33n41, 161n4
Lowrie, Walter, 121–22, 162n5
Luther, Martin, 19n17, 43, 79–80n1, 144, 161

McCabe, Herbert, 161n4
MacIntyre, Alasdair, 28n20

Index of Names

Mackey, Louis, 92n14, 113n22, 148n13
Malantschuk, Gregor, 145n1
Malesic, Jonathan, 57n32
Martensen, H.L., 33n40, 142, 147
Møller, Poul Martin, 20–21, 147n8, 161
Müller, Paul, 104
Mynster, Jakob P., 58n33, 132n6, **142–43**, 147–48, 151

Olsen, Regine, 11n51, 126n84, 132n5, 134, **140–41**, 149

Pattison, George, 40, 102n61, 133
Paul, Saint, 150, 163
Pilate, 65–8, 80
Plato, 97, 118n50
Pojman, Louis, 123
Polanyi, Michael, 33n41, 75, 161n4
Poole, Roger, ix, 32, 115n31, **116–18**, 121, 122n63, 137n31

Rae, Murray, 16n7, 27n14, 41–42, 54n6, 56n23, 57n32, 58n35, 68, 87, 95n25, 101, 111n5, 113n19, 113n23, **122–24**, 132–33, 161n4
Rasmussen, Joel, 12n58, 17n8, 21n30, 44–45n22, 71–73
Ricoeur, Paul, 92n14, 106n81, **112–13**

Schlegel, K.W.F., 71, 155
Schleiermacher, Friedrich, 23n1
Socrates, 3, 20–21, 52–53, 71, 90–91, 93, 147n8.

Thiselton, Anthony, 23n1
Thulstrup, Niels, 86, 122n65
Tolstoy, Leo, 1
Torrance, T.F., 75

Walsh, Sylvia, 30n28, 44–45n22, 85n24, 126n86
Watts, Michael, 121–22
Wittgenstein, Ludwig, 8, 23n1, 39, 105–6, 133n10, 161n4, 162–63